Lorraine

Between You and Me

THE AUTOBIOGRAPHY

Lorraine

Between You and Me

THE AUTOBIOGRAPHY

Lorraine Kelly

headline
review

First published in 2008
by HEADLINE REVIEW
An imprint of Headline Publishing Group

4

Cataloguing in Publication Data is available from the British Library

Hardback 978 0 7553 1784 4
Tradepaperback 978 0 7553 1839 1

Typeset in Aldine by Avon DataSet Ltd, Bidford on Avon, Warwickshire

Printed and bound in Great Britain by
Clays Ltd, St Ives plc

Headline's policy is to use papers that are natural, renewable and recyclable
products and made from wood grown in sustainable forests. The logging and
manufacturing processes are expected to conform to the environmental
regulations of the country of origin.

HEADLINE PUBLISHING GROUP
An Hachette Livre UK Company
338 Euston Road
London NW1 3BH

www.headline.co.uk
www.hachettelivre.co.uk

To my husband Steve and my daughter Rosie,
with love and thanks

Contents

	Acknowledgements	ix
One	A Child of the Fifties	1
Two	Where It All Began	25
Three	On the Ladder	59
Four	The Rough and the Smooth	69
Five	Morning Sickness	129
Six	So That's What It's All About	143
Seven	Run for Your Life	153
Eight	Going It Alone	181
Nine	Beyond Belief	195
Ten	Talking the Talk	209
Eleven	All Human Life	219
Twelve	Reach for the Sky	233
Thirteen	Dragged Through the Mud	253
Fourteen	Homeward Bound	263
	Epilogue	299
	Index	301
	Picture Credits	309

Acknowledgements

A very special thank you to my husband Steve for his patience, help and support, especially when I was writing this book at weekends or late into the night.

To my lovely daughter Rosie who brings so much happiness into my life.

To my mum and dad for being such good parents and for allowing me to tell their story, and to my brother Graham for still talking to me.

To Joyce Woodrow, 'my sister', for all the miles we have covered together.

To Siobhan O'Gorman for her help and for always being there when I need sensible advice; and when I need to go shopping for very un-sensible shoes.

To Jacqueline and Craig Millar and Joan and Hugh Grant for their friendship and their sense of fun.

To Pam Ross for being the bravest woman I know.

To my agent and friend Michael Joyce and to everyone I have ever worked with over the years. Thank you for making it all such a terrific roller-coaster ride.

To Andrea Henry, Bernie Dive, Shona Abhyankar and all the team at Headline for their invaluable help.

And to every single one of you who watch me on TV and read my columns.

Thank you so very very much. I couldn't have done any of it without you.

CHAPTER ONE

A Child of the Fifties

When I remember how young and daft I was as a teenager, I can't believe how well my parents coped with having me when they were just teenagers themselves. Mum and Dad – Anne and John – were only seventeen when they married. My mum was barely out of her convent school and my dad was still living at home on an apprentice's wages.

They look impossibly young in their wedding photos. My dad has a shiny suit and an Elvis quiff and my mum is doe-eyed and gorgeous in her new outfit, or 'costume', as a matching skirt and jacket was known in those days. The bloom in her cheeks and the light in her eyes were probably because I was already on the way. I never could work out how it was that they got married in July 1959 and I was born just four months later. I was told I was premature and a miracle child and, of course, I accepted this explanation without question because we all think the world revolves around us and everyone else plays a walk-on part in the movie of our lives.

My parents were never pushy, but they always told me I could be anything I wanted to be. After all, we were at the dawn of the sixties, and there was optimism in the air. The war babies were growing up, listening to rock-and-roll, and imitating the young Americans they saw in the movies. Those were the years when 'teenagers' were really invented, but my mum and dad missed out on all the fun. With a baby on the way and a wedding to plan, they had to grow up really fast.

When my parents found out they were expecting, my dad went round to his best friend Eddie Barry's tenement flat in the Gorbals to break the news that he was going to be a dad. At the same time Eddie was on his way to tell my dad the exact same thing. He and his girlfriend Flora were also going to be teenage parents. In those days if a boy got a girl pregnant, he married her. Those were the rules and that was your 'punishment' for having sex out of wedlock.

When my mum and dad told her mother, this formidable woman wasn't at all happy and she hatched a plan. She wanted her daughter, my mum, to travel down to the south of England and have her baby there, then immediately put the child up for adoption. No one would be any the wiser and there would be no scandal. My mum's older sisters, Jacqueline and Mary, who lived in England, would organise it all. My mum would come back to Glasgow and forget about her 'mistake'.

My parents were having none of it.

My dad stood firm in his ill-fitting suit, pointy winkle-picker shoes (so cheap that they turned up at the ends and he said he looked like an extra from *Kismet*) and declared they were getting married whether my granny liked it or not. She wasn't used to being disobeyed and there were some terrible rows. She came round in the end and developed a grudging respect for my dad that eventually turned into genuine affection.

The wedding was held at Martha Street Register Office in Glasgow, and because my mum was pregnant, and both of them weren't actually old enough legally to drink anything stronger than Irn Bru or Tizer, the reception was a modest cup of tea, a chocolate biscuit and a slice of wedding cake. In the evening, they went to see the famous Scottish comedian Lex McLean at the Pavilion, and that was that.

The hard-up newly-wed teenagers couldn't even afford a honeymoon, and when they returned to their 'single end' in Ballater Street in the Gorbals, after their one special night at the theatre, they found it had been broken into and all their wedding presents stolen. Imagine the despair of having your first home together trashed, and being robbed of the little you owned. The presents had been scraped together by friends and family: a two-bar electric fire, a kettle, pots, pans, cups and saucers, blankets and towels. This was to have given my mum and dad at least the basics, and it was all gone, along with my mum's precious record collection.

It wasn't the best start to their married life, but they picked themselves up and eventually managed to save enough cash to refurnish their tiny home. These days a 'single end' would be described as a chi-chi studio apartment, but in the Gorbals in 1959 my mum and dad had moved into a cold, dank, ground-floor room with a recess for a bed, and a cooker and sink in the corner. The toilet was outside and shared with four other families. Somehow my mum turned this one room into a little palace. My dad's family helped to paint and decorate, and my mum scrubbed everything clean. Gritting her teeth and holding her nose, she even made that outside toilet sparkle. And that was the home they brought me back to.

I was born on St Andrew's Day, 30 November 1959. My mum was so young and unworldly that she had no idea she had gone into labour, and I was well on the way when they both took the half-hour trolley-bus journey from the Gorbals to her mother's home in Dennistoun. The bus dropped them off at the bottom of one of the steepest hills in Glasgow, and my teenage mum huffed and puffed her way up Whitehill Street to the front door of the tenement flat.

My granny took one horrified look at her and rushed to get a taxi to Rottenrow Hospital in the heart of the city. She was briskly checked in and, less than an hour later I arrived, looking, as my dad put it, 'like a skinned rabbit'.

Of course, he wasn't actually there for the birth. In those days any man who wanted to be by his wife's side to welcome their child into the world would have been chased out of the labour ward by a hatchet-faced matron, so my dad just went back to his work. I think I was filling my lungs for my first seriously big bellow before he had time to jump on the trolley-bus back to the hospital.

They brought me home when I was a week old to a place that was considered one of the most deprived areas in Britain, if not the world, and often compared to the Black Hole of Calcutta, but underneath the shocking headlines of poverty, stabbings and violence there was a close-knit community.

My dad was born in the Gorbals and lived in Mathieson Street. His mum, my granny Kelly, said that all the women left

4

their doors open because no one had anything worth stealing back in the thirties and forties. She had a tough life, bringing up her four kids and losing four more to childhood diseases like scarlet fever, which rampaged through the tenements. My dad John, Uncle Billy, Aunty Lydia and baby Carol all survived.

My gran says that my dad cried for the first two years of his life and drove her and my granda to distraction. When he was still a baby he was taken into hospital with diphtheria and nearly died. The doctors and nurses said they were never so glad to see a baby leave the ward as he constantly yelled and girned.

Money was always tight and although my granda worked hard as a roofer, there was never enough coming in and my granny had her work cut out to feed and clothe her husband and four kids.

Like so many families in the west of Scotland, the Kellys had come over from Ireland in the eighteenth century looking for work. They were originally from Draperstown in Northern Ireland, about forty-five miles west of Belfast. It's a small, quiet village of just over fifteen hundred people, and its biggest claim to fame is that it has the only regular open sheep market in Ireland.

I went back there two years ago when I was tracking my family tree for a feature on GMTV, and it was fascinating to see the place where my ancestors had lived and worked. The village is small, neat and friendly, and the house where my great-great-great-grandfather John Kelly lived is a big, solid building right in the middle of the main street. I can't imagine why he would have left this beautiful part of the world for the slums of Glasgow. They must have been desperate for money and work. His son, also called John, grafted in the Glasgow shipyards as a hammer-man, which was exactly what it sounds like: a man with a hammer who would take on whatever job, no matter how tough. The family huddled in a tiny room in Anderston, north of the River Clyde, before moving to the Gorbals.

The Kelly clan were ordinary working-class people, who worked too hard and died too young. Many of them suffered from the twin curses of poverty and drink. In January 1905 my great-great-grandmother Catherine had to go on 'the parish' and apply for a handout from the local authority in order to survive. There was no welfare state in those days and she couldn't pay her rent. There was huge stigma attached to being 'on the parish', and she would have been deeply ashamed to take the money, but her husband had died, her kids were starving and she had no choice.

Catherine was trying to bring them up on her own and couldn't cope. She tried selling rags, second-hand clothes and old bedding, door to door, but there was never enough money coming in. She suffered with chronic lung disease and took to drink. Her kids were taken away from her and the inspectors found her in her Gorbals tenement in filth and squalor. 'Keeping a dirty house' would have seen her ostracised by most of the other women in the tenements, who battled daily with dirt, disease and overcrowding.

Somehow, against all the odds, Catherine managed to beat the bottle and get her kids back, which must have been incredibly difficult in those days. I admire her guts and determination, something that proud but flawed woman has passed down through the generations to me and my brother, and to my daughter. Too many other men and women in that situation would have given in and either drunk themselves to death or coughed their last on a filthy, damp, dirty and disease-ridden bed.

The Kellys stayed in the Gorbals, living and working and helping to make Glasgow the second city of the Empire, behind only London in generating wealth and allowing the rich to grow richer.

My dad was bright, but when he was young you left school at fifteen and got yourself a job. That was the way things were and there simply wasn't the money for further education. He became an apprentice at Semples, an electrical shop in Dennistoun, which also happened to be the part of Glasgow where my mum lived with her mother and sisters.

My mum also landed a job in Semples in their record department. It was a pretty cool and glamorous job for a sixteen-year-old. All the teenagers came in to buy copies of 'Great Balls of Fire' by Jerry Lee Lewis, Buddy Holly's 'That'll Be the Day', and the mighty Elvis classic 'Jailhouse Rock', but I think they also came in to chat up the curvy beauty behind the counter. The songs they listened to were the soundtrack to my mum and dad's romance when the two of them met and started 'winching'.

My mum also worked at the Dennistoun Palais, serving soft drinks and Coca-Cola to the teenagers who came to listen to up-and-coming bands, and singers like Dorothy Paul – who is a national treasure in Scotland – and to flirt with each other. It might have been his good looks and cheeky patter, but then again my dad *was* in television.

The young apprentice was learning how to fix the massive black-and-white TVs that all families aspired to owning. It was a big status symbol to have a set and to be able to watch shows like *Take Your Pick*, *Double Your Money* and *Emergency Ward 10*.

My mum had spent most of her childhood from the age of five until she was fifteen in a strict convent school with her sisters Helen, Josephine and Patsy. Her parents, Margaret and John McMahon, had split up, which was rather scandalous during the forties, though they never divorced. They had a tempestuous marriage, with endless rows. My grandmother had scars on her legs until the day she died from when he had held her down in a chair and repeatedly kicked her. Eventually, my grandfather John walked out on his wife and his children. The fights played their part but he was also having an affair with a red head waitress, which gave my granny Mac a lifelong loathing of flame-haired women.

She was once travelling upstairs at the back of a bus on the way to one of her many jobs when she caught her husband and his mistress smooching several rows ahead of her. She crept up behind them and banged their heads together. She used to tell this tale often and always with great relish.

Granny Mac gave birth to twelve children, but only eight of them survived because of the virulent childhood diseases that blighted the city. As a single mum of eight children she simply couldn't cope. Despite having three jobs, she was a very bad manager of money and was constantly in debt, preferring to buy an expensive magazine, a bunch of flowers or a new outfit rather than pay the rent or the electricity bill. At one point she had about three catering jobs, but was still hopelessly in the red.

But, somehow, Mary, Jimmy, Jacqueline, Tony, Helen, my mum Anne, Josephine and Patsy all made it through Granny Mac's haphazard child-rearing. The older ones all left home as soon as they could make their own way in the world. The four younger girls were sent away to be educated in a residential convent school, which, while it wasn't exactly the stuff of nightmares, was no picnic either. The nuns were very strict and there were no cuddles, words of comfort or any real affection.

The convent girls were given a basic education and also expected to work for their keep, doing cooking, cleaning and general housework. I'm surprised my mum and my aunts grew up to be such well-balanced, kind-hearted individuals after their strict and loveless upbringing. It made them all very close, especially my mum and her sister Josephine, whose real name is actually Sandra. When my granny went to have her christened in the Catholic church, the priest frowned at her and bellowed that Sandra was no name for a Christian child. As it was St Joseph's day, he declared that she would be called Josephine. In those days if the priest told you to jump you asked, 'How high?', and if he wanted you to name your child Cherry Blossom because it was his favourite shoe polish you did it without any objection.

My parents had a 'mixed' marriage as my dad was Protestant and my mum Catholic. In those days, this was frowned upon in sectarian Glasgow, but although my dad and his brother Billy and most of the Kelly clan were devoted followers of Glasgow Rangers, and my mum had that strict Catholic convent upbringing, neither family was particularly religious. However, some couples found themselves shunned by their families after marrying either a 'Hun' (Protestant) or a 'Tim' (Catholic).

My granda Danny Kelly had no time for organised religion, which he claimed, not unreasonably, to be the cause of all wars and strife. He worked hard and drank hard and was a man of few words, but he did have a cracking sense of humour and when he found something funny, he was a real giggler.

When he had a few drinks inside him for Dutch courage, you could sometimes persuade him to sing at family parties and he had a terrific voice, but it was his sister, my great-aunt Lena, who was the real entertainer. She had been one of the Moxton Girls, a sort of Scottish equivalent of the Tiller Girls but with more sass. Lena had a fine pair of legs and at family parties she would belt out old classics with great gusto.

Everyone would turn up to a do knowing their party-piece, and my shy mum would dread being asked to do a turn. She would cross her fingers that Lena and my granda would get on their feet first, and then she was safe as they could entertain for hours.

My granda's youngest brother, my great-uncle Billy, also had a terrific voice, and listening to them was far better than watching the TV, especially at New Year. This was always the big celebration. In the days leading up to Hogmanay the house, which was already sparkling, would be completely cleaned from top to bottom.

I loved family parties when I was a little girl, especially at New Year when you were allowed to stay up and have a glass of cordial and as much fruit-cake as you could stuff into your greedy little face. The children, especially me and my cousin Danny, ran riot until about 2a.m., and then we just fell down exhausted as the party continued around us.

The next day there would be massive plates of home-made soup, steak pie, mashed potatoes, turnips and cabbage, and my granny Kelly's fruit dumpling, which she boiled in a pillowcase in a giant pan. This plump, steaming fruit-filled ball was utterly delicious and we would queue up for a slice, and then take a big dod home with us. I would have my share gobbled down before we reached the bottom of the stairs and got out of the door of the close.

When I was a toddler the clearance of the Gorbals was in full swing. The old tenements were being demolished and bright new multistoreys – or high-rises – thrown up in their place, but those cheap, nasty buildings were a big mistake. Like the slums they replaced, those soulless monoliths would eventually have to be torn down, but not before they had wrecked communities and separated friends and families for ever.

My granda's mum and dad, Danny and Lizzie, lived well into their nineties, were both as sharp as tacks and had grown up in the Gorbals and didn't want to leave. So my great-granny and granda sadly ended up high in the sky in the notorious Queen Elizabeth tower-block. The architects might have won awards and the planners plaudits for their experiments in 'social engine-ering', but those buildings were a dismal failure and ruined people's lives. The flats were riddled with damp, old people were trapped in their homes because the lifts often didn't work, and there was nowhere for kids to play. Despite the best efforts of the house-proud tenants, the landings reeked of rotting rubbish, boiled cabbage and pee.

Going to visit my great-granny and granda was a bit of a lottery as to whether the hoist – lift – would be working. If it wasn't, you would have to walk up endless flights of stairs, and I was scared of the long black featureless corridors, which made you feel as though you were in a jail.

Once inside, my great-granny, like all decent working-class women, had made the place gleam, but she could no longer hang out of the window to talk to her neighbours, or listen to the motley band of hard-up singers and entertainers who would perform their 'acts' in the back courts of the tenements. People would throw pennies at the poor souls, and more often than not you would hear them yelping in pain because the coins had been heated up in a pan over the fire before they were flung out of the window. That didn't stop them scrabbling in the dirt for the money.

Obviously the old overcrowded tenements had to go, but the planners made an unforgivable blunder by stacking people high in the sky like termites in those God-awful tower-blocks. Lessons have been learned and today the New Gorbals is transformed, with proper houses and shops, and is slowly getting back a sense of pride and community. There are still drug and crime problems, common in every inner-city scheme, but it is light years better than it was.

My mum and dad moved out of the Gorbals altogether when I was three and we went up in the world, but thankfully not to a multistorey high-rise. Our new tenement was in Swanston Street, Bridgeton, in Glasgow's East End, and had two rooms and, oh, joy of joys, an inside toilet. My dad built a small hardboard partition lengthways down one side of the tiny living-room where the sink and the cooker were, and used one of those multi-coloured ribbon-like plastic curtains over the entrance. This meant we had a separate kitchen, and there was still room for a three-piece suite and a small table and chairs in the recess of the living-room.

We had some real luxuries that many other families would have envied. There was a big fridge in the hall (no room in that teeny kitchenette) and we had a top-of-the-range television, thanks to my dad's job as a TV engineer. We were the first in our street to have a colour TV and I'll never forget seeing *Tom and*

Jerry in Technicolor. It was like being at the Saturday-morning 'funnies' and watching a proper cinema screen. Family and neighbours would come round to 'ooh' and 'aah', and we had an even bigger crowd than usual to watch one of Frank Sinatra's many farewell TV concerts.

We also had a radiogram that looked like a sideboard. You lifted up the polished wooden lid to put on your vinyl records. You could stack about half a dozen 45s (or singles) to play one after another. My mum's favourite was Dusty Springfield, and I remember coming home from school and dancing and singing with her to 'Mocking Bird' and belting out 'Son of Preacher Man'.

It was on that radiogram that I first listened to Bob Dylan, the Beatles, the Animals and the Rolling Stones, as well as top crooners Frank Sinatra and, the Kelly family favourite, Matt Monro. As soon as I hear the velvet voice of Matt Monro, I am right back to my childhood. Del Shannon was another big hit in our house and I knew all the words to 'Runaway' when I was two and a half.

I was a very happy little girl until I reached six years old, when something terrible happened to shatter my world.

It came in the form of an 8lb 5oz curly-headed blue-eyed baby boy, my wee brother Graham. My mum came home from Belvedere Hospital with this usurper who took up all her time and energy and whom I instantly loathed. It didn't help that this cherub was like a baby from Central Casting, with his perfect chubby cheeks and placid personality. He would spend all day gurgling contentedly in his pram, whereas I had been a shrieking terror, like my dad before me, who demanded constant attention and caused my poor parents far too many sleepless nights.

I should have loved my baby brother Graham and treated him like my very own real-life dolly, but instead my nose was put of joint as I was no longer the spoiled only child of the family and I was truly horrible to him. I sneakily drank his free NHS orange juice and forced his chubby feet into my tiny dolls' shoes until he yelped. Later we fought like cat and dog, and my poor mother must have wanted to strangle us both as we traded slaps and nips and rolled around on the floor.

Graham continued to be merely my nuisance of a wee brother and I was his intensely annoying big sister until the day we almost lost him. We were playing in the street when five-year-old Graham was chased by his pal into the road. He was knocked down by a car and trapped under the wheel. I will never forget the ambulance taking Graham's broken body away and the utter shock and horror on my mum's face.

I was tortured by guilt because I had never wanted him in the first place and I was sure it was all my fault that the accident had happened. Of course I didn't tell anyone I felt I was to blame, but it did make me realise that deep down I actually loved him very much and I was ashamed of being such a rotten sister.

Graham had to have his spleen removed and he could have died. He was by far the youngest in the ward and the other patients and the nurses doted on him, partly because of his age and cherubic good looks, but mainly because he was also a funny and genuinely lovely little boy. He was given special dispensation to have his talking 'Major Matt' toy by his bedside. This was a truly magnificent action figure of an astronaut that actually spoke when you pulled a cord in his back and he could do a space walk from bed to bed at the same time.

Graham came home bent over like a wee old man and with a

very impressive scar on his belly. He was quite rightly treated like a little emperor and we declared a truce.

My brother and I would never admit it, but we did have a lot in common. We were both sci-fi geeks, mainly thanks to my dad's enthusiasm for science fiction and his deep and lifelong interest in astronomy. He bought me my first telescope when I was five and we pored over his Patrick Moore books and maps of the moon for hours. I knew where the Sea of Tranquillity was before I could point to the Mediterranean.

When the original *Star Trek* was first shown on TV, I was utterly enthralled. I had my first major crush on the half-Vulcan Mr Spock. Like most women who admired this logical green-blooded hero, I thought I could crack through his cold façade. Sitting there watching *Star Trek* for the first time, I obviously hadn't a clue that in thirty years' time I would be interviewing Spock, Kirk and Sulu, and that we would still be talking about that extraordinary series.

Star Trek was well ahead of its time, and it was another two years before fiction turned to fact and we watched Neil Armstrong's flickering image as he took his first steps on the moon. I was ten and Graham was four, and we were both captivated. The whole world held its breath while the astronauts, in little more than a cramped tin can, went round the dark side of the moon and were no longer in communication with NASA.

Years later on GMTV, when I was doing a live link to Houston, Texas, I secretly longed for the satellite to go down so I could dramatically declare, 'Houston, we have a problem', as famously uttered by Jim Lovell from Apollo 13. Sadly the interview went without a hitch.

I still have a newspaper cutting from 1969 in the heady days after the moon landing that proclaimed we'd have a man on Mars by 1984. There is even a drawing of the proposed spacecraft. I'm really disappointed that we didn't boldly go where no man has gone before and continue with space exploration. At the time, we honestly believed the moon landing was the first step towards man conquering space. It was a real-life thriller and mystery. We also wondered whether there would be a red flag with a hammer and sickle flying on the moon. The space race was serious and the Soviets had kept everyone guessing as to whether they had got there first.

As always, Graham bombarded my dad with questions throughout the whole event. I swear my brother came out of the womb asking, 'Why?' It was the first word he ever uttered and the one he used most often.

We both collected models from cornflake packets (long before these were banned as choking hazards) of the spindly lunar module known as the *Eagle* and the command module *Columbia* piloted by Mike Collins that waited to bring Armstrong and Buzz Aldrin home. I had these iconic posters of the moon taken from the *Eagle* and the astronauts planting the US flag on the lunar surface. The *moon*. I looked up into the sky and couldn't believe we had made such a leap.

It was a magical time, full of optimism and possibility, but for my parents the late sixties and seventies were all hard graft. As well as his day job, my dad worked most nights doing 'home jobs', fixing TVs and radiograms. He was determined that his family would always be fed, clothed and want for nothing. This was a time when there was still abject poverty in Glasgow. I saw kids coming to my primary school in tatty hand-me-downs, and one wee soul in my class, who had a pinched white face and scrawny body, used to wet himself repeatedly. There would be a tell-tale puddle under his chair and he would be quietly sent to the nurse for clean pants and trousers and a dose of malt extract from a big brown jar to try and build him up. Then there was the girl who had scabies and went around with big blotches of purple gentian violet on her little shaven head.

Strangely these kids were never picked on, but they weren't fussed over either. They were simply left alone.

We might have had no running hot water, no phone, no bath and no shower, but we were well off compared with most other people in the street. Our home was still basic, though. As well as the inside toilet, we had just two rooms: the living-room, with the sectioned-off kitchenette, and the bedroom, which the four of us shared. My mum and dad had a double bed and Graham and I were in bunk-beds.

We all shared the same small room until we moved house when I was thirteen. It meant we had to be very respectful of each other's privacy, and always lock the toilet door. I didn't think there was any other way to live, because it was the way we were brought up. In any case, we didn't actually spend all that much time inside when I was growing up. We were always out playing, or I was at the Rosebuds, a girls' club and forerunner of the Brownies, which I also joined, and where I became a Seconder of the Scottish Kelpies, and Sixer of the Imps.

My mum and dad only had two children. How families with five, six or even seven kids managed to shoehorn them all into the one bedroom, I have no idea. They must have slept in shifts. I also don't know how my mum kept the place so pristine and how she managed to cook such brilliant meals on that tiny gas, stove. She had to boil kettles for everything and wash and wring out all our clothes by hand; big items like towels, sheets and blankets were taken to the launderette. It was my job to take the washing there in a thick plastic bag and collect it the next day. I hated that task and I used to kick the 'bag-wash' all the way down Swanston Street and into Dalmarnock Road. My mum used to think it was the laundry's fault that the bag got so dirty and full of holes, but it was really me taking out my frustration at having to walk all the way there and back.

As if looking after us wasn't enough, she also had a part-time job in Frasers, the Glasgow department store in Buchanan Street. She was (and indeed still is) a remarkably beautiful woman with a real sense of fashion. I know it pains her deeply that both my brother Graham and I prefer comfort over style.

Graham is a hugely successful award-winning advertising creative director based in Singapore, and my mother would dearly love to see him suited and booted and dressed from head to toe in Armani. He is, however, a chinos and T-shirt bloke, and I don't think he's owned a tie in his life. To be honest, if I didn't work on TV, I would happily live in tracksuits and comfy trousers, and I am more likely to be wearing George at Asda than Giorgio Armani.

Style is about so much more than just having the money to buy designer labels, and my mum always knew how to put an outfit together, even when money was tight. She also knew how to make our home warm and comforting on a shoestring.

The tenement flat in Swanston Street was a real step up from the single end in the Gorbals, but it was still hard work for my mum. Constantly heating water must have been a real chore, but she never complained, even when she once dropped the boiling kettle on to her foot and was badly scalded. Graham was still a baby, and I had to run to my granny Kelly in Dalmarnock Road for help as we had no phone and neither did any of the neighbours. I ran all the way, but it still took me ten minutes to get there.

My poor mum was in agony, but she tried to keep calm so that Graham and I wouldn't be too scared. After seeing the doctor she seemed to get better and a few days later she was well enough to go to the first showing of the big movie in 1965, *The Sound of Music*. It was a real treat and to make it even more special we took a black taxi. My mum was wearing red velvet slippers to accommodate her bandaged foot, and had tied a big bow round her walking-stick. Even when she was poorly she liked to look alluring.

Half-way through the film, round about the bit where Julie Andrews and the children are doing the yodelling puppet show, my mum became really ill and was rushed to hospital and kept in. She had serious blood poisoning and was in a very bad way. In those days kids weren't told what was going on, so we were simply bundled up and distributed like parcels to whichever relative happened to be closest.

I was looked after by my mum's older sister, my lovely kind-hearted aunt Helen. She was confronted by a surly six-and-a-half year old who behaved abominably and threw a tantrum when she tried to wash my hair and look after me. Hair-washing was my mum's job and I would let no one but her do it for me. I was worried sick about her, and I even missed my horrible wee brother, who was being spoiled rotten by my granny and granda Kelly and having the joy of going through my granny's drawers. (Which is not as rude as it sounds.)

My granny Kelly had a sideboard that was filled with

fascinating bits and bobs – old photos, nuts and bolts, tape-measures, bits of string and tons and tons of 'stuff'. We spent hours happily delving into those treasures. At Granny Kelly's you were also allowed to watch loads of TV at night-time, with the curtains drawn and your feet curled up on the sofa and a big fat sweetie to sook.

My mum got better, but she still has the scarring on her legs and foot, and for a long time she was in great pain. She still had to hobble on to the bus with Graham and me to make the weekly visit to the new town of East Kilbride, to which my granny Mac had been uprooted, kicking and screaming, from her tenement in Dennistoun. This formidable woman was shaped like a cottage loaf left too long in the oven and wore her black, waist-length hair in plaits atop her head like a Russian empress. She'd wanted me adopted before I was born, but she completely changed her mind when I came along and I was her spoiled and petted darling.

She did try to bully my mum into calling me Winnie because I was born on the same day as her all-time hero Sir Winston Churchill, but luckily my mum and dad stuck to their guns and named me Lorraine because they happened to like the sound of it.

My granny Mac's house was extraordinary. Every bit of wall space was covered with framed photos of her massive extended family, and above the fire there were horse-brasses and trays that needed to be cleaned and rubbed furiously with Brasso. There were 'wallie dugs' – those sour-faced pottery dogs – at the fireside and books stacked up to the ceiling. You had to tip-toe carefully round all the coffee-tables, leather pouffes and side-tables packed with knick-knacks, magazines and yet more books. For me and my cousins it was a wonderland, and we were allowed to stuff ourselves with cake and sweets and run riot.

My granny Mac was a man's woman and she enjoyed the company of her sons and her sons-in-law, but she was hard on her daughters. The men were poured massive whiskies that reduced them to gibbering wrecks. Her daughters were put down mercilessly, especially my mum who was the one who saw her most and looked after her when she was very ill and dying.

My granny was a very well-read and intelligent woman, who could quote the Koran, the Bible and the latest naughty joke in *Playboy* with the greatest of ease. She encouraged all her family to read and to study, and she created an imaginary world for herself that was much more exotic than her true origins: she grew up in Coldstream in the Borders. Depending on her mood, she would be descended from the kings of Ireland, a rich Jewish family from central Europe who had fled persecution at the turn of the century, or sometimes she would be the daughter of landed gentry fallen on hard times. It was hugely entertaining for all her grandchildren, but rather perplexing when we found the stories didn't quite match up. Did she really cook for Sir Winston Churchill and the Queen Mother? Did she play in the woods as a young girl with the future prime minister Harold Macmillan? Had she really worked for the Labour firebrand Emanuel Shinwell? No one has ever been able to unpick the truth from the colourful tales, but it made spending time with her endlessly entertaining.

She was extravagant, given to flamboyant gestures and equally outlandish costumes. There weren't many elderly women wandering around East Kilbride with their upswept plaited hair fixed with a grand, Russian-style decorated comb and covered with a Spanish mantilla. She wore swishing capes, too much fake tan, white gloves and giant sunglasses. Margaret McMahon should have been a movie star or a grand lady wafting around the Riviera having fascinating conversations with titled and somewhat shady gentlemen.

Instead, she ended up in near-poverty in the East End of Glasgow, stuck in an unhappy marriage to a man incapable of being faithful.

For all his faults, I remember my maternal grandfather with affection. He was the man who gave me my first nickname – the 'Che Baba' – and who bought me my first pair of Jumping Jacks – a popular brand of children's shoes. John McMahon was a head waiter at the Argyll Hotel and very tall and handsome, but he was never really around for his family. He lived in digs in Glasgow, but still came back to his wife every Sunday for a roast dinner. When he became ill with the lung cancer that would kill him, it was my grandmother and his children who took care of him until he had to go into a hospice. Until she died, my granny would visit the cemetery on the anniversary of his death and pour half a bottle of whisky over his grave so that he could have a 'wee drink'. My appalled uncle Jimmy, who would drive her there and back, couldn't believe such a waste of a good malt.

My grandmother died in 1991 from breast cancer. My mum ran herself ragged looking after her and visiting her in hospital. When I saw her shortly before she died, I couldn't believe this frail, tiny woman was the formidable Margaret McMahon. All I could think was, Who is this wee old woman and what have they done with my granny? The nurses said she was no trouble at all and a real lamb. She shrank before our eyes, and towards the end she lost all her spark and fire and became as quiet as a novice nun. She just melted away.

I know she was in her eighties, but I still feel cheated by her death. She was in good health otherwise and so sharp, and I'm sorry she died before my daughter got to meet her. My way of remembering her is to do as much as I can for breast-cancer charities and hope that others will hold on to their loved ones a bit longer.

CHAPTER TWO

Where It All Began

My mum was very particular about everything being tidy and neat, and that included Graham and me. I have inherited her manic tidiness and make Monica from *Friends* look like a slattern. I need everything to be in its proper place, and although being a mum has made me a bit less fussy, I still can't go to bed unless the house is tidy, every dish is washed and in the cupboard, and the bins are put out. It's as if I am worried that the Tidy Police are going to break in and arrest me for violating their code of neatness. I simply can't help it and can only blame my mother for giving me the tidy gene.

She maintained that I always had to look my best as a child, and at night would wrap old tights in my hair so that I would have perfect ringlets. She insisted I spoke 'properly', without using Glasgow slang, so I was branded a 'snob' at Strathclyde Primary School and had my fair share of being bullied. Once I was hit over the head with a Tressy doll – the one whose hair grew out of the top of her head when you pushed her stomach. A whack from that tough little plastic dolly with its pneumatic breasts made my nose bleed horribly and I was devastated at spoiling my favourite pink-and-white checked dress with the velvet rose on the belt.

Going to the toilets was always an ordeal, as that was where you were most likely to be jumped on. Walking home after school was another trial and I always waited for my pal Elizabeth Spark, who lived in the next street, was a year older than me and provided protection.

At the height of the bullying I remember stepping on to a nail on a piece of wood. It went right through my shoe and embedded itself deep in my foot. I was taken to hospital, given an anti-tetanus jab and had a couple of days off school. I sometimes wonder if I stepped on that rusty nail just so I didn't have to go back to the classroom and face my tormentors.

Being bullied and picked on makes you utterly miserable and dominates your life. I would go to school with ice in my stomach, and although I had it relatively easy, I can still remember those feelings of utter helplessness. Even girls you thought were your friends tended to play it safe and go along with the bullies for their own protection. That herd mentality makes you feel utterly isolated. There are usually only one or two ringleaders but they can turn the whole class against you.

It breaks my heart to see how much bullying there is these days, and how it has spread to texting and the Internet. Some young children are in such despair they even take their own lives. I have had to interview too many devastated parents who have lost their child through bullying, and many of them had had no idea it was happening.

I suffered in silence for months before I eventually told my mum, but I remember feeling so ashamed that I wasn't able to handle it on my own and that I had somehow 'let the side down' by not being popular enough. My mum was far too sweet-natured to tackle the problem, so she called in the heavy artillery.

My life at school improved dramatically after my dad's sisters, my aunty Carol and my aunty Lydia, stormed into the playground and warned the bullies that they would *personally* sort them out if there was any more trouble. Carol and Lydia in full flow were truly a sight to behold, especially Carol with her miniskirt and thigh-high leather boots. She was only about eighteen at the time, but after her SAS-style appearance, I was left in peace. Although there were some girls I would never see eye to eye with, I stayed out of their way and they let me be.

Despite that brief period of bullying I loved school. I went there aged four already able to read and write because my mum taught me my alphabet and read me stories every night. There were always books in the house and both Graham and I were encouraged, but never pushed, to read the classics, and spent most of our pocket money on comics – *Bunty*, *Judy* and later *Jackie* for me; the *Beano*, the *Dandy* and then *2001AD* for Graham.

In fact, the first money I ever earned came from selling a badly drawn cartoon to Graham's *Knockout* comic when I was twelve. I had scrawled a crashed rocket on the surface of the moon with two robbers in black-and-white striped spacesuits carrying bags of swag. One is saying to the other, 'Great get-away, boss, but where do we spend the cash?' I'm sure I must have stolen it from somewhere, but I got a postal order to exchange for a whole one-pound note, and I think that was the moment I realised that the media would be a pretty good career if you were given such riches for such a feeble offering.

As part of my mum's ongoing campaign of improvement I was taken to ballet lessons in Glasgow at the top of Sauchiehall Street. The Margaret Hopkins School of Dancing was taught by a wonderfully ancient and rather large woman who looked like a Hungarian countess. She even had a black walking-stick just like the grand ladies in the movies, which she banged on the wooden floor to get our attention. I had all the grace and elegance of a baby elephant, but I loved those lessons.

There was a *barre* at the mirror where we practised our movements. I still remember all the positions, but would end up in hospital in traction if I attempted any of them now. We practised in little purple tunics and green ballet shoes, but were allowed to wear white tutus when we 'performed' at the McLellan Galleries, an exhibition hall just further down Sauchiehall Street where all of us little ballerinas put on a show for our doting parents and family. I still have those tiny shoes. They're all worn and scuffed but very precious to me.

The bus fares, class fees and ballet outfits must have cost my parents a fortune, and it was money they could ill-afford, but I was to have the best and be given every opportunity to shine. The teacher told my mother I had a 'high instep', which was her kind way of saying I was hopeless without causing offence. I had really good fun as an aspiring prima ballerina, although the bit I most looked forward to was after the class when my mum took me to the café downstairs for a toastie and juice while she had a coffee out of a squat glass cup and saucer, considered the height of sophistication in the mid sixties. It was always damp and noisy in the café from the coffee machine and the windows were all steamed up, but I felt very grown-up.

I was also sent to piano lessons when I was older, with a teacher in West Nile Street, in Glasgow. My pal Elizabeth was learning the guitar and was naturally gifted, but I never got past the basics and I really regret not sticking with the lessons. I was more interested in the bar of chocolate we guzzled on the bus back to Bridgeton.

When I was seven years old, my mum and dad and Graham and I went on an impossibly glamorous and exciting adventure. We took the plane from Glasgow Abbotsinch airport to Paris, to visit my aunty Josephine. This was before the days of package holidays, and air travel was only for movie stars or the very rich. Josephine had married a cute German soldier when she was working as an au pair in Paris, and she and her husband Michael lived in Fontainebleau just outside the French capital. My mum and dad saved up hard to pay for the flights, and to buy new outfits for all of us.

In those days you dressed like a toff to go anywhere by plane. Now it's all trainers and tracksuits, but then you got done up to the nines like Lizzie Taylor and Richard Burton. There was even an air-hostess outfit for my Sindy doll just like the glamorous cabin crew on the BOAC flight.

As usual, Graham was a crowd-stopper, and besotted French women squealed and chattered about how utterly 'magnifique', 'incroyable' and 'superbe' he was, and they pinched his fat little cheeks until they were bright red.

Over the years we visited my aunt and uncle in army bases across the Continent, including the HQ of SHAPE (the Strategic Headquarters for the Allied forces in Europe) in Belgium. I couldn't help noticing that while the Americans and the Germans had terrific accommodation and looked incredibly smart in their uniforms, the British were treated a bit like second-class citizens. Sadly, it's still the same to this day. My uncle Michael is a lovely man, who speaks better English than most of us and with a hint of a Scottish accent. He had it tough winning my old granny round. She gave him a really hard time simply because he was German, but even she couldn't withstand his charm and decency.

We are a close-knit family and even had our own daft language. My dad started it when I was really young by calling a kiss a 'Gregory' after the actor Gregory Peck, because a peck on the cheek means a kiss. So we give each other 'Gregories' when we meet or say goodbye; and we also confusingly say, 'See you Oscar', meaning 'see you later'. This was after Oscar Slater, a Glasgow character falsely accused of murder in 1908 and subsequently released. That slang word has been in the family for donkey's years. I won't tell you what 'going for a Lillian' means, but suffice to say it almost rhymes with the name of the silent-movie star Lillian Gish. I think you can work it out.

We are a family of movie buffs and have to be *the* most infuriating people to watch a film with because every actor who appears on the screen causes us all to say, 'Oh, look, it's Franchot Tone/Farley Grainger/Lisbeth Scott/whoever', and then we proceed to name every film they have ever starred in, who they were married to and if there was any scandal attached to them. This can get pretty heated sometimes, and the movie is paused while we consult the Internet or *Halliwell's Film Guide*.

A big treat when I was growing up was to go to the pictures with my dad. We went at least once a week and my favourites were the James Bond films with Sean Connery and any big epic feature. Dad teased me for years after we went to see a rerun of *The King and I* because I sobbed so loudly and hard we were almost asked to leave the cinema. The same thing happened when we went to see the re-release of *Ben-Hur*. I had forgotten a hanky and used the front of my blue-and-white floral summer dress to wipe my tears when Charlton Heston's mum and sister were cured of Hollywood leprosy, which looked for all the world like a minor bout of acne.

As well as the Bond films, my dad and I went to see block-busters like *Zulu* and *2001 A Space Odyssey*. I remember queuing outside the Odeon or the Gaumont in Glasgow as the skies darkened and all the starlings made a real racket above our heads.

I also spent hours listening to music. Through his work, my dad was able to bring home one of the very first stereos, complete with headphones, and played the soundtrack of *2001 A Space Odyssey*, the movie we had just seen and talked about for hours. I couldn't believe what I was hearing. It was extraordinary, just as if the entire orchestra was in our tiny living-room. I would sit and listen to music at Elizabeth Sparks's house at the weekends and all evening after school. T. Rex, David Essex and Alice Cooper's 'School's Out' were the big favourites.

Top of the Pops was absolutely required viewing as everyone would talk about it at school the next day.

One of my pals had a yellow T-shirt with Marc Bolan's face on it, a purple collar and purple elbow patches. I would have sold my brother for that T-shirt. She also had splendid boobs before anyone else. I was still wearing a vest, as flat-chested as a boy, and was pea-green with envy.

Once a week at Strathclyde Primary School the teachers set up showers outside in the playground and made us line up to go for a wash. I thought this was great fun, especially as we didn't have a shower at home and it meant we skipped lessons, but my mother was utterly horrified. She took this as a terrible slur on herself and her squeaky-clean daughter, who was scrubbed every morning and night and went to the public baths in Ruby Street once a week.

I begged her to let me have a shower with the rest of my class. Even though it was a rather grim experience, I didn't want to be left out. All the pupils were given a lump of pink carbolic soap, with suspicious black lines running through it, and were marched into the showers in twos and had to strip off and jump in. Of course, my mum gave me a pristine bar of Pears Soap and a dorothy bag containing all my toiletries as if I was going to an upmarket spa retreat.

I often had to share the pathetic trickle of water with my pal and her wonderful breasts, and with all four of us in that cramped cubicle, I inevitably ended up getting merely damp. I suppose this was all some do-gooder's idea of cleansing the grime from the Glaswegian scruffs, but I would imagine that the chance of kids developing pleurisy and pneumonia from being outside in the freezing cold, and not having a chance to dry off properly, would have outweighed any possible benefit.

At school, I was lucky enough to have one of those truly inspirational teachers who make lessons a joy and fill you with enthusiasm. Miss Speirs must have been only in her early twenties, but she was determined to open our eyes to the big wide world beyond the East End of Glasgow. She brought in a radio so we could listen to plays and music, and she must have been among the first wave of tourists to the Greek islands back in the late sixties. She came back sun-kissed and taught us Greek dancing and Greek history and all about the food and the culture. She would come in with pictures she'd cut from magazines and ask us to write stories about them. She gave me the confidence to scribble away and not to be embarrassed about having an over-active imagination. Together with Miss Ferguson, who wore impossibly short mini-skirts and terrified the life out of me because she was so elegant, Miss Speirs put on fantastic school plays.

One year we did *West Side Story*, and as I had dark hair I was cast as a member of the Sharks gang from Puerto Rico. If the teachers thought this musical would be a bonding exercise they couldn't have been more wrong. The Jets and the Sharks battered lumps out of each other, every chance they had. The banks of the Clyde outside the school were thronged with nine- and ten-year-olds rolling around fighting and shouting in dreadful phoney American accents about 'rumbles' and calling each other 'Daddy-o'.

During school holidays or at the weekends I would go out to play in the morning and only come back when I was hungry or it was too dark to play kick-the-can, two-man hunt or football. I find it immensely sad that today parents are so worried about their children's safety that they aren't even allowed to play alone in their front garden, and my daughter certainly doesn't have the same kind of freedom that I enjoyed as a child. I wouldn't have considered allowing her to go away and play with her friends on her bike for hours on end when she was younger.

Even now Rosie is a teenager, I have strict rules as to when she has to be picked up from shopping in town or from a sleepover, and I make sure she has her mobile phone with her and that she actually remembers to charge it up and switch it on.

I'm not looking forward to when she starts going out to clubs and coming home in the wee small hours, and I can't even think about her moving out altogether. I'll be worried sick about her, but at the same time I know you have to let your children spread their wings and make their own mistakes.

Our tenement building overlooked an abandoned railway yard and we had hours and hours of fun playing over there, especially as it was the one place we were forbidden to go. There were piles of rotting timber, empty oil-drums, bits of glass and twisted metal everywhere. It was fantastic. My cousin Danny and I would use our duffel coats as capes and swoop up and down pretending to be superheroes like Batman and Superman.

My favourite game was playing 'shops' in the back courts of the tenements. We would gather up bits of glass to use as money and old tin cans filled with dirt as the 'stock'. A cardboard box was the counter and we'd use newspapers to wrap up the 'messages' – our shopping. Sometimes we filled the tins with clabber, or mud, but that was a bit messy.

I spent hours on end, especially during the summer, playing at wee shops. Eventually, thanks to my fastidious mum washing out tins and giving us old cereal packets, we had a very clean, well-run shop without a hint of clabber. We would also jump from the dikes containing the 'midgie bins' – the sheds where the rubbish was stored.

You had to jump from the sloping roof down to the ground and once, while I was being Catwoman, my feline skills deserted me and I tumbled about eight feet and knocked myself out cold. I landed on my head and gave my mum a terrible scare, so I was banned from trying to fly from one bin shed to the next. I still did it, though – you risked being branded a jessie and socially ostracised if you didn't take part in all the 'dares'.

I had permanently skinned knees from falling off my home-made 'stilts'. These were two old bean cans with string through them as handles. You clutched the string and shuffled along, but I never had the knack. I also loved to watch girls play with rubber balls against a wall. I was completely hopeless at this Olympic-standard skill of dexterity and coordination. You had to bounce the ball according to very strict rules, while singing a particular rhyme. I never got past step two, but there were awesome girls who could do 'wee burlies' and 'big burlies' without breaking sweat. This involved bouncing the ball, squatting down and even turning round and still managing to catch it.

They were the same girls who were experts at 'elastics' – multi-coloured elastic bands strung together to make a sort of skinny stretchy rope. They could effortlessly jump over every single stage of the game, even when you held the elastic up above your head and stretched on your tippy-toes. They could also jump in and out of a skipping rope with two girls at either end 'cawing' so fast their hands were a blur. One of my favourite rhymes for skipping went like this:

> Ma maw says I wis tae go
> Wae ma daddie's dinner-oh,
> Champit tatties
> Beef and steak
> Wae a wee bit currant cake.
> Came tae a river,
> Couldnae get across,
> Paid ten boab for an auld done horse,

Jumped on his back,
His bones gave a crack,
Played the fiddle tae the boat came back.
The boat came back,
We aw jumped in,
The boat capsized
And we aw fell in . . .

I also played at 'schools' during the summer on the steps of our tenement where it was cool and away from the heat of the sun. I would be the teacher and give everybody a test and then there would be a prize-giving. I spent all my pocket-money on the prizes and the kids only tolerated my bossiness because there was the chance of winning the top prize of a Mint Cracknell, which was dark chocolate with bright green mint puff candy inside; the runners-up received an Aztec Bar (a cross between a Mars Bar and a Milky Way). Both of these sweets are no longer with us, along with Tarzan Bars, Spanish Gold and Tobermory Tatties.

Tarzan Bars were coated with chocolate and came in orange, coconut and strawberry; they had different pictures of Tarzan on the front. Spanish Gold was basically a sweet that looked like tobacco. It was made of coconut strips dipped in cocoa powder and sugar and was sold in the same sort of packaging as grown-up baccy.

I also *loved* chocolate cigarettes, which came in a similar soft carton to real posh cigarettes. They were sticks of chocolate covered with thin white paper to look like fags. It took ages to unwrap them and they were far better than the cheaper kind of sickly white sugar ciggies, whose packets sometimes contained cards you could collect.

Grandaddy of them all was the Tobermory, or 'lucky', Tattie, a flat, rock-shaped brown lump of chewiness, dusted in cinnamon, with a teeny-weeny plastic toy embedded in the middle. Not only could you lose your fillings or your baby teeth on the chewy bit, but the toy was just the right size to choke a small child. Nowadays those sweets would have health and safety executives reduced to quivering, outraged jellies.

We also spent *ages* trading 'scraps'. You would beg, steal or borrow a big fat book and fill it with cut-out 'paper pictures' that could be bought in a sheet from the shops. They were usually big fat cherubs on clouds, angels in flowing robes or old-fashioned Santas. You and a pal would sit down and look through each other's books and 'swap scraps'. It was a serious business. If you fancied one of your pal's scraps you would stick it out at the top of the page, and the two of you would take part in the ritual of 'swapsis'. One of the aims of the game was to build up 'sets' of scraps, which was basically the same scrap in lots of different sizes, which you proudly displayed on the same page. I had a truly magnificent collection of chubby brown-haired cherubs on blue clouds. The biggest was the size of my head and the little one as tiny as a baby's fingernail. I was so proud of my collection – I wish I'd kept it for Rosie.

When I was twelve I had to make the move to secondary school, but it wasn't as traumatic as it might have been. The whole class simply shifted *en masse* from Strathclyde Primary to John Street Secondary School, so I had the same pals, we sat in the same seats and nothing much changed. It was a fifteen-minute trek across some of the busiest streets in Bridgeton, including Main Street, but in those days everyone walked to school. If your family was lucky enough to have a car your dad would be taking it to his work and certainly not clogging up the school entrance.

I remember my dad being all proud of his turquoise Zephyr with its black roof, which he had bought as a 'bargain'. One day, when we were driving back from one of our Sunday trips to the seaside in Ayr, the bottom fell out of the whole car, and he and my uncle Billy were like Fred Flintstone and Barney Rubble as they tried to 'walk' the car to the side of the road.

We had some wonderful holidays and days out on the Ayrshire coast. Our favourite place was Seamill, where we always went to the same sandy spot, put down our tartan rug, ate my mum's picnic of chicken sandwiches and hard-boiled eggs, and ran in and out of the freezing sea. During the summer we would go to a bed-and-breakfast for a week in Troon or Ayr. I remember it being sunny all the time, but it must have rained now and again. Graham and I spent ages and all our pocket money bouncing on the trampolines on the seafront. I entered the talent competition, trilled a very off-key version of 'Puppet on a String' and won 10p for my efforts, which I'm sure the organisers only paid as a bribe to stop caterwauling.

I only had a year at John Street Secondary School before we were told we had to move house. It was 1973 and some eejit thought it would be a good idea to knock down all those splendid sandstone tenements in Bridgeton and split up the close-knit communities by sending them to schemes like Blackhill, Nitshill and the new town of East Kilbride. A busybody with a clipboard and a constipated expression came round to everyone's homes to assess if they were good enough to be allowed to move up the hill to East Kilbride. My mother, quite rightly, took this inspection as an insult to her immaculate home and fat-cheeked children. We passed their stupid test, were given the rubber stamp to go to East Kilbride, and so began packing for our new life.

My grandmother and my uncle Jimmy already lived there, so at least there would be some family close by, but I was devastated. How would I cope without my pals Kim and Linda Johnston and Aileen Gallie? I had already lost touch with Elizabeth Spark as she and her family had moved to Irvine New Town on the Ayrshire coast. It might as well have been Vladivostok. We didn't have a phone, and although we wrote to each other for a while, it just wasn't the same.

Where else would I witness such colourful events as being woken up in the middle of the night and peeking through our letterbox to see a horse clattering up the stairs? The family above us were gypsies who didn't take well to living in one place all the time, and when their horse needed shelter, she was brought into their small flat. No one turned a hair.

I would miss everything. The corner shop where I was sent for Askits and Abdines, which were cure-alls for anything from a hangover to influenza. There I bought Spangles and MB Bars (a bit like a cheap Fry's chocolate cream) and stood with my finger in my mouth inwardly debating what to buy from the penny tray that patient Mrs Graham held for hours on end for all us indecisive kids.

Then there were the lunchtimes when I went to Kim and Linda's house to watch *The Jokers* and *Crown Court* on TV because they lived just across the road from our secondary school. I also loved going to Ruby Street public baths for a long hot soak in those enormous tubs, just round the corner from the library where I had first borrowed the Malory Towers and St Clare's books by Enid Blyton and chortled at the adventures of *Just William* by Richmal Crompton.

I had just started working my way through bought and borrowed classics like *1984* and *Crime and Punishment*, two books I still have at my bedside to this day, when I was told we were finally leaving. I would have to change schools, which really terrified me. As always I consoled myself by listening to music, especially a new album I had bought by Queen. *NME* had voted them the best upcoming band at the start of the seventies and I played that album, especially the tracks 'My Fairy King' 'Keep Yourself Alive' and the instrumental version of 'Seven Seas of Rhye', almost constantly during that time of upheaval.

We were allocated a three-bedroom house in Turnberry Place, Greenhills, East Kilbride. I have never ever been as cold in all of my life as I was in East Kilbride that first winter, and I've been to Alaska and Lapland, which were positively balmy by comparison. Some genius had decided that in such Arctic conditions what we needed to keep our homes warm and cosy was hot air. They had installed a truly rubbish system that cost a fortune and didn't work. The ceiling was as hot as hell because, as any little kid knows, hot air rises. The rest of the house was bitterly cold. It didn't help that my mum had painted the walls white and we had an ice blue carpet in the living-room. It was like living in a very cold igloo.

We ended up buying one of those oil heaters that look like a Dalek and constantly wheeze out smoke and foul odours, and sat watching TV in our sleeping-bags during the winter months, which generally lasted from September until early May.

There were obviously advantages to living in East Kilbride, and I'm very grateful that I spent my teenage years there because it was also where I had my big career break. For a start, in our new home I had my own room. No more sharing with my brother and my mum and dad. We had a bathroom upstairs and a separate toilet downstairs, so no more queuing.

My mum finally had a proper kitchen with a washing-machine, and we even had a garden. Well, we had a patch of solid clay with one of those whirligig washing-lines wrapped in plastic by the back door, but we had big, big plans. Inspired by Tom and Barbara from *The Good Life*, my dad and I announced to the rest of the family that we would grow carrots and potatoes and be self-sufficient in vegetables. We were so excited to plant our rows of carrots and overjoyed when the first shoots appeared, followed by lush green foliage.

Unfortunately, when we dug them up, the carrots were maggot-sized pale pretenders and the potatoes were small pebbles and as hard as rocks. My old granda thought this was utterly hilarious. He sneaked up to the house one day and buried tins of peas and carrots in the tiny vegetable patch and giggled with glee as my surprised dad dug them up.

We did plant a lawn of sorts and it was my job to mow it. It didn't take long to cut our grass as it was about eight feet square, but that tiny patch of green nearly killed me. I had to use a second-hand machine that was probably one of the first ever electric mowers to be invented. It was massive and made a noise like a jet engine in trouble and was clearly on its last legs. One day the handle fell off exposing the bare wires and, without thinking, I tried to fix the blasted thing without switching it off first. I just remember a flash and a loud bang and being thrown forward on to the path.

When I woke up I looked as if I'd gone ten rounds with

Muhammad Ali. My nose wasn't broken but it wasn't pretty and I had two black panda eyes and a swollen face, but at least I was alive. The force of the shock had flung me on to the concrete path head first and broken the circuit. My hard head had saved me. I had powder burns down to the bone on my right hand. To this day one of my fingers remains deadened and goes waxy-white in cold weather. But otherwise I was OK. I've never mown a lawn since.

At that time we were pioneers in Greenhills. There were no schools, shops, pubs or any sort of community centre. There were just lots of half-built houses and a great deal of mud, glorious mud. There was one tiny Portakabin that sold the basics, like milk, bread and sweeties, but it was a bit like being on holiday in a particularly miserable campsite. My mum was used to going shopping in Dalmarnock Road every single day and buying fresh fish from the fishmonger, meat from the butcher and everything else from Curley's, the grocery. This was a shop where butter was kept in a giant lump on the cool marble counter and carefully patted with big wooden paddles into small portions for each customer, and ham was sliced to order. It was only when my mum moved to East Kilbride in 1973 that she was taken to the town centre for her very first trip to a supermarket and the experience of the 'weekly shop'.

When we moved into our new house the buses didn't even go to the top of the hill. We were dropped off at the bottom and really struggled that first winter with the horizontal rain, hail, snow and sleet beating down on our faces. You had to stick to the pavement or you were in big trouble. I once tried a short-cut home, and went thigh-deep into a quagmire of oozing black mud. I thought I was done for. I lost one of my shoes and hirpled home, cursing the day we had moved to 'Mudhills', as we inevitably rechristened our new home, and griping that we might as well be hippos for all the wallowing we were being forced to do.

Eventually, after about a year, as more families moved in, Greenhills supermarket was built and bus drivers were finally coaxed into driving up the forty-five-degree hill, things improved dramatically. The mud was transformed with trees and grass, and I was even starting to enjoy going to my new school, although I found it hard at first to fit in.

Claremont High School was absolutely enormous, about twelve hundred pupils and I didn't know a single one. The school was a half-hour journey away by bus, and for the first couple of weeks I palled up with the 'naughty' kids at the back, who tried to be cool by smoking and uttering the occasional swear-word. My attempts to join their gang were doomed. Much to their disgust, and even though I was from Glasgow, then an exotic den of iniquity to most of the people of East Kilbride, I didn't know any new swear-words and was hopeless at smoking. I made the end soggy and blew out without inhaling, just like Bill Clinton with weed.

So, for a while I was a bit of a loner, especially as I had decided to study Russian as well as maths, physics, chemistry, English and French. I acquired a reputation as being a bit of a swot, which was socially the kiss of death. Out of the whole school, only three of us studied Russian. We had the undivided attention of our teacher Mr Porter and his assistant Madame Desilu, but it also meant we might as well have tattooed 'nerd' on our foreheads.

I had long been something of an idealistic 'Red', and when I went through to Glasgow on Saturdays for my piano lesson I always bought a copy of the *Soviet Weekly* from the same little man at the corner of Argyll Street. I was fascinated by the Soviet Union, although not so starry-eyed that I didn't realise Stalin was a monster up there with the likes of Hitler, Pol Pot and Mao Tse-tung.

Funnily enough, after being bullied at primary school in Bridgeton because I was 'posh', I was now looked down upon by some of the snobbier elements in the school for being from the East End of Glasgow. It was all a bit baffling.

Once again I was lucky with my teachers. Miss McPhedran instilled a love of Shakespeare that has lasted all my life and Miss Sommers dragged me kicking and screaming though a maths O level, then a Higher (the Scottish equivalent of an A level). She gave all her pupils the golden advice to eat a bar of chocolate before an exam to calm their nerves.

I had a fearful crush on physics teacher Hamish Sommerville and used to blush bright red every time I saw him, then run away from the poor man.

Eventually I found a circle of friends, including Janice Harridan, a stunning girl with a figure to die for and a great sense of humour. We really hit it off, and the highlight of our week was a disco on a Sunday night at the local parochial church hall where we boogied to Ike and Tina Turner's 'Nutbush City Limits' and the likes of Status Quo, Be Bop Deluxe and Hot Chocolate. Our dads took turns to pick us up at 10p.m. sharp and no arguments.

You had to learn specific dances for specific songs and there was a strict dress-code. Janice and I wore high-waisted flared dark blue jeans with a turn-up at the bottom that had to be just half an inch; any more or less and you would be laughed out of the disco. You also *had* to wear a thin red belt and a striped T-shirt with a red kerchief tied at a jaunty angle round your neck. We must have looked like a couple of cheeky boyish sailors.

Janice and I went to see Steve Harley and Cockney Rebel, and her dad even made us bowler hats with the same design as the charismatic Mr Harley. Watching that concert in the old Glasgow Apollo, I would never have dreamed that one day I would be interviewing him.

When David Bowie brought out a new album I played it over and over again until I knew every single word. I still know every breath of *Hunky Dory* and *Ziggy Stardust*. I was entranced by David Bowie's rendition of 'Starman', which we re-enacted over and over again in the school playground. I loved Bowie's music and he remains at the top of my fantasy interview wish-list, but I know I'd be a gibbering wreck if he ever happened to appear on my sofa. I bought all of his albums and learned every single one of the lyrics although they didn't make a blind bit of sense to me or, indeed, to anyone else.

When Bowie released *Aladdin Sane* in 1973, I painted on my bedroom wall the front cover's iconic image of a red and blue lightning streak down his face. My mum was really good about it. She said as long as we kept our rooms reasonably neat we could do what we liked. Graham promptly painted three of his walls pitch-black and the other lurid purple. I can only apologise to the people who moved in after us.

For a bit of extra pocket money I applied for a special work permit (because I was under sixteen) and at just fourteen years old I had a Saturday job in Chelsea Girl, a chain of 'boutiques' for trendy, fashion-conscious girls of the seventies: the decade style forgot. I was given an outfit of a short brown A-line skirt and a white blouse with red cherries on it that had an enormous collar and massive puffed sleeves. I don't know how any of us got through the door with those big blouses, and in a high wind with those collars we could have taken off like kites.

I started at twelve noon on the dot, finished at four and received a crisp one-pound note in my very own pay packet – 25p an hour was considered pretty good money for a teenager back then. All I had to do was basically tidy and re-tidy the rails and look out for shoplifters. Those four hours crawled past, and I got to know every note of Pink Floyd's *Dark Side of the Moon* and *Songs in the Key of Life* by Stevie Wonder, as the two albums were played on a continuous loop.

I always had a Saturday job. It wasn't just the Calvinistic work ethic. I needed to top up my pocket money to buy LPs, sweeties and *NME*, the essentials of teenage life. After Chelsea Girl I graduated to British Home Stores, where they put me on the sweetie counter and I got into terrible trouble for giving OAPs giant bags of chocolates and only charging them about 3p. I was moved to the tights department and spent hours arranging all the stock into colours and sizes. I would growl and scowl at customers who actually dared to buy a pair and mess up my display. This was in the days where every counter had a salesgirl – it was always a girl – to help customers. It was mind-numbingly dull, and sometimes when I looked at the clock it seemed to be going backwards.

In order to make a bit more cash, I also had a stall in the Barrows in Glasgow for a short time, selling unwanted jumble that our mums, aunties and their pals donated. This market-place, home of the famous Barrowland Ballroom, was where I spent many of my weekends hanging out when I was a kid. You could buy anything from fish-hooks to curtains, and it was worth going just to hear the patter of the salesmen. Country-and-western music blared out into the street, and you could enjoy a deep-fried 'Danny's Delicious Donut' or boiled whelks in a brown bag with a long pin to dig the little buggers out of their shells. The air smelled of vinegar, boiled cabbage and burned sugar.

Janice and I didn't have a regular stall, but would turn up early on a Saturday morning, unload the car of whichever long-suffering dad had been blackmailed into giving us a lift, and wait to see if there were any free spaces. We paid a small fee for a pitch, then set about arranging our junk. That first day we made over thirty quid, which was a fortune, but all the best stuff had gone first, and we'd been charging stupidly low prices. In fact, some of the other stall-holders had been snapping up our stuff and selling it on their pitches for more than double what we'd charged them.

We lasted about a month, until our supply of jumble was cut off. To be honest, I think I blagged and sold some stuff that my mum had probably wanted to keep, but it was great fun, and the extra cash meant I could go away on my first holiday without my parents. Janice was going off with her family, so along with my pals Joyce Woodrow and Lynn Young, I went youth hostelling. We bought one of those rail tickets that gave teenagers unlimited travel for a fortnight. It cost about twenty pounds, a huge sum of money, but it meant we could go wherever we wanted, all over Scotland.

First stop was Edinburgh. It was only about twenty miles down the road, but to us it was a huge adventure. We were far too young, and too young-looking, even to attempt to get served in pubs, so the highlight of our day was a visit to Clarinda's tea-room at the bottom of the Royal Mile for coffee and a slice of home-made cake. We walked for miles around the city with our rucksacks on our backs, but for sixteen-year-olds we were shockingly naïve. None of us had a steady boyfriend (I was a really late developer in that department) and teenagers of today would have hooted with laughter at our lack of makeup and hair products. We didn't even have a hair-dryer between us.

Generally we wore cords, desert boots, tartan shirts and big jumpers. If we were going out to a disco then it was a below-the-knee skirt with an eye-watering stripy pattern and a shirt with an enormous collar and puffy sleeves. This ensemble was topped off with a clingy jumper, usually in a dingy colour, and clumpy T-bar shoes. Although I hated the music of the Bay City Rollers I did have a pair of white trousers with tartan turn-ups and a black Ben Sherman shirt with tartan trim. I thought I was gorgeous but I must have looked like a right wee hairy – Glaswegian for ladette – and the trousers were so wide round my ample hips that you could have shown movies on my backside. My mum and dad used to clutch each other and giggle helplessly when they saw me and my pals walking out the door thinking we were 'pure it'.

There were no CDs, Walkmans or iPods in those days, so teenagers actually talked to one another. We spent that whole holiday, blethering, laughing our heads off, or grumbling about the rain and lack of food. We took the train all the way up north to Thurso and sat by the sea looking out to the glorious Orkney Islands. I vowed I would visit them one day, and I've been lucky enough to travel to this magical part of Scotland many times, but in August 1977 they were out of my reach as our budget didn't stretch to the cost of a ferry trip.

Money was the only thing that caused any ruffling of feathers between us. I was in charge of finances and to this very day Joyce reminds me that I wouldn't allow her to buy a KitKat or any sweeties because we simply couldn't afford it. We were so hard up that when Joyce poured sugar on to her fish and chips by mistake in a café she had to eat it or go hungry.

Half-way through the holiday, thanks to the magic of our rail ticket, we all went home, gave our mums our dirty washing and set off again the next day. Despite a successful attempt to buy three half-pints of lager shandy in a pub in the Highlands it was a really innocent holiday. Just three pals seeing a bit of their country and having a giggle.

When we got back, it was time for big changes. We were all swotting hard to win a place at university and had decided to stay on and do sixth-form studies. When we were seventeen, Joyce and I planned to study languages, but before I could put in my university application, I saw a small advert in our local paper, the *East Kilbride News*, for a trainee journalist. Even back then I was a news junkie, and a huge admirer of the late great *Daily Express* columnist Jean Rook, a witty, waspish writer who had the most brilliantly incisive turn of phrase and carried out revealing interviews with notable figures of the day. There never has been and probably never will be, anyone to equal her. I thought it would be the most exciting and satisfying feeling to be able to air your views and opinions to millions of readers and have their feedback.

If you had told me then that one day I would be writing weekly columns for the *Sun* and the *Sunday Post*, I would have never believed it possible. I applied for the job, and my chance at least to put a toe on the bottom rung of the journalistic ladder, and somehow managed to persuade Scottish and Universal Newspapers to take me on. I learned later that my mum and dad were disappointed that I didn't go to university, but they never said a word and wished me all the best in my new job. Thankfully, a few years later my clever brother went to Edinburgh University when he was only seventeen, so they had a photograph on their mantelpiece of a child in a funny hat clutching a scroll on graduation day.

For my first real job my mum gave me money for a new outfit and my aunty Carol bought me a necklace in the shape of a reporter's notebook. Her partner, my uncle Neil, insisted on called me 'Scoop' and I bought new pens and pencils, which I sharpened to lethal points in anticipation of front-page leads. On my first day in my first proper job I was up early feeling sick after worrying all night. I was also in agony because of my new clothes. The cowboy boots were too tight and killing me, and I was hot, itchy and sweaty, thanks to my brand-new woollen polo neck and tight fawn cords. This ensemble was topped off with a thick (and somewhat whiffy) second-hand Afghan coat. It brings me out in hives to just to think about it.

The office was quite dark, smoke-filled, and all you could hear was the clacking of typewriters and the thud of darts hitting the board. Through the gloom I saw two figures hunched over their desks, engrossed in typing out their stories, and two men playing darts with fierce concentration. No one paid me any attention at all, even though I looked as if I was walking on broken glass while suffering the effects of a virulent fever. They weren't being unfriendly, just working to a deadline, and the darts game was being played for serious money.

If you have seen one of the many adaptations of *A Christmas Carol* featuring a certain Ebenezer Scrooge, you'll have a flavour of what our working conditions were like. Everything was a dingy brown. The walls were stained from years of inky-fingered hacks smoking like chimneys. The desks were chipped and battered, and everything was dusty. It smelled a bit like the inside of an old man's underwear drawer.

Our boss was no Scrooge, but we were all rather scared of him. Mr Barr (never Eric unless it was Christmas or New Year) locked himself into his office and only emerged to growl at us, but he was a softie at heart, as he proved time and time again, and a man who really loved his job and his patch. I was also extremely lucky in my workmates. Chief reporter Jim Morrison, Joanna McKerragher, Mike Barr (no relation to the editor) and Graham Crawford taught me interview techniques and how to write a gripping opening paragraph, but most importantly they instructed me in the ancient art of poker, and how to drink everyone else under the table.

The *East Kilbride News* is a weekly paper and was 'put to bed' on a Wednesday. Mr Barr would collect all the copy we had painstakingly typed on small bits of paper, mark it up, and take it twenty miles down the road to the printing presses at Bathgate. Then we had to start work on next week's issue, but not before we'd had an afternoon of card games with a giant-sized bottle of Hirondelle wine.

Mike Barr had composed a little rhyme:
'Hirondelle, Hirondelle,
It's the drink that goes down well.'
Not exactly Shakespeare but it was undeniably true.

Sadly the poker school was shut down when I won fifty quid off the editor. By then I had acquired several nicknames. One was 'Poker-faced Annie', for obvious reasons, but I was also known as 'Hollow Legs Kelly' and 'Gantry Lil' for the amount and the variety of booze I could put away on a night out without getting completely guttered. This was because I was a teenager and had the constitution of a Shetland pony. There's no way I could get through even a tenth of that amount now – nor would I want to.

Like every teenager, I had done a bit of under-age drinking, but not to any great extent. Lack of money and opportunity meant that a night out would be spent nursing a half-pint of cider. Now I was working as a journalist I met my contacts in the pub, crafted my stories in the pub and socialised in the pub. Basically the pub was my second office. This was long before mobile phones and if you needed to interview someone you did it face to face, usually in the pub.

Working on a local newspaper you have to cover local crime and local politics and I have sat for hours in council offices wanting to scream with boredom. The policy and resources committee of East Kilbride district council filled me with dread. I would occasionally find a nugget of a story among all the gobbledegook and jargon, but it was a damned hard slog. I would sit there feeling a tight band across my chest and fantasise about leaping on to the table and bursting into a chorus from *Gypsy* or *Calamity Jane*.

Shortly after I started my full-time job, my mum and dad realised that they could trust me to take care of their home and of my little brother and they went on holiday for two weeks. After all, I had just turned eighteen and was a responsible adult. Big mistake. I decided to invite a couple of pals over and have a party. What should have been half a dozen mates sharing a bottle of Pomagne (a posh kind of cider in a 'champagne' bottle) and giving each other face-packs turned into a complete disaster. A gang of boozy teenagers I didn't even know gatecrashed and trashed the house. I should have called 999, but I didn't want a big fuss and knew my mum would be *mortified* to have the police at her door. Eventually the gang grew bored and scarpered, leaving behind devastation. There were beer cans everywhere, toilets overflowing and cigarette burns on my mum's carpets and treasured sideboard. A window had been kicked in and the kitchen was like a landfill site.

With Graham helping me, I managed to tidy up most of the debris, but there was nothing I could do about the burn marks or the window. Luckily my editor, Mr Barr, showed his cuddly side. He called in a favour with the council, and the window was fixed the day before my parents were due back. But I couldn't hide from my mum and dad that the equivalent of a drunken tornado had rampaged through their house.

When they arrived home, all tanned and relaxed, I really did just want the ground to open up and swallow me. If they had ranted and raved and given me a well-deserved boot up the backside it would have been better, but they just looked so upset and disappointed, and my mum burst into tears. I felt like the lowest worm. My dad had worked really hard to buy decent furniture and my mum took such care of our house but I had just dismissed all of their hard graft. I was forgiven, but it was a major breach of trust and they never left me in charge again.

Part of the deal of my working at the *East Kilbride News* was that I went to college in Edinburgh for three months of the year. This meant I could enjoy student life without the worry of having to find a job at the end of it. I stayed with Nancy and Colin Walker, two of the best people I have ever been lucky enough to meet. Nancy was the cousin of my first boyfriend,

Brian Kennedy – a smashing bloke, who was not only as cute as a button but really made me laugh. We went out with each other for about two years, but when I started work on the newspaper we drifted apart. We stayed friends, though, and he put me in touch with Nancy. She and Colin made me so welcome, and it couldn't have been easy for them, having a daft teenager bouncing around in their gorgeous new house and coming home late after a boozy session in Edinburgh's notorious Rose Street. I ate them out of house and home, played Elvis Costello too loudly, and was basically a terrible nuisance.

It was at college that I went though a pretendy punk phase and would buy black tights, rip them carefully and try to copy Debbie Harry's wardrobe. I once went out in a black bin-bag tied at the waist with a red scarf. I used about two cans of hairspray to keep my hair in a gigantic bird's nest and way too much eye-liner and blusher. I loved the Specials, Elvis Costello and Madness, and I was as thin as a rake because of all that running around on the dance-floor to 'Too Much Too Young' and 'One Step Beyond'. It was the days of ra-ra skirts, Spandau Ballet and boys having to tuck everything into their trousers: vests, shirts and even jackets. I swear there was a boy who tucked his duffel coat into his trousers in a bid to look trendy. The sleeves of your ill-fitting jacket had to be turned up to the elbow, and the shinier the lining the better.

There were about a dozen of us on the course at Napier College in Edinburgh, from all over Scotland, working on papers like the *Dumfries and Galloway Standard* and the *Shetland Times*. We all went to classes in shorthand, public administration (just as boring as it sounds) and Scottish law. We learned how to put together a story from respected journalist Bill Allsop, who ran his classes like a proper newsroom. He was the editor and we were his reporters, and when he gave us an assignment he wanted it good enough to print. He inspired everyone to go out and be the best they could.

Back at the *East Kilbride News*, I had a chance to put all I'd learned into practice. On a local paper you can sit on your bum and rewrite press releases from the council, or you can get out and about and meet members of the community who might one day tip you the wink about a good local story. During my time at the paper I had to cover a charity event that turned into a big adventure for me. The British Heart Foundation decided to launch a competition called 'The Queen of Hearts'. This was in 1980, long before Princess Diana laid claim to the title. The idea was simple. Women from all over Scotland would be asked to raise funds and awareness of heart disease and the winner would be crowned Queen and given a prize.

I had already done some work with the British Heart Foundation and thought this would be a bit of a fun, so I decided to enter the contest. I knew I would have to do something different to impress the judges, so I came up with the idea of a sponsored walk from the 'heart' of East Kilbride to the Heart of Midlothian in Edinburgh. A heart-shaped mosaic is actually embedded in the Royal Mile, the road to Edinburgh Castle, just outside St Giles Cathedral. Apparently it's good luck to spit on it, but I just thought it was a perfect journey's end for my charity walk.

My plan sounded good enough to me, but over a few drinks, my journalist colleagues declared that a walk was simply too dull and I had to do something extra-special to stand out from the rest of the contestants. Someone – I'm sure it was Mike Barr – came up with the idea that I should roller-skate the fifty-odd miles from East Kilbride to Edinburgh. We all agreed that this was a truly splendid idea. The next morning I woke up and realised I couldn't actually roller-skate the length of myself. A pair of skates was borrowed and it soon became clear that there was no way I'd pull this off. Bambi was steadier on his legs on that frozen pond. But I had already announced in the paper that it was going ahead. I could either call it off and look stupid, or go ahead and risk breaking my neck.

There was no choice. I went ahead. I borrowed a pram, one of those big old-fashioned ones, and used it like a Zimmer Frame to enable me to stay on my feet. It took me nearly two days to hirple to Edinburgh. Going uphill was a real struggle as I had to dig in with the front of the skates like a mountaineer going up Everest. I vowed never again to do anything so completely daft. How was I to know that I would go on to complete three marathons and six twenty-six-mile walks more than a decade later?

The stunt worked and I was voted Queen of Hearts, complete with a tiara and a sash. My prize was a ten-day trip to Rio de Janeiro, in Brazil, staying at a hotel on the Copacabana beach. I took my mum with me for a girlie trip, and as we touched down at the airport there was a gaggle of photographers and camera crews. I thought this was a bit OTT for a girl who had simply won a competition in Scotland, but they were actually there to interview Ronnie Biggs, the infamous Great Train Robber who had fled to Brazil to escape British justice.

The notorious robbery had taken place in 1963 and Biggs was sentenced to thirty years in jail, but escaped from Wandsworth prison two years later and ended up in Rio. He was hitting the headlines again because of a failed attempt to kidnap him, and had managed to return to Brazil.

When the mass media heard my mum and me asking what was going on, they realised we were from Britain and turned to us for a comment. My mother delivered the kind of soundbite that makes reporters want to kiss an interviewee. She was brilliant and appeared on news bulletins in Brazil and the USA, giving a deep and meaningful insight into the mind of the Great Train Robber whom she had never met in her life, and a potted history of the entire event in a crisp twenty seconds. I obviously inherited my sense of ease in front of the camera from her.

It was an incredible holiday, even though I almost drowned while I was *paddling*. A giant wave knocked me on to my backside and I couldn't get up again. I eventually staggered back to my sunbed with a bum full of sand.

The time we spent in Rio gave me a real taste for travel, and now we blow most of our money on holidays. I don't go to fancy resorts and wallow in five-star luxury at the kind of place where you find celebs in their glitziest swimwear, hitting the beach with perfect hair and makeup and sucking in their bellies for the paparazzi they know full well are lurking in the sand-dunes. My best holidays have been whale-watching in Alaska, shopping in Japan and going on safari in Botswana. I enjoy travelling to places where you aren't cosseted, but have to struggle a bit with the language and make an effort to do some independent sightseeing. It is my dearest ambition to go to Siberia and to Antarctica one day.

Spending time in South America with my mum helped me get to know her a lot better, but I also realised that it was about time I gave her and my dad a break, cut the family ties and moved into a place of my own.

CHAPTER THREE

On the Ladder

In the autumn of 1983 I was on the bus back to East Kilbride after a night out in Glasgow when I noticed that the patch of land opposite the bus station had a sign saying 'flats for sale'. Although they weren't even built yet, you could buy a piece of the sky that would come fully carpeted throughout and with a fitted kitchen. It wasn't cheap. The total cost of this one-bedroom rabbit hutch was more than £20,000, but it was right in the heart of the city and, being so small, required very little in the way of furniture. There was a brand-new cooker and a fridge, and a washing-machine and all included in the price, as well as carpets throughout. It was a hell of a lot more than my mum and dad had had when they'd first started out.

They were brilliant, and said I could take all the furniture from my bedroom with me to save on buying new stuff. Once my dad and my uncle Billy had put the bed in place, there wasn't any room for anything else in the bedroom apart from my chest of drawers, which, thankfully, was rather narrow. My parents also bought me a TV, and my great-uncle 'Big Billy', or 'BK', fitted a shower in the bathroom.

I bought a leather sofa for a tenner from the Saturday 'snips' in the *Evening Times*, a coffee-table with a dent in it, and a damaged tiny round white dining-table and four chairs that cost all of fifteen pounds in the MFI sale, and I was all set.

The day after I signed the papers on my 100 per cent mortgage, and worked out that if I ate nothing but air every other day I would just about be able to afford my monthly repayments, I got a call from the BBC to go in for a job interview for a new show they were launching. I had been pestering the Beeb for at least a year and a half, applying for every single job I could find in the *UK Press Gazette* and the in-house magazine, *Ariel*. I had travelled all the way up to Aberdeen for an interview to be a farming correspondent, and impressed the board no end with my shocking lack of knowledge of all things rural. I sat and blithely lied during interview after interview, saying that I was born to be a sports/politics/economic/industrial/cookery expert. I had a fistful of knockbacks, but I thought that eventually they'd be so fed up with seeing me they'd cave in and give me a job.

And that was what happened. After the interview, I was asked if I wanted to join BBC Scotland as a researcher for *Sixty Minutes*, which would replace *Reporting Scotland*. The show didn't last very long but, of course, I didn't know that then. All that concerned me was that I would be working on TV and for the British Broadcasting Corporation. As you can imagine, I was beyond excitement.

I loved working on the *East Kilbride News*, and by then I had my own page, which I wrote, subbed and laid out, and was considered one of the 'old hands'. Fresh-faced teenagers were coming in and snapping at my heels, and I knew it was time for me to move on at the grand old age of twenty-four. The bad news was that the Beeb didn't exactly shower you with money when you started as a lowly researcher and my salary was around four grand a year, over a thousand pounds less than I was being paid on the newspaper, and I was already stretched to the limit with the mortgage on my new flat. It was, however, an offer I couldn't refuse and I would just have to find another way of making money.

I knew my mum and dad would help if I asked them, but I wanted to stand on my own two feet and they had given me more than enough over the years. Rescue came in the form of the most delightful, camp, sweet man in Glasgow. Gary Woffenden was the manager of Charlie Parker's diner and offered me a job as a waitress at the going rate of a pound an hour. Gary was a true character, who would answer the door of his flat dressed as Mary Magdalene and expect you to belt out the first few lines of 'I Don't Know How to Love Him' before you were allowed inside.

He also went through a *Midnight Express* phase, and if you have seen the movie you will know what was expected when he invited you to 'walk the wheel' with him as you came into the hall. He had marked out a large circle in the centre of the floor and you had to trudge round it with him, pretending to be a prisoner in a Turkish jail, just like in the movie.

During that summer Gary decided to have a 'garden party' in the tiny patch of communal scrubland at the back of the block of flats. A garden party meant that we drank our lager from a glass, rather than the tin, and the crisps were in bowls instead of being eaten straight from the packet. Gary was very, very strict on dress-codes at his parties. He issued an edict that everyone had to wear shorts to this particular do. Those turning up in trousers were given the choice of either going home to change or cutting the legs off their jeans. It was up to them how skimpy they wanted to go, but no shorts, no entry. Of course, everyone shrieked and giggled and went ahead and cut up their trousers anyway.

Gary was a flame that burned very brightly and, sadly, he died far too young. He was a kind and generous man and gave me a lifeline with that waitressing job. Not only would a pound an hour come in very handy, but I would also be eating at the restaurant so I was guaranteed at least one good meal a day. Also, Charlie's was just off George Square and less than five minutes' walk from the flat, so I had no transport costs.

Only one snag. This was one of Glasgow's trendiest bars and eateries and I didn't really fit its image. The other waitresses were tall, long-legged blondes who looked sensational in the uniform of grey and purple shorts and shirts. They glided from table to table in high heels, their hair and makeup immaculate.

I was a small, round, bespectacled figure, whose idea of putting on slap was to pinch my cheeks, throw on some mascara and a slick of ChapStick. There was no way my bunions would cope with even five minutes in a pointy stiletto, so I was given special dispensation to wear flat shoes and not required to tuck my blouse into my shorts. I was permanently covered with bruises on the outside of my thighs from banging them on the corners of tables. I only ever worked in the diner and never in the bar, which I was very glad about as it was filled with yuppies throwing their money around and drinking overpriced bright blue and green cocktails topped off with cream.

Waitressing is bloody hard work, and I don't think I've ever grafted so hard for so little for so long. The hours were tough, but I was young, and after work at the weekends I usually headed to Bennet's nightclub for a quick drink and a boogie to unwind. As it was a gay club, you knew the music would be good and you could let your hair down without having to worry about being chatted up. We danced to the Human League, Grace Jones and Heaven 17.

I would have certainly been the worst waitress in Glasgow if my best pal Joyce hadn't narrowly beaten me to the title. She went to Strathclyde University during the day, worked at the Spaghetti Factory at night and also suffered from bruising of her outer thighs. When I went to the restaurant where she worked while on a first date, expecting to be fussed over and perhaps even get a free drink, she managed to spill an entire bowl of grated Parmesan into my open handbag. It still smelt of baby-sick a year later.

My first day at the BBC was utterly terrifying.

Whenever you start a new job there's that horrible lost feeling of not knowing where the toilets are and not being able to find the canteen and not having a clue who's an arsehole and who's a good egg. I had left a job where I was a vital part of the team and had juniors asking for my help and advice, but now I was the lowest form of human life and it was a bit of an adjustment to make.

Four of us had been taken on as researchers: Alan Little, Connie Henderson, Dorothy Parker and me. The others seemed far more efficient and confident than I was, apart from Alan who looked as though he'd slept on the floor all night and hadn't quite woken up. We were all soon to discover that there was a lot more to this intelligent young man, and he was clearly on a fast track to becoming one of the Beeb's big stars. Indeed, he has gone on to be one of the best and most highly respected journalists the Beeb has ever produced, and his reports are outstanding.

Alan is also the partner of Sheena Macdonald, a towering presence in British journalism, who fought her way back to health from a near-fatal accident in 1999, when she was hit by a speeding police car and suffered severe head injuries. Her recovery has been extraordinary and inspirational.

Back in 1984, the four of us found ourselves in a tiny room with one phone between us and no idea what the job entailed. We soon discovered that, basically, we were to be used like terriers, sniffing out stories and making them stand up. We also had to check on events like press conferences or PR stunts and see if they were worth covering. Everything had to be checked and rechecked, including travel distances, the best person to interview, and even whether or not there were sockets to plug in the lights. Woe betide us if we told the reporters we'd found an excellent interviewee who then clammed up in front of the camera or turned out to be less than articulate.

During my short stint at the BBC, I watched the beginning of a hugely successful broadcasting career. Kirsty Wark was one of the most highly rated young producers at the time. When a studio revamp was under way and they needed someone to sit behind the newsdesk to check the lighting, Kirsty happened to be on site. She was drafted in and did a dummy run for the technicians. She was so outstandingly good that the bigwigs knew they had found a star.

Meanwhile I was throwing a party at my little flat in honour of a very important event of my own. A small salary rise had allowed me to buy some curtains, those pink velveteen affairs from the back of the Sunday supplements that cost about £1.99 a week for around three months. There was a slight hiccup on the evening when Joyce and I scraped together enough money for a couple of bottles of wine and she was sent to the 'offie' to buy them. She came back with the alcohol-free kind by mistake, and we were in a real panic. Thankfully, a gaggle of delightful queens turned up with sparkly Cava and Twiglets, so the party was saved.

I spent my first six months at the BBC in a state of rigid tension, terrified out of my wits of doing something wrong, until I came across a cutting in a local newspaper all about a farmer whose cows had started dying, and who blamed it on a nearby chemical company. This story was made into a documentary for a programme called *Focal Point* – inevitably referred to by us lowly hacks as *F★★k-all Point* – and fronted by David Scott, a legendary reporter and producer who taught me so much about how to cut through bullshit and get to the truth, and how to put a story together.

I didn't do much more than shadow David, but when the documentary was complete, there on the screen was my first ever credit as a researcher. It gave me a lot of much-needed confidence to work with someone like him and so, a couple of weeks later, when I was called into the big boss's office I thought I was going to be promoted and maybe even allowed to do some on-screen reports.

I had been sent out a few times to do 'vox pops', where you accost members of the public and ask them a daft question, usually for the 'and finally' slot at the end of the programme. I asked traffic wardens what their romantic secrets were for Valentine's Day and policemen about fashion trends, and was generally thought of as someone the public would happily talk to. So, I went into the meeting with high hopes.

The boss, George Sinclair, looked at me sternly over the top of his glasses and I could tell right away that this wasn't going to go well. He told me in no uncertain terms that he thought my accent was horrible. I was too 'Glasgow' and would never make it in broadcasting if I didn't go for elocution lessons.

Although it sounds very odd now, back in the mid-eighties it was most unusual to hear a regional accent, even on BBC Scotland. The reporters either had a posh Edinburgh twang or a kind of Scottish lilt that didn't really exist anywhere but on the telly. Certainly no one spoke like me. There were no Geordies, Liverpudlians or people from Yorkshire on network TV. Most TV stars, like Sue Lawley who was brought up in the West Country, worked damned hard to erase every trace of their native accent, because it was the only way to get any work. I was devastated, but George had actually done me the biggest possible favour and I will be for ever in his debt.

I also received the best possible on-the-job training at the BBC and will always be grateful for the months I spent there. Without that, I would never have had my career in television. But realising there was no future for me at BBC Scotland, I looked around for another opportunity.

It just so happened that TVam were looking for a Scottish reporter. Unlike many, who dismissed breakfast TV as fluff that no one would be bothered to watch, I thought TVam was exciting and exotic. I didn't find out until much later that, until I joined, the finest hour of the Scottish outpost was to have booked a man who sang into his own washing-machine, but by then I was utterly committed to early-morning TV.

I picked up the phone and asked if I could speak to the boss, Greg Dyke – who went on to become Director-General of the BBC – and asked him to give me a job. Where I got the nerve to just call him up out of the blue I'll never know. It's certainly not something I would be able to do today.

I was asked to come down to London on 16 August 1984 for an interview. All the way down on the sleeper I went over and over what I was going to say and didn't sleep a wink. Mind you, no one does on those trains unless they've at least a few nips of the finest malt inside them, but I wasn't going to risk turning up for the biggest interview of my life with a raging hangover.

Since I had spoken to Greg Dyke, he had been replaced by Bruce Gyngell, a charismatic and eccentric Australian who would come to be known as the 'Pink Panther', thanks to his fondness for all things pastel. I went into the interview armed with a list of Scottish stories that I would have put forward for that morning's edition of TVam if I'd been working on the show, as well as a fistful of feature ideas. That had been part of my job remit at the Beeb and the panel seemed impressed. I was then asked to do a dummy report about a train crashing into the studio in Camden Lock, and I must have bumbled through it somehow because they offered me the job.

When I asked Bruce if my accent would be a problem he looked at me as though I was plain daft. 'You are bloody Scottish, aren't you?' he bellowed. Bruce always sounded as though he was shouting into a gale. 'What the hell else would I want you to sound like?'

I realised then that this was my kind of place: honest, down-to-earth and sparky.

CHAPTER FOUR

The Rough and the Smooth

Although I would be working from a small studio in Glasgow, which just so happened to be two minutes from my city-centre flat, my first week on TVam was spent in London getting to know everyone and watching the show going out live.

On my very first day Anne Diamond and Mike Morris were interviewing Bette Davis. This wasn't long before Bette died. She was a tiny bird-like figure, recovering from a stroke so her face was all twisted, but she was *Bette Davis* and I was breathing the same air as a genuine Hollywood legend. I just couldn't believe I was within touching distance of the diva who had enthralled me in classics like *Now Voyager* and *All About Eve* as she lit up the screen with dialogue that crackled and eyes a man could drown in.

Even in the eighties, you weren't allowed to smoke in a TV studio, but Bette very slowly took out a cigarette, lit up and puffed away in that terrifically affected style. A nervous producer asked Anne through her earpiece if she could tell Bette to stop smoking. Anne, quite rightly, ignored the instruction. No one told Bette Davis to stub out her fag.

In those days, the big stars came over from Hollywood and were wheeled into the TVam studio. If they wanted to promote a film or a book, there weren't that many TV outlets, so we had the pick of the crop. Often they would be flown over at huge expense by the makers of *Wogan* and we'd nab them the next day before they flew back to LA. So the likes of Sammy Davis Junior, Gregory Peck and Lauren Bacall all appeared on the sofa to talk to Anne, Nick Owen, Mike Morris and Richard Keyes.

I had five days in London and even made the air with a voice-over report on unrest at the Ravenscraig steelworks in Motherwell, a story I was to cover extensively over the next few years. I also booked Julie Newmar, who played Catwoman in the cult US TV series *Batman*, to come into the studio and sit on the sofa. I had a long chat with her on the phone, but didn't let on that I used to dress up as her as a kid, using my duffel coat as a cat-cape. I wrote a brief for the presenters, sorted out her hotel, wake-up call and car to the studio, and would even have fed her a bowl of Kit-e-Kat and double cream should it have been required.

I turned up to meet her the next morning, with my stomach in a knot in case she was late. I finally relaxed once she was on the sofa and telling stories about Batman and Robin.

My first days at TVam in Glasgow were a huge learning curve. The crew, cameraman Pete Caldwell and soundman Angus Hunter, weren't quite sure what to make of this fresh-faced rookie. They were both very experienced BBC technicians and I knew I would have to win them over if I was to have any chance of doing well in this demanding job.

The senior reporter was also a new recruit. Ian Kellagher was a damned good journalist and a fund of knowledge, especially about Scottish history. On the days he wasn't filming, he would disappear out the door at midday to pick up the *Evening Times* and 'have a wee sharpener'.

Essentially, Ian and I were salespeople. We basically 'sold' Scotland to our newsdesk in London. We would get into the office really early, phone our contacts in the police and other organisations, scour the papers and listen to the bulletins. Then we would make a list of all the news and sports stories in the order we thought most important, and have four or five ideas for features in case none of the news stories grabbed our editor. This was before computers, the Internet, email and satellite TV, never mind 24-hour news channels. There were only four TV stations in the UK at that time, and in the morning you had a choice of BBC *Breakfast*, TVam's *Good Morning Britain*, the Open University on BBC2, and *Channel 4 Daily*, a serious news programme that was eventually axed to make way for *The Big Breakfast*.

I was a woman on a mission, and for me a programme without some sort of input from Scotland was a failure. If it was a big story we would spend most of the previous day filming and updating the piece. It seems hard to believe now, but in the very early days before we had our own editing suite, and if we were shooting a straightforward feature or sports story, I would pop the tape in a brown envelope and drop it at the British Airways or British Midland desk at Glasgow airport, and a friendly pilot would take it on the last plane, then give it to a courier at Heathrow. Can you imagine any airline in these security-conscious days happily accepting such a package? But this was a different world, long before the terror attacks on New York and London. The tape would be rushed to TVam in Camden Lock where they would edit it overnight. Obviously, if it was a massive story we would book a line in the studio and send the pictures direct, updating them through the morning.

I could also appear live in our little studio, which looked like those Photo-Me booths in railway stations where you go to get your passport picture and always end up looking like Myra Hindley's granny. All of the studios outside London, including Manchester, Belfast and Cardiff, had exactly the same layout, with an uncomfy little cream sofa and a plastic aspidistra in the corner. We tried to jazz up our set by hiding toy animals in the dusty foliage, including a little koala bear Angus had received from a grateful Foster's lager company. I don't think anyone ever spotted our non-speaking 'tree guests' but they were there every single time we did a live link.

As a reporter, I found there was no such thing as a 'normal' day. I might have to fly to the North Sea to cover an accident, or wait outside the High Court for hours on end to film a five-second shot of the accused walking in, or spend the whole night outside a siege-hit prison. My granny Mac would see me doing my one-minute news report from half-way up a mountainside that had taken us all day to film and half the night to edit and she would always say, 'I saw you this morning on the TV and I have to wonder what you do with yourself for the rest of the day when you've done that wee bit.' She honestly thought that all I did was that one minute's bulletin in the morning, when in fact I was working my butt off. It was a brilliant job, but it did take over your whole life.

The newsdesk in London was often shockingly and woefully ignorant about Scottish news, politics and, most of all, geography. Times without number I was asked to 'pop up' to Inverness as though it were just round the corner, and I used to get calls in the middle of the night asking if I could get to Shetland in under an hour.

The whole time I worked at TVam I never owned a car, mainly because I couldn't afford one, but also because I preferred to walk the three and a half minutes it took to get down to the offices and studio in Queen Street from my wee flat. When we needed to go out filming, I would jump in the crew car. It meant we didn't have the disadvantages of travelling in a convoy and always managed to get to the location without any fuss.

About a week into the job, and with my feet barely under the table, I had my first major test. My bleeper went off in the middle of the night, and when that happens, you know you aren't going to be doing a story with a happy ending. I scrambled the crew and we headed for Glenrothes where there had been a fatal shooting.

In 1985 any sort of gun crime was a major news event and this would be leading the bulletins. As we drove to the scene I made calls to the police and scribbled down questions and ideas for my piece to camera – or ptc. There wasn't much to film in the darkness, but we got a statement from the police and enough general views – or gvs – to cobble together a 90-second package. All we had to do was record my ptc.

We only had about five minutes to get it all on tape and rush back to the studio to send the pictures down the line to London so they could be aired on the 6a.m. bulletin. As there weren't many pictures to be had, my ptc was vital. The ptc is very useful when there is nothing much to film. It is usually done as a sign-off at the end of a report with the correspondent's name and location ('Lorraine Kelly, TVam News in the Cairngorms, chilled to the bone, utterly miserable and in need of a hot chocolate . . .').

For this particular story with such a lack of footage I would have to deliver about forty-five seconds of calm, authoritative commentary straight into the lens. I was tired, freezing and wracked with nerves. My first attempt was a disaster and so was the second. I went for a walk and recited my 'lines' over and over again. I went back, took a deep breath and somehow managed to get all the words out in the right order. Sadly, there was an eejit in the background waving at his mum so I had to do it all over again. The clock was ticking, but I used all my powers of concentration and managed to nail it.

We drove back to the office just in time to feed through the pictures and commentary to be edited and on screen for the start of the programme. I felt fantastic, but it was months before I stopped suffering from those horrible nerves and started to enjoy the job.

I was also scared stiff before going off on a story, especially if it was a bad one involving loss of life. Somehow I always managed to get through it, but I worried terribly about arriving too late, missing a vital interview or not realising what the main angle was. The advice I received as a teenager from Bill Allsop at college in Edinburgh helped me enormously, as did that training at BBC Scotland, and I was lucky to have an instinct for what makes a good news story, which is something you can't really learn.

Around the time I started, TVam had their knuckles rapped by the Independent Television Commission, who used to regulate TV stations, for not having enough material from 'the regions'. Of course, we in the Scottish outpost were 'black affronted' – a wonderful Dundonian expression meaning so much more than 'outraged' – at being classed as a mere 'region', but TVam took their telling-off very seriously and immediately instigated a new policy that resulted in what the London newsdesk called 'regionnaire's disease', as bosses demanded more and more news stories and features from outside the capital.

This was a great opportunity for me to get on air and highlight some of the most quirky and interesting stories Scotland had to offer, and I was lucky that it happened just as I arrived. We were given free rein to cruise the country in search of interesting tales when we weren't filming the miners' strike clashes, poll tax demos or prison riots. Our first big trip was to the island of Barra at the bottom of the Outer Hebrides. The news angle was that Barra was in the short-list of the most beautiful islands in the world competition, so I had the perfect excuse to visit the jewel of the Hebrides. Barra is the only place in the UK where your flight times are subject to the tides, as the plane lands on the beach.

It was a perfect spring day and, out of the window of our tiny plane, it looked just like the Bahamas. The sea was clear and turquoise and the sand was pure white sugar. I was enchanted by Barra and, full of strong hot coffee and bravado, we even went swimming in the Atlantic, shouting, 'Next stop America!'

I also travelled to Islay to report on the whisky industry. I left my cameraman and soundman in one of the distilleries while I went through some questions with the manager and came back to find their eyes rolling around in their heads. The mischievous distillery workers had given them a wee nip of the whisky in its raw state and they were having difficulty standing up.

We went to Orkney to report on the world's shortest scheduled flight from Westray to Papa Westray, which takes about fifty-seven seconds. The pilot does his landing checks before he takes off and we put a clock in the corner of the screen to show how fast the flight was.

Working as a TVam reporter meant I had no social life whatsoever and I inevitably lost touch with a lot of my friends, but I never lost sight of how lucky I was to have such a plum job. At the time I was going out with a brilliant young lawyer called Cameron Fyfe. We had met while I was working at the *East Kilbride News* and instantly hit it off. He was funny, charming, handsome and great company. He is now one of the most respected lawyers in Scotland and a true champion of the underdog. He was, and is, a terrific bloke, but we didn't stand a chance.

It's tough to have a relationship when you can never guarantee that you'll be around. I lost count of the times I had to cancel dates, special occasions and functions because my bleeper had gone off and I'd had to go and report on a story because there was no one else to do it.

By this time Ian Kellagher had left and I was on my own with the crew and our secretary Elizabeth. As we were such a small team, we all had to muck in. If the newsdesk in London needed a Scottish guest in the studio, I would often book their taxi, write the background brief and get into the office in the wee small hours to let them in, make them a cup of tea and hand over a bacon roll I had picked up from the all-night café on the way in.

I would go over the questions, the guest would be miked up, plonked in front of the sad aspidistra full of furry animals and would have to deliver the interview right down the barrel of the camera lens to the presenter in London. It was difficult for people who hadn't been on TV before to cope with not seeing who they were talking to and only hearing them through an earpiece. They often looked like startled rabbits. After their four or five minutes of fame, I'd give them a pep-talk, another cup of tea and send them off in a taxi.

We'd then go off and shoot whatever big news or sports story was developing. It was hectic and demanding, but I had tons of energy and enthusiasm and didn't mind going without proper sleep for weeks on end.

I had great fun receiving the mail that came in to us at TVam. There would be letters addressed to the Head of News/Sport/Politics/Forward Planning/Features – and they would all be for me. I was once invited to a very high-powered evening at Edinburgh Castle, hosted by the then Scottish secretary Malcolm Rifkind. The big cheeses of the BBC, STV, Grampian, Channel 4 and their deputies were all in attendance, along with the supreme head of all things at TVam in Scotland, a twenty-something junior reporter.

I had been filming all day, but in a plastic bag I had my new posh frock, some mascara, lip-gloss and high heels. I got to the castle with about ten minutes to spare, rushed to the ladies' loo and gave myself a quick wash with liquid hand soap and paper towels. I've done this so often before a big, glamorous evening after I've been working, and have wondered wistfully what it must be like to have a stylist to buy your dress and someone to anoint your body with oil, then do your hair and makeup.

Anyway, I poured myself into my dress, but I hadn't realised when I grabbed it in the shop that it was scandalously low-cut at the back and I was in real danger of bum cleavage. It was also covered with glitter, which rubbed off on everything and everyone. In my haste to get ready, I ripped my tights and managed to poke myself in the eye with my mascara brush. So, half-blind, walking at a funny angle to disguise the ladder on my shin and scattering a trail of glitter, I barely made it to the before-dinner drinks.

I would love to be able to tell you that I stunned all of those bigwigs with my witty repartee, and made them all gasp with admiration at my grasp of the Scottish media and political scene but, truth be told, I felt very shy and out of my depth, and said barely a word. This was one of the few 'glam' nights, and indeed one of the very few nights out, I was ever able to have when I was working as a reporter.

Just as well, as I have never been all that comfortable at formal occasions and still find them a bit daunting.

About ten years ago I was asked to a dinner at St James's Palace in aid of the Prince's Trust, and was horrified to look at the seating plan and discover that I would be sitting right next to the Prince of Wales himself. It wasn't that long after the death of Princess Diana and rumours were rife about his relationship with Camilla Parker Bowles.

There were so many questions I would have *loved* to ask him, but you can't exactly barge in and ask the heir to the throne about his sex life over the organic salmon starter. I actually felt really sorry for him. He had the saddest eyes of any person I had ever met. We ended up talking about Scotland. I have been to the places in Lewis and Harris in the Outer Hebrides that he loves so much, and somehow the time passed, but I couldn't wait to get home.

It's just as well that I don't really enjoy getting all done up and going for big nights out, because once I started working in breakfast television I had the kind of job that simply would not have allowed me to be a party animal, even if I'd wanted to be one. I was on call twenty-four hours of every single day. I didn't even have so much as a small glass of wine of an evening because I never knew when I might get bleeped and have to rush off on a story. When that bleeper went off I had to respond instantly.

In 1986, when I had been in the job for about eighteen months, we were very excited to be given a car phone, which was 'mobile' in the sense that you could remove it from the vehicle and carry it around – if you were a weight-lifter. As well as being unbelievably heavy, it was also pretty useless as it didn't work in most parts of Scotland.

Around the same time as the mobile phone arrived, something far more important walked through the door of our tiny office. Stephen Smith from Dundee joined the crew and I instantly knew he was 'the one'. We hit it off right away because he possessed the most attractive feature of all. He made me laugh. I think we were both a bit wary of acknowledging our feelings because we were working together in such a small office and didn't want any awkwardness. Also, I think, we didn't want to spoil our friendship. It was, however, inevitable that we would be together, especially after Steve invited me on our first date to go and see Dundee United play Hearts at United's home ground, Tannadice. As a chat-up line it was original and it worked. I fell in love with the man, the team and the city.

I have always been a football fan. My dad used to take me to see Glasgow Rangers when I was a pup, and I watched legends like John Greig, Sandy Jardine, Derek Parlane and Derek Johnstone when he was a skinny wee boy. As a teenager I lost interest, mainly because of the ludicrous sectarianism of football in Glasgow. Back when I watched Rangers, they still refused to sign Catholics, and fans chanted about a battle that had taken place in 1690 between a Dutchman and an Englishman in a river in Ireland. To this day, certain Rangers supporters still chant 'No surrender' about Protestant 'King Billy' who defeated his father-in-law, the Catholic King James II, all those years ago. Then there were certain sections of the Celtic fans who openly supported the IRA and waved the tricolour Irish flag.

It made no sense to me then and it makes no sense to me now. With my parents' marriage being a mixed one, in that Mum was Catholic and Dad was Protestant, I wasn't brought up with that sort of bigotry, but I do remember one Rangers-daft girl in my class who, I kid you not, refused to go on Glasgow Corporation buses because they were painted 'Celtic Green'.

These old, old grievances are brought to the fore every time Rangers face Celtic. Efforts have been made to clamp down on this senseless bigotry, but scratch a bigoted Rangers or Celtic supporter and it still lurks there, a horrible, dank and sinister shame.

When I was growing up in Bridgeton, the build-up to 12 July, when the Battle of the Boyne was commemorated, saw Orange marching bands in the street. I had no idea what it was all about and just enjoyed the stirring music, and marvelled at the cocky young boys who twirled the massive mace and threw it high in the air before catching it expertly, and the drummers who were so dedicated they beat their drums until their hands bled.

I went to a non-denominational school, but there was a

Catholic school a few streets away and they were our sworn enemies, although no one could tell me why. There used to be regular fights and skirmishes between the two primary schools, but just before 12 July they became more serious. It was bonkers.

I firmly believe that all children should be educated together, and if they do have special religious needs these can easily be met with different morning assemblies. To split kids up from their pals at five years old only leads to conflict and suspicion. It gives bigots a chance to pollute the minds of impressionable young-sters, and until that stops you will never stamp out the scandal of sectarianism, and the deep divisions between all religions. Football pundits, especially in England, wax lyrical about the Old Firm Rangers and Celtic fixtures, and talk wistfully about the electrically charged atmosphere, when in fact this is largely down to pure, blind, blinkered hatred.

It wasn't for me.

I regained my passion for the beautiful game when Steve asked me on that first date to the Dundee United v. Hearts match. In 1986 United were the classiest team in Scotland and, under the management of Jim McLean, part of the formidable New Firm alongside Alex Ferguson's Aberdeen. McLean was a brilliant manager and his team line-up in the eighties was astonishing. He might have called United the corner shop in comparison with Rangers and Celtic, who were Tesco and Asda, but in terms of talent and ability United were fighting well above their weight.

In 1987 I watched the most perfect moment of football I think I will ever witness, when our striker Kevin Gallagher scored at home against the mighty Barcelona, with less than two minutes on the clock. The crowd did indeed go wild and the 1–0 victory was made even sweeter when we went on to beat Barcelona at home in the Nou Camp stadium 2–1. The Spanish side was managed at the time by Terry Venables, and his multi-million-pound squad included Gary Lineker and Mark Hughes. The wee corner shop had taken on Harrods and thrashed them.

It was obvious United were on a roll and playing some incredible football, and I asked my TVam bosses if I could continue to follow their European progress and send them reports on the games. Not many women covered football in the eighties and I don't think any other station would have sent such a blatant fan to follow her club around Europe, but TVam were always mavericks and this appealed to their style of broadcasting. My boss Bill Ludford gave his blessing, and I have to say that I filed some of the most biased football reports ever seen on British TV.

After we beat Borussia Mönchengladbach in the semi-finals, I was so excited that my report was a kind of high-pitched squeak that only dogs could properly register. I don't think all that many football reporters run on to the pitch and joyfully hug the players, the ref, the mascot and even the local police. Sadly, we lost the final to Gothenburg and I had to do my report through a haze of tears.

In the eighties the city of Dundee was beginning to fight back. It had been badly served by a corrupt local council who had knocked most of the beautiful buildings down to build hideous concrete carbuncles, and they had also ineptly missed out on the oil boom of the seventies and eighties that had so transformed the fortunes of Aberdeen, just an hour up the road. But there are few cities in the world with such a breathtaking setting, and that view from Dundee across the Tay lifts your heart. I loved it right from the start.

Yes, there were eyesores in the city centre, and not nearly enough decent restaurants, although that's all since changed, but there were warm and friendly pubs, and Steve had a thriving social life with some terrific characters who will always be our pals.

While we began our romance and beavered away at work in Scotland, there were rumblings in London, which led to the ACCT technical staff taking industrial action. TVam camera crews from all over the UK, in Glasgow, Cardiff, Belfast and Manchester, were also on strike. There was no question in my mind of us hiring freelances or crossing a picket line, so I obviously couldn't do any filming in my patch, and neither could the other journalists. The management's way round this was to scatter us overseas. In the London studio, office staff manned the cameras, which meant watching *Good Morning Britain* was a queasy experience. Anne Diamond linked to a lot of cartoons but she still interviewed guests while stoically having to cope with Bruce yelling in her ear: 'This is bloody boring. Wrap it up and introduce Batman.'

I was dispatched to Los Angeles to interview newly-released American hostage David Jacobsen. He had been held in Lebanon and freed due to the efforts of the Archbishop of Canterbury's special envoy Terry Waite. Since Jacobsen's release, both Terry Waite and John McCarthy had been taken hostage and TVam wanted to highlight their plight as part of the campaign for their release.

It was my first time in America and I was, frankly, terrified and overwhelmed. I didn't have a credit card in those days and wandered into the fancy-smancy LA hotel with a brown envelope stuffed full of dollars. The receptionist looked at me as though I was a barbarian.

I sat on the beach at Malibu talking to Jacobsen, a thoughtful but rather haunted man, and tried to imagine what Terry and John were going through. Years later I was able to report on their freedom but at that time Jacobsen didn't hold out much hope for their chances. I didn't even see the Hollywood sign before I had to jump on another plane and fly across the States on a red-eye to cover the Broadway opening of a new Andrew Lloyd Webber show starring Michael Crawford, which had already been a big success in London's West End.

The Phantom of the Opera is now the longest running show in Broadway's history but back in January 1988 no one really knew whether or not it was going to be a hit. I had to interview a not-surprisingly jittery Michael Crawford in his dressing-room before the opening night. The whole thing almost got off to a catastrophic start when the American soundman went to shift the iconic white phantom 'mask' from its place on the shelf. A dismayed yelp from Mr Crawford, who superstitiously didn't want anyone to touch his prop, averted a scene and we went outside to record my piece to camera. It was done in one take and I was all set to go off and have something to eat, until the cameraman shook his head, looked grave and said there was a problem.

I thought there must be a major camera fault, or perhaps we had a sound problem on Michael Crawford's interview, but apparently it was even more serious. The agonised cameraman said my hair was a bit messy and we would have to do a retake. It was windy on Broadway that night and my hair was moving around a bit. On American TV not a hair on the head of a reporter would ever have the audacity to be out of place and they are caked in Pan-Stik, lip-gloss and blusher – and that's just the boys.

I was so relieved that I could only laugh and tell him that in the UK it was all right to look less than perfect and that it was a wrap. I took them all to the nearest restaurant, which happened to be the world-famous Sardi's, and we threw vast quantities of pasta down our necks.

I hadn't slept since leaving Scotland fifty-five hours ago. I had spent just eight hours in LA, a day in New York, and now I had to get on another plane to Washington to interview a senator about abortion clinics being bombed in St Louis. A mixture of fear, adrenalin and black coffee kept me going.

After a disturbing set of interviews with the senator and concerned campaigners, who were convinced someone was going to get murdered by the fire-bombers, I headed back to the TVam bureau where the whole team were excitedly quoting lines from *Broadcast News*, the new movie starring William Hurt and Holly Hunter they had all been to see that night, which depicted the sweaty, stressful world of American TV news. I felt even more of an outsider as I hadn't seen the film and the US-based TVam gang were impossibly glamorous and sophisticated.

I had to jump on another plane to St Louis to interview the doctors at the fire-bombed abortion clinic and a very scary Pro-Life man – why are the spokespeople of these extreme anti-abortion organisations always men? – who didn't get the irony that he was trying to kill fellow human beings in order to 'save' babies from being aborted.

When I got back to Washington after recording my voiceovers and pieces to camera on Capitol Hill, I flopped into bed and slept solidly for ten hours. I went back to the office to the most terrific surprise. Steve had jumped on a flight from Scotland and come all the way to Washington just to spend a couple of days with me.

I had never doubted that he was the man I wanted to spend the rest of my life with, but one look at his crumpled wee face after that long overnight flight and I knew we were destined to be together.

When the TVam strike was finally over, we went back to work and into a series of massive stories, which began in 1987 with unrest in jails throughout Scotland. I seemed to spend most of my nights in the freezing cold outside Perth or Peterhead prisons. The siege at Peterhead was the more sinister. After a riot at the jail in October, a hard core of lifers took fifty-six-year-old prison officer Jackie Stuart hostage and threatened to cut his throat. Wearing balaclavas, the prisoners took to the rooftops and the siege lasted more than a week.

We spent all that time outside the jail, filing regular updates for our news bulletins, living on junk food and coffee. We had to do the night shift, and because at that time there was no twenty-four-hour rolling news, it was vital we had the overnight developments. Much to the relief of Mr Stuart, his family and the authorities, the siege was eventually resolved when the SAS stormed the prison and we headed back to Glasgow for a shower and a much-needed change of clothes.

I honestly don't think I ever completely relaxed during all the years I worked as a news reporter, because you simply never knew when your bleeper or your phone would go off and what would unfold. You could go from filming a rather dry industrial dispute, to flying up to Shetland to cover their world-famous Up Helly Aa fire festival, to a major disaster.

In the wee small hours of 6 July 1988 I got a call that there was a fire on an oil-rig in the North Sea. Piper Alpha was ablaze and it looked serious. We immediately headed up to Aberdeen and to

My mum, Anne Kelly – a doe-eyed beauty on her wedding day, 25 July 1959.

My dad, John Kelly – impossibly handsome and *so* young.

My formidable granny Mac – what style!

My favourite picture of all time. My dad and my uncle Billy in the Gorbals of the 1940s.

My granda Kelly, during the Second World War.

My granny Margaret Kelly, in her heyday.

My dad, Uncle Billy, Aunty Lydia and Aunty Carol and their pal in the Gorbals.

My dad as a baby – not crying for once. He had to be tied on to that chair with a rope because he wriggled so much.

Me and my daddy.

I am my dad's double: we both have the Kelly 'baw heid' (football head).

How cool is my mum? Look at her fabulous beehive.

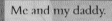
y dad striking a pose on the beach in 60. As always my mum looks chic.

Me with a greetin' face. The water would have been freezing.

My utterly adorable brother Graham who I loathed at first sight.

With Mum and Graham in Rouken Glen Park, Glasgow.

Graham aged three.

Graham and me in 1967 – my mum had cut my fringe.

Christmas morning 1969 with Dad and Graham – and our presents.

Me aged five. I loved that dress.

With my granny Mac, aged 11.

On a school trip to what was then Leningrad in 1975.

With Aunty Lydia and Aunty Carol.

The newly crowned 'Queen of Hearts' with Aunty Carol.

Graham Crawford, Joanna McKerragher, Jim Morrison, Mike Barr and me all hard at work on the *East Kilbride News*.

My granny and granda Kelly.

My granny Mac in her amazing living-room in East Kilbride.

My cool brother graduating from Edinburgh University.

My lovely mum and dad on holiday

The usual crowded TVam sofa: Mike Morris, Joan Rivers, Tom Jones, Ivana Trump and me.

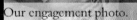
Our engagement photo.

Just married, 5 September 1992.

Our wedding day, surrounded by the TVam gang – Liza Aziz, Mike Morris, Kathryn Holloway and Katy Tayler.

My angel at just two weeks old.

I love this photo of Rosie – so cheeky

My friend Pam, the bravest woman I know, and her daughter Alison.

Steve, Rosie and me in Majorca.

Rosie as Mary in he school Nativity play

the headquarters of rig owners Occidental to find out more, and to file a news story for the next day's programme. It was quickly apparent that this wasn't just a serious fire: it was a disaster. Of the 230 men on board the oil-rig, 167 were killed.

A gas leak had caused the massive explosion that ripped through Piper Alpha. Most of those who died didn't stand a chance and were suffocated by toxic fumes. We waited anxiously in Aberdeen for the survivors, who told me stories that chilled the blood. I interviewed oil worker Mark Reid in hospital. He was badly burned and he had seen men dying all around him. Mark had tried to keep away from the ferocious heat by hiding behind a container full of tomatoes. Frantically he and the other survivors squashed them over their heads and faces to try to cool down. Eventually Mark had had to jump hundreds of feet from the heli-deck into the sea to escape the fires raging on the rig. The water was covered with boiling oil, but somehow he lived through it.

He was astonishingly brave and only concerned about other injured colleagues and the men who had died. I wanted to give him a hug but there wasn't one part of him that wasn't bandaged or burned. A few days later we hired a helicopter and flew over what was left of Piper Alpha. It was nothing more than a piece of twisted, blackened metal, impossibly fragile, and I was astonished that anyone had got out of there alive.

I honestly thought that covering the world's worst offshore oil disaster would be as bad as it would ever get, but at 10p.m. on 21 December 1988 I had a call at home from a contact to say that a plane had crashed near the border.

I knew from the start that this was going to be a bad one.

Steve and I were living together by then, so we quickly picked up fellow crew member Paul Pentland in Glasgow and drove south to Lockerbie. Reports on the crash were sketchy and we needed to get more information from people at the scene. As we got closer to the town it became obvious that a real disaster of almost unimaginable proportions had occurred.

I became aware of ambulances and saw that veteran members of the rescue services looked utterly shell-shocked. There was the smell of smoke, aviation fuel and something else too hideous to contemplate. The fleets of ambulances had nothing to do. Later they would be used to remove the dead.

We walked to the field where the nose of the plane had broken off and embedded itself in the ground. We could see clearly its name on the side: *Clipper Maid of the Seas*. This was the cockpit of Pan Am Flight 103, which had been headed for New York's JFK airport from Frankfurt via London Heathrow. The flight had been delayed at Heathrow for twenty-five minutes. The bombers had planned for the plane to explode over the Atlantic leaving no trace and no evidence. Instead it had blown up over Lockerbie.

We had arrived so quickly the police hadn't had time to set up barriers. There were dead bodies scattered everywhere and the only reason we didn't all break down was because it looked and felt like the set of a disaster movie.

This was so alien to any experience any of us had ever had that it felt completely unreal. I think that saved us all. I recorded a piece to camera beside the broken cockpit. We filmed as much as we could, then went to the burning houses in Lockerbie where debris from the explosion had rained down.

At least two houses had vaporised and others were on fire. As long as I kept filming, asking questions, interviewing local people and emergency workers, I didn't have to think about the horror of what had happened, and the sheer scale of the human tragedy. Two hundred and fifty-nine air passengers and crew had perished and eleven residents of Lockerbie had been killed in their homes.

Later, at the inquest, we heard that a few passengers had very briefly survived the explosion, decompression and disintegration of the aircraft. A mother was found cradling her dead child, two friends were holding hands and some others were discovered clutching crucifixes.

I know that somehow I put a story together, and that Steve, Paul and I drove to Carlisle to feed the pictures to London.

I know we had to stop to change a tyre that had burst on debris from the explosion that littered all the roads in and out of Lockerbie.

I know we checked into a hotel and didn't sleep for at least four days, but I honestly don't remember any of the details.

I think your mind protects you from the most hideous and gruesome sights. One scene does stick in my mind, though: we filmed residents taking down their Christmas decorations. There would be no celebration in Lockerbie that year.

We stayed in Lockerbie over Christmas, but my dad came to pick me up and take me home for the afternoon of Christmas Day. I had been keeping the horror to myself, but on the two-hour journey home I didn't draw breath, just poured out all the shock and horror of covering such an enormous tragedy. I kept thinking about the young American students on their way home for Christmas, and the crew looking forward to a break. Then there were the people of Lockerbie who had died on the ground, watching TV and never suspecting what was about to rain down on them from the sky.

While I was doing my job, it would have been unforgivable of me to be crying for the dead or becoming angry at the vile bombers who murdered so many people, but I certainly grieved and raged behind closed doors. For a long time, I had flashbacks to that first night and to the grisly sight of bodies scattered in fields around Lockerbie, but when you're a news reporter you have a job to do and it would be highly inappropriate and self-indulgent to be overwhelmed on air, or to break down.

That doesn't mean you can't be compassionate. Michael Buerk's deeply moving reports from the famine in Ethiopia, which sparked Live Aid, show the power of pictures combined with exactly the right words.

As is often the way in TV, my coverage of the Lockerbie disaster led to me becoming a presenter, and it is something that still makes me uneasy. Out of death and destruction, I received a big break and eventually went on to win my dream job. It didn't feel right then, and it still doesn't feel right today. I had the lead story on every TVam news bulletin, and did live reports throughout the morning from Lockerbie for weeks.

In January 1989, just over a month after the disaster, I was asked down to present the 6–7a.m. 'Daybreak' slot on TVam on my own. Although by then I had a lot of live reporting under my belt, this was a whole new ball game. I flew to London the day before and ran through possible items with the day team, then went back to the Holiday Inn in Swiss Cottage. I asked for a 3.30a.m. alarm call as I needed to be in the studio by 4a.m. to go through the papers, look at tapes and scripts and discuss the running order.

Of course, being a worrier, I didn't sleep a wink and tossed and turned all night, terrified I was going to make an absolute fool of myself in front of the entire nation and that I would either freeze on air or start burbling utter nonsense. When I got to the studios, I had the whole hair-and-makeup experience. As a reporter I would run a comb through my hair, slap on some powder so I didn't have a shiny nose and maybe a slick of lip-gloss and a smudge of mascara. I was simply too busy to bother with what I looked like, and wore clothes that were practical, comfortable and warm. Throwing a reasonably decent coat on meant you could get away with wearing fleeces and trackie bottoms and you always asked your cameraman not to show your tackety boots.

It being the eighties, makeup was a serious business, especially in a TV studio. *Dynasty* was the most popular TV programme in the world at that time and everyone wanted to look like either simpering blonde Krystal or bitchy, ballsy Alexis, as portrayed by the legendary Joan Collins. The makeup team at TVam were brilliant. They had to work at a time of day when people aren't exactly at their best and try to transform them into human beings basking in the 'eternal sunshine' that Bruce Gyngell demanded.

Brenda Yewdell and Simon Jay were miracle-workers, but in keeping with eighties' trends, they had to plaster on the slap. And when they had finished with my hair, it looked as it had been ceremoniously lowered on to my head. It was a gigantic football, thick with enough lacquer to create its very own hole in the ozone layer. Seeing photos of myself as a girl in her twenties at the fag-end of the eighties, I honestly think I looked a hell of a lot older than I do now.

Women on TV were into that whole 'power-dressing' thing. Those bright, big-shouldered jackets with buttons the size of dinner plates, tight black pencil skirts and high heels, combined with the thick makeup and immovable hair, were horribly ageing. I was given a gorgeous if eye-popping canary-yellow suit that cost more than my entire existing wardrobe as a TV reporter, and a pair of uncomfortable high-heeled black court shoes that made me walk like Dick Emery. Thank God I would be sitting down for the duration of the show and not have to do the ridiculous 'standing news' of today that makes me yell, 'Sit down!' at my TV.

I read through the newspapers and marked out stories that would be good for the papers' review, and reread my notes and all the questions I had written down for the guests. This is a typical rookie mistake and one I quickly discarded. If you write your questions down you're tempted to read them out to your guests rather than just talk to them in a conversational way. You will also be tempted to stick to the order of your questions, another big no-no. These days I might write a couple of words down to jog my memory, but my golden rule is to *listen* to what the person is saying to me, whether it's George Clooney or the man with the world's biggest marrow. I know that sounds ludicrously obvious, but you would be surprised at the number of TV and radio hosts who don't open their ears, and it makes for a very self-indulgent and rather dull interview.

So there I was with all the copies of that day's newspapers, my copious notes, my big hair and bright red blusher, and my stomach doing its best impression of a washing-machine. I had heard people say that your knees knock together with nerves, but I'd never really believed them until then. I was glad I was sitting behind a desk so that people couldn't see me shaking and quaking.

On a live TV news programme you need to wear an earpiece so that the producer, director and production assistant can talk to you. It's called 'talkback' and you can have it open so that you hear absolutely everything, including the director talking to the camera operators and the runner asking what everyone takes in their tea and what sort of choccie biccies they'd like. You can also have switch talkback so that you only hear what you absolutely need to and the director and producer can switch you on and off.

I prefer 'open' as I like to know what's going on in the gallery, and it means they can't talk behind your back and snigger about your bright yellow outfit or scary hair.

At that time, I'd had some experience of talkback as a reporter, when the director gives you a cue to let you know you are on air and the PA gives you a time count and tells you to wind up and stop talking, but I'd never experienced it in the studio. It takes a bit of getting used to, but now I find it easy to listen to people talking in my ear while I'm on air even while I'm asking a question or listening to the answer. It's also useful to get a heads-up when a link to LA or New York has gone down, or if a guest is stuck in traffic, or a piece of tape isn't ready. This kind of thing happens virtually every day, but hopefully you will never know because we just juggle the items and move on to something else.

Do, however, watch out for me wittering on about *Coronation Street*. I might have a smile on my face, but this is very, very bad. It means we have no guests, no tape that works and no live links, and that I'm frantically filling in time until we can safely go to a commercial break. It happens more often than you'd think. I believe, however, that it's far better to acknowledge there's been a balls-up if it's patently clear that something is amiss.

When I was interviewing our showbiz reporter Jackie Brambles, who was in Cannes for the film festival, there was a naked man in the background of the live shot. Clearly it would have been ridiculous for me not to mention to Jackie that there was a man waving his willy around and mooning behind her. We made a joke about it. I told anyone of a nervous disposition to avert their eyes, then changed my mind and said there was nothing much to see anyway.

Being able to cope with open talkback is a very useful skill. It drives my husband crazy when I'm watching TV or reading the paper and can conduct a conversation with him but not miss anything on screen or on the page. It's also very good for earwigging on other people's conversations in restaurants or at functions.

TVam believed in giving people a chance to prove they could cope with the demands of a live TV show, and if you wanted to be a presenter, you would eventually be given an opportunity. I had fallen into sitting in the hot seat because of my Lockerbie coverage and because regular presenters were on holiday. I would either sink or swim, because everyone was far too busy to hold my hand.

That first morning is a bit of a blur, but I do remember talking very fast and galloping through the items far too quickly. I think I went to the 6.30 news at 6.15, and I'm pretty sure we had to steal at least one guest from later on in the show because I had romped through all my interviews at a head-spinning rate of knots. After I had chirpily thrown to the main show with Mike Morris and Kathy Tayler, I found I could hardly stand up. My legs were wobbly and I was so tense that even my hair hurt. Everyone was really kind to me, but it was clear they thought I'd be on the first plane home to Scotland and, to be honest, I completely agreed with them. Although I hadn't made any major *faux pas* or fallen off the air, it wasn't exactly an award-winning performance.

Still, the bosses saw something they liked, and although there were quite a number of complaints about my accent – many from fellow Scots scandalised that a Glaswegian was being allowed to pollute their airwaves – most of the viewers seemed to like me. I was, however, amazed when they asked me back to finish the week, and over the next few months I filled in for the regular presenters when they went on holiday. Gradually the nerves eased off and I began to enjoy myself.

I was allowed the luxury of making my mistakes and learning the job on air. I made myself slow down and talk less quickly.

I have always made a point of trying to meet my guests before the show and telling them to treat the interview as a conversation with me, and ignore the cameras and crew if possible.

It's not just members of the public who get nervous. When famous actors are confronted with live TV they sometimes dissolve into quivering jelly. I had to cut short an interview with Ralph Fiennes because he was so uncomfortable with being asked questions about his film. He was a really lovely bloke and very apologetic, but when not playing a part he was a mushy bag of nerves.

Anyway, as far as the bosses were concerned, I must have done something right. I was told I had 'likeability' and that I also was very natural in front of the camera. As with the instinct for a story, I don't believe that's something you can learn. You either have it or you don't. So that summer I was asked to stand in for the host on TVam's flagship Sunday show while he was on holiday.

As this particular presenter just so happened to be the legend that is David Frost, this was an exciting if sphincter-nipping prospect. Along with Geoff Mead, who is now a stalwart of *Sky News*, I would be hosting for six weeks the Sunday news and current affairs show *Frost on Sunday*.

Geoff was brilliant to work with, a real newsman through and through but with a good sense of humour, and he was someone you could utterly rely on.

The 6a.m.–7a.m. Daybreak programme had been a big enough challenge, but this show was more than two and a half hours long and we would be tackling some really heavyweight issues. I don't think I've ever prepared so much for any programme in all my life. I read and reread my briefs and scripts and laboriously prepared all my questions. Again, there was a sleepless night and I was ready and waiting for my 3a.m. car, feeling I had done all I could to get ready for the show.

We were in makeup when our producer came through to tell us to throw away those carefully prepared scripts. There had been a major disaster on the Thames. The *Marchioness* pleasure-boat, jam-packed with young people enjoying a night out on the Thames, had been smashed into by a dredger. Details were sketchy but there were reports of bodies being pulled from the river. We would be going on air with no scripts, no guests and scant information. It was real seat-of-the-pants stuff, but the team worked very hard to make sure we quickly had eye-witness reports and reaction from rescue teams and survivors.

It was an appalling human tragedy, and all the more difficult because most of the victims were so young. In the end fifty-one people died and eighty survived. As had happened when I was covering the Lockerbie disaster, it was only afterwards that the reality and the horror sank in properly. At the time you're too busy trying to make sure you're giving out accurate information that is easily understood and asking the questions viewers need answered. It is only after the show is over that you can allow yourself to think about the young people who died and about their grieving relatives and friends. Otherwise you couldn't possibly function.

When our stint was over for the summer I went back to shuttling between Scotland and London. There was huge speculation in the press about who was ultimately going to be crowned the new 'Queen of Breakfast TV', as Anne Diamond had decided to move to her own weekend morning show and her day job was now up for grabs.

To be honest, it passed me by. I was too busy getting on with my job, but an article in the *Daily Mail* made me recoil in horror. Over the centre pages they had photographs of all the potential successors to Anne Diamond, in a sort of TV equivalent of the Grand National. There were even descriptions of our 'form' with hot favourites newsreader Liza Aziz, weather-girl Ulrika Jonsson and presenter Kathy Tayler apparently battling it out for that place on the sofa. In fact, Kathy was completely happy with her *After Nine* slot, Liza was our top newscaster and Ulrika had many other irons in the fire. She would soon leave breakfast TV to host the Saturday-night show *Gladiators*, but the press wanted a catfight and were very disappointed when none of us would play their silly game.

I was described as having the looks of a forties film star – although they didn't say which one, I suspect more Elsa Lanchester than Rita Hayworth – and being a strong contender for the 'Diamond crown'. And, in the end, I landed the job, mainly thanks to TVam's head of programmes, Bill Ludford, a gruff, no-nonsense former newspaper man who wanted a journalist in the job and was impressed by my work ethic as the Scottish correspondent.

A man of few words but with a soft centre behind that tough façade, Bill knew I had mixed feelings about being a presenter and did all he could to make it easier for me. I wasn't at all sure about moving south and perching on the sofa. I genuinely loved my job in Scotland, even though it was constantly demanding and gave me no time for any social life. And I was lucky enough to be going out with the only man who would understand when I had to leave my house at 2a.m. to go and shoot a news story, because he would be there too, operating the camera.

I have never run away from a challenge so I decided to give the sofa job a go for six months and see if it worked out. I knew there were people at TVam who didn't like my accent and even considered me rather common. People like Bill were canny enough to know that being 'common' was actually the key to my success on breakfast TV. I had the ability simply to be myself on telly and *Good Morning Britain* was one of the few shows where that was not only acceptable but a positive advantage. Back then there really wasn't anyone else who sounded like me, even in Scotland. Newsreaders and presenters were all rather posh.

Our boss, Bruce Gyngell, wasn't initially convinced that I was the right woman for the job, but he couldn't have been more generous or supportive. He sorted out a flat for me in Kensington, and kindly paid for my flights home to Scotland at weekends. It was a very strange situation for Steve and me. We went from living in each other's pockets twenty-four hours a day and working closely together to seeing one another for a couple of days a week. I would arrive home on Friday evening completely exhausted and have to go to bed at about eight o'clock like a toddler. We would have Saturday together and just be getting back to normal when I had to fly to London on Sunday afternoon. My mum said that if we managed to survive both extremes we'd be fine, and we did, but it wasn't easy and we missed each other.

During the week I had the social life of a nun. I got up at 3a.m. to go to work and usually got back to the flat about lunchtime after the show and the post-mortems. These were lively affairs with everyone chipping in on how they thought an item had gone and how it could have been improved. Everyone had a chance to air their opinion, and some of the daftest and the most successful ideas for shows would come out of these meetings.

We had three and a half hours of TV to fill every single day of every single working week and the show was a relentless machine that gobbled up ideas and energy. I always tried to go out for a long de-stressing walk in the afternoons and, as the flat was right opposite Kensington Palace and half-way between Holland Park and Oxford Street, I got to know central London really well. I was usually in bed by nine o'clock each night. If I did venture over the door it would be to a TVam event. Bruce loved the ballet and would take all his 'girls' out and book us the best seats in the house. There would be champagne and smoked salmon at the interval, but I always felt I was there under false pretences, and that the doormen wouldn't let me as I was too working class. It's really silly, but I'm still not entirely happy about going into posh boutiques or hotels, and feel horribly uncomfortable if I'm fussed over in restaurants.

Bruce was a real character. I was always a bit afraid of him, but he was an extraordinary person. He arranged free shiatsu massages for all of us, and he's the only man ever to have yelled down the corridor at me demanding that I follow his example and have colonic irrigation, then describing the process and the aftermath in more detail than I will share with you now. He could be utterly ruthless, but if you were in trouble he would do anything to help. I have known many an employee with a drink or drugs problem whom he paid for to be placed in a very posh spin-dryer to be detoxed, and he took a genuinely caring interest in any of his staff having a tough time. I remember him being very angry with me when I didn't take enough time off after the death of my grandmother. My way of coping was just to continue working, but he always said you needed time to grieve when you lost someone.

One thing that would drive him absolutely berserk was if we strayed from his rule of wearing ultra-bright, preferably pink, clothes. I remember our newsreader Jayne Irving once wore a navy-blue jacket. You would have thought she had gone on air stark naked. Bruce went completely ballistic. Likewise when I wore a black camisole under an eye-wateringly neon lime-green top he was not at all amused. He wanted the whole studio to convey that atmosphere of eternal summer, which was why we were attired like dolly-mixtures and had bright orange faces.

I was lucky enough to work with Mike Morris and Richard Keyes, who is now a top sports presenter at Sky. I did most of my shows with Mike, who was one of the most quietly professional and vastly underrated presenters on TV. He was dismissed by a lot of the critics because he didn't look like a matinée idol and just quietly got on with the job. What they failed to realise was that his real talent was in making it look easy. He had the knack of making guests relax. He is a true professional and incredibly easy to work with.

We had a system whereby if I was kicking off an interview and he wanted to ask the next question he would tap me on the leg. I would lean forward ever so slightly if I wanted to do a follow-up question, or back a bit to let him know to go ahead. No one noticed these subtle gestures, but it worked well and meant we didn't talk over one another. I learned a lot from Mike. He wasn't a show-off or an arrogant bighead and I hated it when the critics had a pop at him, because he took it very much to heart. We all did.

The late great Jean Rook, my role model from all those years ago, once said I had a voice that sounded like a glass of the finest malt whisky and I was thrilled to bits, but a couple of weeks later she said I should be sacked because I made a noise like out-of-tune bagpipes. I was really upset because I admired her so much and that sort of comment cuts you to the quick.

As a presenter at TVam I was treated extremely well. We each had a bright, comfortable office where we could answer letters and catch up with scripts and briefs, and we shared a secretary. We also had lovely dressing-rooms, which were small but so well designed that there was room for a bed, a bathroom with a shower and lots of space to hang up those brightly coloured clothes.

I never really appreciated how lucky we were until I moved to GMTV, where conditions are rather more Spartan for everyone from the big bosses to the runners. I now share a teeny room the size of a phone-box with Fiona Phillips and Kate Garraway, a couple of rickety chairs and a carpet that smells of cat wee.

At TVam, I was almost paranoid about getting my six hours'

sleep every night, and because of the crazy hours I was a real lightweight (or a one-pot-screamer, as they say so descriptively in Australia) when it came to booze. I simply didn't have a drink when I worked for all those years as a reporter and now that I was a presenter I was tucked up in bed when most people were just getting ready for a night out. The days were long gone when Hollow Legs Kelly could have drunk her way through the gantry.

There was just the one occasion when I fell off the wagon with a spectacular thud. I knew actor John Hannah (star of *The Mummy* and *Four Weddings and a Funeral*) from Claremont High School in East Kilbride. When I was in sixth year he was a blue-eyed curly-haired angel in first year and I used to take his class for registration. We met each other years later when he was on the same flight as me, on his way up to Scotland to star in an episode of *Taggart*. (If you are an actor with any connection at all to Scotland it is the law that you *must* appear in *Taggart* at least once.)

Back in London, the next week we went out for lunch with a bunch of his pals. We were still sitting in the restaurant when it grew dark, and decided to go back to John's house. We all had coffee and talked for hours. By 3a.m. I had completely sobered up and realised I needed to get to work, but I was exhausted as I hadn't had any sleep. Any normal person would have called in with 'food poisoning', but my Calvinistic work ethic ensured that I would never miss a day's work unless I was dead. I called a cab, left the rest of them still blethering and went to work.

My hangover had well and truly kicked in by the time I arrived at the studio and I was white-faced and miserable as I sat in the makeup chair and poor Brenda Yewdell had to make me look presentable.

Those two hours on the sofa were torture, but I gave an Oscar-winning performance and no one noticed that I wasn't firing on all cylinders. When we came off air Mike Morris made me a medal out of silver foil and yellow Post-it notes for performing under pressure. It was the one and only time I have ever gone on air with a hangover and it will never, ever happen again.

Being on such a successful show as *Good Morning Britain*, I was beamed into people's kitchens, living-rooms and bedrooms on a daily basis. I started getting recognised when I was out doing my shopping or waiting at the bus stop. I have always been very lucky that when people come up to me and say hello they are really friendly. They feel as though they know me, which I take as a massive compliment. I was also being asked by magazines to do photo-shoots, and they wanted to know the contents of my fridge or what I kept in my handbag. It was all very odd.

In the first proper photo-shoot I did, I was wearing a Scotland football strip and boxing gloves and pretending to thump our weather-girl Ulrika. She was clad in a Swedish strip because our teams were facing each other in the World Cup in 1990. We did a funny photograph, with the two of us pretending to box each other's ears. It made the front cover of the *TV Times* and was the very first time I had ever been a cover-girl. My mum went into John Menzies and covered up every single other magazine with that issue and bought at least a hundred copies for all her 'closest' friends. (For the record, Scotland beat Sweden 2–1, with goals from Stuart McCall and Mo Johnson.)

My next front cover was a corker. Forget *Vogue*, *Vanity Fair* and *FHM*. I was on the front of the awesome *Knitting Now ... and Crochet Too*, wearing a homemade knitted jumper and matching hat. I was as chuffed as if it were the cover of *Tatler*. I've been lucky enough to appear on the front of lots of magazines and it is a real buzz to see your fat face on *Best* or *Woman and Home*.

One of my most favourite ever photo-shoots was for *Boyz*, a fabulously flamboyant and camp magazine aimed fairly and squarely at broad-minded gay adults. It was a chance for me to get in touch with my inner diva as I was swathed in fabulous fabrics, painted, primped, preened and bejewelled, then wafted in front of a wind machine. I got to raid the dressing-up box and wanted to take everything home with me, especially the tiara and the fake-fur wrap.

I am delighted that so many gay men have watched me over the years; and was very touched when one young boy wrote to me that he wished I was his mum because he could have come out to me without being scared. He said I would have understood, totally accepted him, given him a cuddle, and then we would have gone shopping for shoes. I thought that was adorable, and I don't understand why there is still prejudice against gay men and women or transsexuals, or anyone who happens to be a bit different.

One of the most touching interviews I have ever done was in 2008 with Jan Hamilton, who used to be a paratrooper called Ian. Jan is funny, articulate and actually looks a bit like the sister I never had. She told me she had been watching me for years and that when she was learning to talk like a girl she used my voice as a sort of guide. I was really flattered. Jan is a very strong woman who has been through hell and has since become a good friend. Her interviews with me attracted a huge response and she has helped many transsexuals with her common sense and compassion.

The *Boyz* crew were hilariously funny and cheeky, but my mum caused a bit of confusion when she went into John Menzies and WH Smith looking for a copy of the magazine. At that time you could only get *Boyz* in gay bars or clubs and it was just full of willies of all shapes and sizes. It was an education for me – and, indeed, for my mum when she finally got her hands on a copy.

I did get into a bit of trouble after an interview with another gay magazine. *Attitude* did a very tongue-in-cheek chat with me and I was probably a little more forthcoming than I'd meant to be. When asked if I had ever tried 'poppers' (a concoction of amyl nitrate that can be bought in sex shops and is alleged to enhance orgasms), I replied that, years ago, someone at a night out had a little bottle of the stuff and asked me to have a sniff. I thought it smelled like nail-polish remover. I told him it was horrid and that he would be better off having a glass of *vino* or a voddie. When I was then asked if I had ever had sex outdoors, I said many years ago when Steve and I were 'winching' we might well have indulged, but just the once and it was a bit cold.

I thought no more about it until a couple of days later when Steve and I were driving up to Scotland for the weekend and he stopped at the garage to get the papers. He told me I was on the front of the *Daily Record*. Now, in our family this usually means that there's a picture of a monkey on the front of the newspaper.

Let me explain.

To this day Steve goes through the Sunday papers and will say, 'There's a lovely photo of you in the *Sunday Times*', and I will look up and ask to see it, and it will *always* be a photo of an orangutan or a chimp. So when I smiled and said, 'You aren't catching me out this time. What particular ape or monkey is adorning the front of the paper?' he looked a bit grim and said, 'No, you really are on the front, and I think you'd better read it.'

The headline was a lurid one along the lines of 'Lorraine Kelly's Sex and Drugs Confession. Turn to page three for more in-depth revelations.' When you turned to page three you swiftly found out that the 'confession' was that once someone had waved poppers under my nose and I had slept with my husband on a hillside. It hardly made me Ozzy Osbourne or Paris Hilton, but it was hugely embarrassing, especially for Steve and my dad.

It was my own fault. I had given the newspaper the ammunition with my *Attitude* interview and had only myself to blame. Their interpretation was a bit naughty, but it was my own silly fault for being so candid.

Even the *Daily Record*'s leader page said I was so squeaky clean that my sex romps were marital and I hadn't even tried anything illegal. Still, the damage was done with that front page and I was lambasted by some viewers, and teased by my friends, who thought it was hilarious that someone so strait-laced could have generated such saucy headlines.

You have to be very, very careful when you talk to the press, especially these days when so many of them are vying for a story. As I am a journalist myself I can usually spot what's coming and manage to tippy-toe through potential minefields, although I clearly failed miserably to do that when I was interviewed by *Attitude*.

One innocent remark can land you in real hot water, and you even have to be careful what you carry under your arm as you leave the studio. I was snapped looking like a bag-lady leaving work recently with a copy of the *Daily Record* under my arm. As I have been working for the *Sun* since 1999, this was a very bad move, a bit like Jamie Oliver being photographed shopping in Tesco when he advertises Sainsbury's. I now make sure that I have the 'Currant Bun's' logo well to the front if I'm ever carrying newspapers just so I'm not caught out. I don't think attention from the press is something you ever get used to. I remember being on holiday in Sri Lanka and seeing myself on the front cover of an old edition of *Woman's Weekly*, which was utterly bizarre.

Another of the joys of working on TVam, apart from the brilliant breakfasts in the canteen and the real sense of 'family', was that we were light years ahead in the ratings and stars were falling over themselves to perch on our pink sofa. One of the first A-listers I had to interview was Kirk Douglas. I was beside myself at the thought of talking to the star of *Spartacus* and *The Bad and the Beautiful*, one of the most searingly honest films about Hollywood ever made. Kirk was still a man in his prime and he was on the show to promote his latest project, a rather racy novel that had left me a bit pink-checked. *Dance with the Devil* was about a Hollywood director who had survived the Holocaust and was rogering his way through Tinsel Town. It was a pot-boiler, but a very well-written one, full of thinly disguised Hollywood grotesques and raunchy sex scenes.

Like all true stars who have nothing to prove, Kirk was delightful. He was funny, witty, polite and a joy to talk to. When I ventured that his book was a bit 'naughty' he was highly tickled, and he took great pleasure in copying my accent. Over the years I have found that being Scottish is a real asset, especially when talking to American movie stars. They invariably have an aunty from the Outer Hebrides, or a genuine and deep devotion to golf and/or whisky. I had to travel to Paris for TVam to interview Bette

Midler, and spent the whole time in our posh hotel suite telling her all about the best places to go on holiday in the Highlands with her husband and young daughter Sophie. She must have listened to my advice because they were all spotted enjoying the delights of Inverness shortly afterwards.

That interview gave me one of those 'moments' when you have to hug yourself and giggle because things are just too mad and fabulous to be true. After the show, I was whisked to Heathrow airport to catch a late-morning flight to Paris. I was wearing a Louis Vuitton suit I had bought in the sales (because it was eye-watering canary yellow and nobody other than a breakfast TV presenter could wear it). It fitted perfectly and for once I wasn't carrying any extra poundage. My hair had just been cut and my makeup was spot on. I sat in the back of the limo and looked out at the sights of Paris and couldn't believe how lucky I was. Bette was a joy to interview and I was back in the limo, on the flight to London and in my pyjamas watching the nine o'clock news that evening and wondering if I had simply dreamed my Paris trip.

Another fantastic experience I had at TVam was working with one of my favourite bands of all time. The Cure were off on a tour of America and their record company wondered if we would be interested in filming them. I volunteered for the job even before I was told the added bonus that the boys were travelling on the QE2 to New York because they hated flying. The combination of the Cure and the QE2 was unlikely but irresistible.

The band, led by Edward Scissorhands lookalike Robert Smith, might have looked a bit scary with their black outfits, spiky hair and white faces, but they were adorable, and really polite and well-mannered.

The *QE2* was a joy. At the end of a voyage, everyone waddles off the ship carrying excess baggage around their waists, thanks to the quality and vast quantity of the food on offer round the clock. The boys spent most of the day napping, then came out at night, a bit like bats. One of the all-time truly surreal experiences of my life was standing at the bar in the *QE2* disco with the Cure and watching lovely sixty-something ladies in sparkly tops shaking their groove to 'The Lovecats', one of the band's biggest hits.

I saw the band in concert in New York and Rhode Island then had to jump on a plane and fly to LA to interview Curtis Stigers. We did the whole interview playing his favourite game, Frisbee Golf, which I'm surprised hasn't caught on over here, because it was really good fun.

It was a mad, crazy time and I loved every minute of it.

After about a year in the job, I was told that I had made the shortlist for an award. The TV and Radio Industry (TRIC) awards are highly prized and you are judged by your peers, so I was extremely flattered, but thought I had no chance. The bash was held in the posh Grosvenor House Hotel in London's Park Lane.

TVam had taken two big tables and Bruce had insisted that my mum fly down for the event. That was typical of him, and a lovely, generous gesture. My mum was beside herself in a room packed full of celebrities, and I could see her storing up all the bad frocks, dodgy facelifts and fake sincerity so that she could have a right good gossip with her pal Betty Crawford when she got home.

The great thing for breakfast TV presenters is that the TRIC awards are always held at lunchtime, which means you can actually enjoy yourself without panicking about getting home early enough to go to bed. I was convinced I had no chance of winning, hadn't prepared any sort of speech, and was really just there to enjoy the lunch, have a proper catch-up with my mum and do some star-spotting. The event was hosted by David Frost and the award winners included David Suchet for ITV's *Poirot*, Bruce Forsyth was top BBC Personality, and Sir David Attenborough's *The Trials of Life* was voted best science-based programme of the year. This was 1991, and they are all still as popular and successful to this day. The best newcomer of the year was announced by Kevin Whately, a star of the classic comedy *Auf Wiedersehen Pet*, the sublime *Morse* and now *Lewis*. I really couldn't believe it when my name was called.

My heart was thumping so loudly I couldn't hear anything else, and I went up to the stage in a blur. I gabbled something inane, thanked the gang at TVam, cried like a baby and went back to my table in a daze. I had never won anything like this before and it really meant so much to me.

Years later, in 2006, I won the RTS best presenter award and that was another huge surprise. It was a brilliant night, made even more special because all of my team, including my producer Sophie Hodgkins and director Michael Metcalfe, were there to share it with me. Those who say awards don't mean anything are kidding themselves. It's a total blast, hugely exciting and a wonderful excuse for a party.

TVam was an extraordinary place to work and there were some legendary howlers over the years. My particular favourite, although it was very sad, involved a brave St Bernard dog. It had performed a heroic rescue of a child and was booked with its owner to come on the show. The researcher sorted out the travel arrangements and a hotel room. Sadly, on the morning of its TV appearance the shock, stress and nerves must have been too much for the poor animal, which rolled over and died in the room.

Frantic producers were up against it as the story had been trailed all morning and the nation was waiting to see the 'Bravest Dog in Britain'. There was a lot of gnashing of teeth and tearing of hair until one genius (you know who you are) decided that if the dead dog was carried into the studio and plonked on the sofa no one would realise it had expired and would just think it was either very well behaved or asleep.

This idea was actually debated for a few minutes, but thankfully dismissed or the presenters would have been interviewing a corpse. They just moved a few items around and did an extra-long newspaper review instead.

TVam used to run a 'Caring Christmas' Campaign when viewers were asked to donate a present to people in need. It was a massive success with the British public, who, as always, responded with huge generosity. During December, celebrities who appeared on the show were asked if they could bring a Christmas present with them for the campaign. The canny ones donated their latest CD or book, thus ensuring a big fat close-up of their product while appearing generous at the same time.

Those who had forgotten a gift or couldn't be bothered to bring one along, were handed a 'prop' present from a cupboard where we kept a supply in case of such emergencies. Inevitably it led to crossed wires. The French pianist Richard Clayderman hadn't quite understood the whole 'caring Christmas' premise.

As he was being miked up, a harassed researcher thrust a

pressie into his hands. The poor man obviously thought, not unreasonably, that he was being handed a gift for appearing on the show. Lots of TV shows do give out goodie bags. If you appear on *The Paul O'Grady Show* you stagger out of the studio with flowers, chocolates, champagne, Jo Malone perfume and a Buster nodding dog. Along with the sheer joy of being interviewed by Paul, it's one of the reasons people love doing his show.

Anyway, the bemused Mr Clayderman failed to hand over his gift, but instead thanked everyone for his present and walked off the set with a toaster under his arm. I'm sure he was bewildered when he got home and unwrapped it.

People often ask whether things go wrong while presenting a TV show. The answer is 'all the time' but, hopefully, you will never know. I inadvertently and unknowingly 'did a Judy Finnegan' and flashed to the nation. It was in May 2003 and I was wearing a pink top made of pretty flimsy material. The weight of the microphone caused it to slip down and reveal my bra, and a lot of my boobs, to bleary-eyed viewers.

I was talking to Trudi Goodwin and Mark Wingett, who were on *The Bill* at the time, and had to interrupt the interview to apologise for giving everyone an eyeful. My director had told me, laughing, through my earpiece that I was exposing myself to the nation and to cover up. Trudi and Mark thought it was hilarious because we had been talking about her character, Sergeant June Ackland, having been transformed into a 'sex siren' by having an affair with Mark's character, PC Jim Carver. So we had a giggle about both being strumpets, I pulled up my top and after the show put it in my pile for the Oxfam shop.

There were more bare boobs during London Fashion Week in

September 2003. Mark Heyes, *LK Today*'s brilliant stylist, and I had no idea that we had plonked ourselves right in front of the area where all the models were changing. Our viewers were treated to a gaggle of bare-breasted models blithely stripping off and clambering into designer creations.

In 1992 the whole franchise fiasco reared its ugly head. This was a truly bonkers piece of legislation masterminded by the then prime minister, Margaret Thatcher, whereby all UK TV stations had to win the right to exist by making a bid for their own air time.

Some stations were safe and wouldn't attract any bidders, but TVam was making a lot of money and attracting interest from other broadcasters and investors, who were salivating on the sidelines and waiting for the chance to compete for this juicy bone.

The deal was that this would be a silent auction and no one would have any idea what the other bidders were putting into the pot.

From the day of the announcement, the strain on everyone at TVam was horrible. We all tried to get on with the job, but always at the back of our minds was the fact that, in less than a year, we could be on the dole. We thought we were coping well, but then we started getting ill. I developed shingles, Ulrika had a suspected stomach ulcer, and everyone had aches and pains. Even stalwarts like Richard and Mike were feeling the pressure. We loved our jobs, the show was a big success, yet everything we had worked so hard for was under threat.

One by one people started to drift away. Ulrika landed her *Gladiators* prime-time Saturday-night show and Richard won his dream job of top sports presenter at Sky TV. The rest of us waited and hoped, as TVam made a bid to hang on to its very existence. Our bosses reckon they could afford a maximum of £11 million and still be a viable company. There would probably have to be cuts, but they had done the sums and that was as high as they could go.

I gave Bruce my granny's lucky sixpence and crossed every part of my body as we waited for the news. It was delivered in a terse fax. The magic sixpence had failed. We'd lost. The winners, Sunrise, had bid more than £36 million and the government had grabbed the cash. I knew that in a year I would be out of a job.

I cobbled together a tape of my 'best bits' and, armed with my showreel, did the rounds of all the TV stations and basically said, 'Gizza job.' I didn't care what was on offer, and I wasn't bothered about being on screen. I just wanted a job, any job. It was a bit humiliating, and some of the bosses I spoke to took great delight and glee in informing me that they had nothing on offer.

At BBC Scotland I was asked if I could speak Gaelic (unlikely in a woman brought up in the East End of Glasgow). They shrugged their shoulders and said that unless I could speak Gaelic there was really nothing they could do for me. I had to fix a bright smile on my face, thank them politely and walk out the room trying to hold on to my dignity. It was only when I got outside that I allowed myself to cry.

I had a couple of months of writing letters, making calls, banging on doors and having them shut firmly but ever so politely in my face before rescue came in the shape of producer Peter Bazalgette. This delightfully posh, lanky and enthusiastic man later brought us *Big Brother*, but in October 1992 he was my knight in shining armour. His company had been asked to produce a show called *Top of the Morning* for Sunrise, which had by now changed its name to GMTV. It would be broadcast from 8.50 to 9.30a.m., five days a week, and the new bosses wanted me to be the presenter. The show wouldn't be on air until about a year later, in January 1993, but this offer was a lifeline. I would have job security and would still be working on breakfast TV where I felt I belonged.

TV is a funny old industry. It can chew you up and spit you out, and I was all too well aware that plum jobs like mine did not come along often.

When I got home, I realised I would still be working at TVam while preparing the new show for the people who were effectively the 'enemy'. They had told me I was their 'secret weapon' to retain loyal TVam viewers, which made me feel like some kind of double agent from MI5. I had mixed feelings about it all and worried myself sick. I was rather sheepish when I told the gang at TVam the next day and almost felt like I was betraying them – but they were genuinely pleased for me, and I discovered I wasn't the only one who had been picked off by GMTV. Many of our contributors and experts, including Dr Hilary Jones, were asked to join the new show, and the company had also been canny enough to persuade a lot of our producers and technicians to jump ship.

Those were very strange months when I had to present the show on TVam in Camden with Mike, then cross London to the South Bank for rehearsals for *Top of the Morning*. Although I felt as if I was leading two very odd lives, I had some of the best fun I've ever had on telly during that last year at TVam. Because we only had a short time left to do the show we could take risks and experiment, and having the axe over our heads led to a strong camaraderie and a certain gallows humour. We all got on well anyway, but it really was 'us against the world' that year. Viewing figures had never been better and guests were queuing up to be on the 'doomed' show because it was such a hoot.

A cartoon in the *Sun* at that time showed Mike and me lounging with our feet up on the sofa. He is wearing his pyjamas and is unshaven and I have my curlers in and am wearing a nightie and fluffy mules. Underneath it says, 'They just don't seem to care any more.' It was a very funny cartoon, but the truth was we cared more than ever. There was a real Dunkirk spirit to the show, and although we were now haemorrhaging staff, who were slowly but surely finding new jobs, we were determined to go down with our heads held high.

One very happy result of TVam losing the franchise was that Steve and I decided to get married. The end of the TV station where we had met each other and where we both still worked meant we needed something positive to look forward to. We both *knew* we would get married one day and have a right good party for all our friends and family, but we had never really got round to talking about it or setting a date. It was a weekend and I remember we were watching an old film. I had just come out the bath and was in my favourite old dressing-gown when we both said it was probably about time we got hitched, and that was that.

Steve is one of the funniest men I have ever met and he charms everyone he meets. He is a decent, straightforward, utterly loyal friend as well as being my husband and I am just glad he walked through the door of that TVam office all those years ago. He is also really thoughtful. The most romantic thing he has ever done for me involved a five-foot-tall emperor penguin.

Let me explain.

I am hugely interested in anything to do with polar exploration, especially Antarctica and the South Pole. I have a massive collection of books and memorabilia on my hero Sir Ernest Shackleton, a chippy Irishman who was one of the bravest men ever to have lived. Sir Ernest first headed south in 1901 with the ill-fated Captain Scott in a ship called *Discovery*, which was built in Dundee.

They failed to make it to the Pole; Shackleton was struck down with scurvy and almost died. The two of them became rivals, and most observers at the time thought it would be a straight fight between them both to see who would be first to reach the South Pole. No one had counted on the wily Norwegian Roald Amundsen, who told everyone he was heading north but swerved south with his pack of lean, fit dogs that would drag him all the way to the winning-post.

Shackleton almost made it to the Pole as leader of his own 'Nimrod' expedition in 1908, but knew that if he didn't turn round he and his men would surely die. He reckoned that his wife Emily would have 'preferred a live donkey than a dead lion'. Scott and his men made it to the Pole in 1911 but they all perished on the way back.

Shackleton embarked on another ambitious expedition to trudge across the Antarctic continent, and set off on his ship *Endurance* at the start of the First World War. The ship became trapped in ice in the Weddell Sea, 'like a raisin in a wedding cake', and was crushed to matchwood. Shackleton and his men used the lifeboats to sail to Elephant Island, a god-forsaken uninhabited lump of frozen rock in the middle of nowhere. He left most of his party there and, with five of his men, sailed eight hundred miles in mountainous fifty-two-foot waves and freezing temperatures to South Georgia, where they knew there was a whaling station. It was an astonishing feat of seamanship and bravery.

After sixteen days they made it to South Georgia, but they were on the wrong side of the island. Shackleton, Frank Worsley and Tom Crean hiked over unexplored mountains, exhausted, starving and bone-weary. The thought of the twenty-two men stranded on Elephant Island kept them going on that thirty-six-hour march to the whaling station at Stromness Harbour. 'The Boss' went back to rescue his men on Elephant Island and they all survived, thanks to his extraordinary powers of leadership. He is buried on South Georgia and, one day, I will visit his grave and pay my respects. This quote from Raymond Priestley sums up the man: 'Scott for scientific method, Amundsen for speed and efficiency, but when disaster strikes and all hope is gone, get down on your knees and pray for Shackleton.'

The *Discovery*, which took Scott and Shackleton on that first journey south, is now Dundee's most famous landmark. The ship has been restored and sits proudly on the river Tay at Discovery Point where there's also a brilliant museum. You can visit the ship and even hire it for special occasions and eat a meal at the table where those brave Antarctic explorers once dined. Right in front of Discovery Point there are four statues of emperor penguins with their beaks tucked under their wings as though sheltering from the icy blasts of a polar winter. I love them.

As a big surprise, Steve tracked down the artist Tim Chalk in Edinburgh and got him to make me one as a birthday present. My penguin is unique because he has his head pointing upwards and looks noble and proud. The reason Tim had to design the penguins outside the *Discovery* with their heads bowed was because Health and Safety officials were worried an inattentive passer-by would be impaled on their beaks.

No such danger with my penguin. He is my best ever pressie, even better than the gorgeous diamond ear-rings and lovely Tiffany cross Steve bought me, and even more precious than the beautiful diamond ring he gave me for my fortieth birthday to replace my original wedding ring, which had cost a hundred quid and made my finger turn green. We couldn't afford a more expensive one back in 1992.

I know people assume that those lucky enough to work in TV take their wages home in a wheelbarrow, and although we were doing fine, we were just like every young couple getting married and we had to save up our pennies. I still wear my original wedding ring: it means more to me than any number of diamonds which, after all, are just bits of squashed carbon.

I don't wear designer clothes, I don't drink fancy booze and I think paying a fortune for a handbag is completely insane when there are so many good high street 'homages' around. I love flowers and scented candles, but it's hard work to come up with a gift I really like, which is why Steve has to be so inventive.

We went all the way to Edinburgh to 'pick up my penguin' and even when we went into the artist's studio I had no idea what the present was. I thought for a horrible moment that Steve had commissioned a sculpture of me, but there in the corner was my glorious penguin. He is in my garden now, facing south as is only right and proper, and he stands guard over the fishpond. In the summer we give him oversized comedy glasses, a hula skirt and a garland of flowers; in the winter he wears a scarf emblazoned with snowmen.

I think that's real romance.

When we decided to get married in 1992, on the Monday morning Mike and I were doing our usual catch-up on air about what we'd got up to at the weekend and I told him we'd decided to get hitched. I had no idea there would be such an overwhelming reaction. This was in the days before email and texting, but lots of viewers phoned in to wish me all the best and I received so many cards and letters in the next few days offering congratulations. I was overwhelmed. You perch on your lumpy sofa wearing clothes so loud people ask you to turn them down, and you don't really think about the number of people who are watching. Our press officer, Janey Ironside-Wood, was inundated with requests from newspapers and a very reluctant Steve and I ended up posing for a photo-shoot just outside the studio on the canal.

Although I was doing such a high-profile job this was the first time I had faced a barrage of cameras and it was very odd, rather scary and not something I would go out of my way to do on a regular basis. Steve is much happier behind the camera and I'm glad the fuss didn't make him head for the hills. I remembered sitting in the presenters' office the year before, watching Lisa Aziz plan her wedding, and being amazed at the amount of work she put in with her folders and binders and colour charts.

Of course, I hadn't realised that organising a wedding is probably one of the most stressful things any woman can ever do and, like Lisa, you needed to be organised and have steely determination. I decided to do the planning by myself and I made some huge mistakes. The biggest one was the guest list.

I wanted a relatively small wedding with close friends and family. The venue, a castle in Dundee just a couple of miles from Steve's house, could hold sixty for the ceremony and reception, then another hundred for the evening party. When I drew up the list of those I wanted to invite, I completely forgot to include a couple of my cousins. In my defence, I hadn't seen them for ages, and it was a genuine mistake, but it caused a huge fuss with their mother, my aunty Jacqueline, taking umbrage and refusing to talk to my mum. This was grossly unfair as Mum had had nothing to do with drawing up the list – but then has there ever been a wedding that didn't cause some sort of family fall-out?

The dress was easy. My friend Joyce and I saw an advert in the paper for one of those wedding fairs being held in a Glasgow hotel with massive reductions on bridal gowns. We battled our way into the room where wild-eyed gibbering harridans were feverishly grabbing frocks. I saw one I liked, which had been marked down from £2,000 to £750, which I still thought was way too expensive for a frock you would wear only for a day, but I tried it on, it fitted perfectly and we hightailed it out of there.

I organised everything locally in Dundee during the weekends when I was home: the flowers, the cake, the cars, the kilt hire, the venue and a hundred and one other details. We had chosen Mains Castle in Dundee, which is a really popular venue for weddings, with a lovely courtyard and a little burn with a bridge for photos. It was built in 1562 and although it's now on the edge of a housing estate it's really tranquil and peaceful. The owners took care of the booze and food and decorated the little 'church' inside, which was a big load off my mind. I had the invitations printed in Dundee, and then I bought lots of little blue-and-white tartan bows and spent hours sticking them on individually. The Reverend Bob Wightman from the Church of Scotland – a lovely man with a face like a happy baby – agreed to marry two heathens.

I always think that when the bride and groom are having their photos taken the guests never know what to do with themselves, so my pals 'The Clan' from East Kilbride offered to provide entertainment. They are an amazing bunch of people who re-enact old battles, and long before the movie *Braveheart* they were committed to keeping the spirit of William Wallace alive.

The day before the wedding it poured with rain, but on 5 September 1992 we woke up to brilliant sunshine. Steve and all the boys had been sent away to a local hotel for the night and the house was turned into a girly sanctuary. In charge of the bedlam we had the unflappable Brenda Yewdell, our brilliant hair-and-makeup artist from TVam who gave me the best wedding present of all: makeovers for me, my mum and the bridesmaids, so we would look gorgeous for the big day. She excelled herself with my hair, sweeping it up and threading real roses through the tiara and veil, and she did my makeup so beautifully that I cried with happiness and she had to do it all over again.

I had originally told my bridesmaids, Joyce and Steve's sister Margaret, that they were wearing shiny peach taffeta with puffed sleeves and ultra-wide skirts like Anna in *The King and I*, so they were relieved and thrilled with their simple blue shot-silk dresses. I actually bought them in the sale at Harrods really cheaply, and made them weddingy by adding a big fat detachable tartan bow at the back, so they were able to wear them again.

My flower-girls were my cousin Danny and his wife Anne's

two daughters, Joanna and Carla, and I think everyone thought I had hired them from Central Casting for the day. Not only were they as cute as buttons but so well behaved. I'd had their little dresses specially made for them by designer Spencer Ralston in Glasgow. Everything else had come in under budget so I wanted to splash out a bit and make them feel like princesses.

My mum looked amazing in her new suit and hat, more like my younger sister than mother-of-the-bride.

The wedding wasn't until three o'clock but Brenda made us start getting ready at nine. She worked like a woman with six arms, and had me, Joyce, Margaret and my mum all sorted and stress-free by lunchtime with a glass of champagne in our hands. I did have one wobble in the morning when I decided that I had to go and cut down all the foliage at the front door as I was convinced I wouldn't be able to get out and down the path in my wedding dress. Joyce found me outside in my new underwear and my veil, with a lethal pair of shears in my hand, and gently explained, as though to a toddler, that we were actually going out of the back door where the car would be parked. I was talked down from the pre-wedding jitters and, thanks to Brenda, we were all ready on time.

The girls left for the ten-minute journey to Mains Castle and my dad arrived to take me in the car. He had a tear in his eye when he saw me in my dress and he said I looked like a movie star. He had a swift brandy – for his nerves – and we set off.

So many people had turned out to wish me well – little kids gave me silver horseshoes and homemade cards and good-luck charms, and all the Scottish papers were there to take photos. It was all really relaxed and joyous and the way I wanted it to be.

I know that a lot of celebs sell their weddings to glossy

magazines, but then they have their big day taken over. The brides are smuggled into the venue like criminals so that no other publication gets a photo of them in their dress, and the wedding car has the windows blacked out. Guests are even told they can't take snaps and all personal cameras are actually banned. Most of my favourite photos from my wedding are those unposed, funny, touching snaps taken by grannies, aunts and uncles.

I would have felt really uncomfortable telling my friends and relatives not to bring their Instamatics, and I would certainly not have wanted my wedding hijacked by a magazine. The trouble is, they pay an awful lot of money for the event, which means that the celebs can have the very best food and drink, flowers, wedding dresses and even a gospel choir if they so desire, but of course there's a price to pay and you aren't in control of your own wedding day.

Inside the Castle were all my friends and family, and a piper played 'Bonnie Dundee' as my dad walked me down the aisle.

It was a fantastic day. The Clan were a huge success with their blood-curdling battle-cries and fierce fighting. They also gave my aunties a thrill when they fell over 'dead' and their kilts went above their heads. These boys are true Scotsmen, wear no knickers, and I was told it was all most impressive.

My dad's speech was one of the highlights. I'd had no idea that he was so nervous about it, but he's actually rather shy and had never done anything like it before. My brother Graham, who came all the way from Singapore to be at my wedding, realised how worried he was and had a really good idea. He had one of the then newfangled camcorders and filmed my dad making his speech in the kitchen, and then they both watched it. Graham reassured him that he wouldn't make a show of himself, or embarrass me in any way (not that I would have been bothered, but he didn't want to let me down on my big day). This gave him the confidence boost he needed. It was a lovely speech. Short, sweet, straight from the heart, and really moving.

He thanked everyone for coming, especially those who had travelled so far, like Graham from Singapore and my aunt Josephine, uncle Michael and cousin Anthony from Germany, my cousins Jasmine and Maya from London and all the TVam gang from England. He welcomed Steve to the family and said he was very proud of me and that he loved me and I looked beautiful. I know my dad loves me, but he is a typical Scottish working-class man and doesn't do 'mushy stuff'. That's why it meant so much.

In the evening we had local singer Lorna Bannon and a fantastic band to entertain everyone, and my friend Allan Bryans stood up to sing a song for Steve and me. He did a blistering version of 'The Wind Beneath My Wings' that only a boy who had been a member of a band that had bid for Eurovision glory could perform.

I know the bride is supposed to leave early, but Steve and I stayed to the bitter end, waving most of our guests away, until my mum rightly pointed out that we had an early flight to catch to the USA the next day. We went back to the Sandford Hotel, across the River Tay near the hamlet of Wormit, and promptly fell fast asleep, fully clothed, on top of the bed in the beautifully decorated bridal suite.

We woke up the next morning with about ten minutes to get ready. I still had my hair up in what was now an Amy Winehouse rat's nest and there was confetti in every orifice. We were on our way to the Florida Keys for our honeymoon, the plane was on time, but it was soon clear something was wrong.

We were flying into hurricane Andrew, the second worst hurricane in US history. It killed sixty-five people and caused 27 billion dollars' worth of damage. It was, as you would expect, a pretty bumpy flight. The airport was organised chaos, and I think our hotel had been blown away, possibly to somewhere in Oklahoma, but we were offered the alternative of a rented villa in Kissimmee near Disneyland and jumped at it.

I *adored* Disneyland. I bought into every single bit of this insane, contrived, soppy, sentimental alternative universe. I loved queuing for the rides, eating junk food and meeting people dressed as mice and ducks with no trousers on. (Why *is* Donald Duck bare from the waist down?) I also thought the Disneyland idea of celebrating New Year every single night was inspired. I loved the giant burgers, turkey legs, vats of Coca-Cola and ice-creams as big as your head.

We had saved up for the honeymoon and thought we would have more than enough money for our two-week holiday, until on 16 September we went to change some sterling into dollars and found that the pound in our pocket wasn't worth the paper it was written on. A bungled economic policy by the Tory government under John Major had meant sterling was with-drawn from the European Exchange Rate. 'Black Wednesday' effectively killed off Chancellor Norman Lamont and the Tories but it hit Steve and me hard in Disneyland where our money halved in value. Sadly, I wasn't able to buy the kitsch Snow White outfit or bridal Minnie Mouse ears complete with veil, which was probably just as well.

During our honeymoon, and being a square-eyed TV addict,

I spent hours zapping on our giant US TV screen. In the UK we still only had four channels and I was transfixed by a procession of insincere Americans trying to sell me haemorrhoid cream or begging me to send them all my money so they could buy bigger, gaudier churches and larger, stretchier limos. In return they would pray for me. A twinkle-eyed pixie called Richard Simmons sobbed with enormously fat people and promised to make them thin with his 'Deal a Meal' plan, and the New York fire brigade had to knock down a morbidly obese man's house around his ears so they could crane-lift him out of the building.

I know this is all very familiar to British TV viewers today, but back then it was a ghastly revelation. I watched in open-mouthed horror as a smug host called Jerry Springer ringmastered a never-ending procession of the vilest, most foul-mouthed and utterly repellent people ever to have stunk up a TV screen. I consoled myself that it could never happen at home . . . could it?

CHAPTER FIVE

Morning Sickness

When we returned home from our honeymoon, we decided that there would be no more commuting for me, and that Steve would move down south. He had built up a very successful career as a freelance cameraman in Scotland and it was a big decision for him to give all of that up and start again in London, but we decided to give it a go. He has always been really supportive of me and I don't know what I would do without his steadying influence.

So we began house-hunting. It soon became apparent that the sale of my little flat in Glasgow and Steve's much more expensive house in Dundee, plus all our savings, would probably buy us a rabbit-hutch in most parts of central London, so we looked further afield. Ulrika Jonsson and Kathy Tayler lived near each other and I had visited them often and really liked where they had chosen to settle, close to Marlow on the banks of the Thames.

Kathy and her husband Olley had been particularly good to me when I first came to TVam and didn't know a soul. Along with Bob and Cynthia Merrilees, who also worked at TVam, they had taken me under their wing and winkled me out of the house to go for dinner and socialise during the week, and I will always remember the kindness they showed me.

Steve and I eventually found a cute little house – Chalkpit Cottage – in a Berkshire village that looked like the set of *Midsomer Murders*. In fact, some of the filming for the series actually took place in Cookham Dean, at the top of the hill. It really is a gorgeous part of the world, and our little whitewashed cottage came complete with low oak-beamed ceilings, a wishing-well and roses round the door. It was idyllic, and as soon as I stepped inside I knew it was the right house for us.

The only problem was that I was leaving TVam, starting at GMTV and moving house all in the same week, which was really bad planning. Although I can soak up stress like a sponge, this was probably at least one major life change too many. We were in our new house, sitting on deckchairs because the sofa hadn't arrived, and living on crisps and takeaways during that last week of TVam.

Although we knew it was the end of the show, somehow it didn't seem real, and even as we all cleared our desks and packed up our belongings something didn't ring true about the whole process. I think up until the very last day we expected Bruce to call us together and tell us there had been a terrible mistake and that things would be going back to normal. It just seemed completely crazy that a successful show could be killed off.

The last day of TVam was bittersweet. All the gang were there and it felt like the end of an era. Mike was brilliant and held everything together, but when it came for me to say goodbye I looked behind the cameras to where every single member of staff had gathered for the farewell party and burst into tears.

Presenter Kathryn Holloway had one piece of good news for us: she announced that she was pregnant and that really lightened the atmosphere and put everything into perspective, but it was so sad to think that we were being split up and would probably never all work together again. I would even miss that lumpy, uncomfortable, grubby pinky-peach sofa, which had had some of the most famous bottoms in the world making a dent in its cushions. Most of us didn't stay long at the farewell do as no one was really in a party mood. I left the building for the last time feeling very deflated.

Just two days later I was in a studio on the South Bank, hosting *Top of the Morning* on GMTV. The build-up to the launch of GMTV had included a lot of talk about something called the 'F Factor', which was the bizarre idea of viewers 'fancying' the presenters. The women apparently had to be sexy and glamorous.

Luckily I was well out of all of that. My *Top of the Morning* show had its own titles and identity, and as it was being made by an independent company we were pretty much left to our own devices. It was more of a lifestyle show, with lots of celebrity interviews, fashion, cookery and human-interest stories.

That first morning at GMTV was a very strange one. As I was doing the newly created ten to nine slot I didn't have to be in the building until seven, which meant leaving home around six. This should have meant an extra hour or two in bed, but of course I didn't sleep much that night due to my usual fretting and worrying. I was apprehensive about what sort of response the new programme would have, and whether the viewers would accept me in the new show. It was a cause for real anxiety, because they, of course, had no say in all of these changes, which had seen TV companies like TVS (Television South, which covered the south-east of England) and TSW (Television South West, which operated out of Plymouth in Devon) and the mighty Thames TV simply disappear overnight.

GMTV had rented a couple of floors of the LWT multistorey building on the South Bank. It was the studio that had been used to broadcast *The Saint and Greavsie* – a Saturday-afternoon light-hearted look at the world of football, which I'd never missed. Now their set had been ripped out and transformed into someone's idea of an 'ordinary' living-room, complete with a sad little pretend flickering gas fire and some distinctly odd soft furnishings. It was trying to be warm and cosy, but it didn't come across that way: it reeked of trying too hard.

Everyone, from the bosses down to the runner, was horribly tense, and this showed on air. Presenters Michael Wilson and Fiona Armstrong were consummate professionals, but at times they looked decidedly uncomfortable with the mixture of hard news and showbiz silliness. It reminded me of the disastrous launch of TVam back in 1983, with the 'Famous Five' – Michael Parkinson, David Frost, Robert Keyes, Anna Ford and Angela Rippon. Those shows had bombed and it had taken TVam years to achieve the difficult balance between news and entertainment. It's not easy to go from a disaster to an item on fashion, but with confidence and experience you can set the right tone and you can do almost anything you want without it being eggy or toe-curling.

Guests that first morning on GMTV included Ken Morley, who was a huge hit in *Coronation Street* as Reg Holdsworth, and

Rachel Hunter, the then Mrs Rod Stewart, giving her first ever TV interview. Linda Lusardi had been hired as the station's fitness queen, and she launched her 'healthy hunks' spot with Paul Gascoigne, in the days when he was a slightly pudgy but genius footballer. The teenage McDonald twins, Steve and Andy, from *Corrie*, took part in a daft competition to see who could build the highest tower made of toast and poor Fiona Armstrong had to measure their efforts with a plastic kipper.

I had a bit of a mix-up at Security when I arrived for my first day on air and was told I wouldn't be allowed in as I didn't have the right sort of pass. At TVam we knew all the boys on the door, who would give each of us a cheery wave and a 'good morning' so this was rather different. My sense of unease heightened when I thought I wouldn't even make it into the building. Eventually, after a bit of a stand-off, I was allowed in and headed for the makeup room to be turned into a human being.

To my great relief, there was Simon Jay, the miracle man with the powder puff who had been working at TVam alongside Brenda Yewdell. Seeing a friendly face really helped me that first morning, but for the first time in years I was very nervous about going on TV. I knew the critics would be sharpening their knives, but far more importantly the viewers would be making up their minds about whether to keep watching. I've been pretty lucky over the years – bad reviews are usually about my weight or my accent. I escaped the most vicious criticism initially levelled at GMTV because I was essentially doing a separate show with a different name, and everyone was concentrating on the new presenters. The old TVam gang sent a good-luck message and Bob Geldof's hugely successful *The Big Breakfast* on Channel 4 sent a crate of champagne and hot sausages.

Those first couple of days we were given a reluctant C minus by the critics, and there was to be no honeymoon period for GMTV. Fiona Armstrong unfairly bore the brunt of the criticism and was accused of looking glum and not chirpy enough. Bosses immediately told her to smile more, which was leaked to the press who started campaigns to 'cheer up Fiona'. It was all horribly unjust and it must have affected her confidence.

I liked Fiona a lot. She is a really good broadcaster, but breakfast TV is very different from reading the news and doing current affairs, and she was clearly uncomfortable with all the media attention. Being told by one boss apparently to 'stick a hanger in her gob and smile', combined with having to commute to Scotland where her husband and baby daughter lived, meant that it was never going to work for her. No one was surprised when she decided to leave after a couple of months in the job. GMTV was in freefall.

Breakfast TV has a unique relationship with viewers. People watch while they're in bed, getting dressed or brushing their teeth. They want stability and, like it or not, GMTV had 'robbed' viewers of their pals. Where were Mike Morris, Richard Keyes, Liza Aziz and Lizzie Webb? Where was the squashy pink sofa, and the comfortingly naff plastic set, with its fuzzy background and fake pastel bricks? The public just weren't happy and were switching off in droves. Things had to change.

The original management team was axed after just a few months and I found myself in the new boss's office to be told that I was being pulled from my cosy *Top of the Morning* show and parachuted back on to the early-morning sofa. I was very reluctant to make the move and not just because it would mean going back to getting up at 4a.m. I was really enjoying working on my own show with my own team. We had launched some interesting features, including our childcare 'Tots of the Morning' slot in which we planned to follow six babies all the way through until they went to primary school, and our Dating Agency had taken off like a rocket. Thanks to the three cookery items every week, I was finally learning my way round a kitchen – I felt as if I was attending my very own cookery master-class. I was working with a young, enthusiastic team and we were just getting into our stride.

I had no choice, though. I was told in no uncertain terms that the station was going down the toilet and if I didn't want to help then I was part of the problem instead of part of the solution.

Michael Wilson was given his own early-morning slot from 6 to 7a.m., and I was teamed with Eamonn Holmes, who was then presenting GMTV on Fridays and Sundays alongside Anne Davies, from 7 to 9a.m.

It wasn't the easiest set of circumstances for either of us. We felt very awkward to be replacing our colleagues, and were most uncomfortable to have the weight of rescuing the show on our shoulders. Luckily we are about the same age, although Eamonn takes great glee from the fact that I'm older than him, even though it's only by three days. It meant we grew up watching the same TV shows, listening to the same music and experiencing the same big news events. I also think Belfast and Glasgow are very similar cities, so we shared the same sense of humour and sparked off each other. But those early days were pretty grim, not just for us but for everyone at GMTV.

The station felt under siege after relentless battering by the press. My way of dealing with any kind of unpleasantness is to retreat into my shell. The papers were full of praise for the sassy, risk-taking *Big Breakfast* and GMTV was accused of being dull and dreary in comparison.

I just put my shields up, my head down and ploughed on. On the outside I looked as though I hadn't a care in the world, but I was going to work with ice in my stomach. Ratings were terrible, the atmosphere was horrendous, and it looked as though the station would collapse. I was constantly worried about what would happen if I lost my job. Steve and I had a huge mortgage on our little house. He tried to reassure me and told me not to worry, but he might as well have told the tide not to come in.

It didn't help that we had guests like the insufferable Freddie Starr, whose idea of fun was to spit water on Eamonn and inform me that I was as 'ugly as Quasimodo' before jumping on top of me. Then I had pompous Tory MP Toby Jessel inform me in withering terms that he couldn't understand my accent when I asked him a question he either didn't like or couldn't answer. Despite all the fuss and negative press over my accent when I had first joined TVam, this issue hadn't reared its head since. I was very polite and repeated the question, but was again dismissed in a most high-handed fashion.

I was really touched to see that morning's duty log – the phone calls from viewers, which are noted down and passed along to us while we are on air. It was chock-full of viewers expressing their outrage on my behalf.

The pressure at that time was truly horrendous, but we had to sit there smiling and joking and hoping that somehow we would be able to turn the ship round. It was blatantly obvious that this wasn't going to be easy, and although I wanted to help, it was clear at that time there was a culture at GMTV that dismissed presenters as mere bubble-heads and autocuties. It was an attitude I was determined to overturn.

At TVam presenters had been expected to attend debriefs and planning meetings and to come up with ideas. It was a part of the job that I really enjoyed, and still do. At *Top of the Morning* it was a real team effort. We were a strong group and, even over those few short months, had built up a real bond. We always had an informal discussion after the day's show to throw around some ideas. This is vital to the success of any show and really important that everyone has a chance to have their say about a programme you have just done, especially if you're doing the daily grind of a live news/current affairs and lifestyle show. Some of the best ideas have come out of those sessions and usually from the younger and least experienced members of the team.

After that first GMTV show, when I popped my head round the door and cheerily asked if this was where we were having the debriefing, you would have thought I'd taken all my clothes off and demanded a tattoo on my left buttock. There was a deathly hush, a distinct frost in the air, but I took my seat, smiled sweetly and would not be moved.

After a week, debriefs and meetings involving all the presenters were the norm, but I had to pretend to have the hide of an elephant that morning while shaking in my shoes.

You should always have some sort of post-mortem – no matter how brief – to sort out any problems, flag up any weaknesses and, most important of all, give praise to someone who has worked their bottom off persuading a reluctant guest to come on, or been up half the night editing a piece of tape. It is also invaluable to get feedback from everyone involved in the show and essential in establishing team spirit.

After the re-launch, viewing figures started to rise, slowly but surely, and everyone became cautiously optimistic. As the show gained in ratings, the rest of TV Land started to pay GMTV presenters a bit of attention and we were invited to appear in other shows. I was intrigued to be asked to take part in a very special skiing programme that was aimed at beginners and was sure to be a big success. I agreed to come along and do some filming for a pilot that would be shown to the bosses at the BBC to see if this was a series that they would commission. The fact that I knew nothing about skiing and had never even tried on a pair of skis was considered by the producers to be a huge advantage. I would come along with an open mind and the show would follow my progress and that of other beginners.

I hoped we might be filming in some gorgeous alpine village in France or Switzerland, or the beautiful Cairngorms in Scotland, so I was slightly befuddled when I was told to meet the crew in High Wycombe, not too far away from where I lived. I was sniffily informed that there was a dry ski slope there and that snow machines were being brought in at huge expense. Suitably chastened I went to meet the star of the show and my instructor, Jean Claude.

I was more than surprised to see a very fat, obviously unfit, chain-smoking bloke with the worst wig I had ever seen. It looked as if a jet-black, rather damp otter had curled up on top of his head and fallen asleep. He also had the most appalling fake French accent and was a real diva, demanding fags, croissants, coffee and brandy, and shouting at everyone at the top of his voice. He put me through some stupid exercises, in which I had to waddle like a duck, jump in the air like a starfish, then cover my face in brightly coloured sunblock.

Of course, Jean Claude was no more French than my cat, but he was part of an elaborate hoax set up by Noel Edmonds for his 'Gotcha' segment of the hugely popular Saturday-night *Noel's House Party* prime-time TV show. I only twigged when Noel himself, heavily disguised as a bearded snow-machine operator, covered me from head to toe with white foam. The bleep operator had to work overtime when I found out I was the victim of a 'Gotcha', but it was bloody funny.

That Saturday night I had to appear live on the show, and felt more than the usual fluttery nerves while I waited at the top of the stairs to make my way into Noel's 'Crinkly Bottom' manor house. My stomach was in turmoil. My boobs were painful, I was putting on weight and felt a bit sick. I'd gone along to *Noel's House Party* with my mum and she had a fantastic time in the green room listening to Tony Blackburn tell her that when he lived in Cookham it was a riotous place abounding with wife-swappers and swingers.

Sadly I had to drag her away as I felt so nauseous, and not just because of Tony's reminiscing. I think my mum suspected what was wrong with me, and on the way home to Scotland she asked me to phone her if I had any news. I was on my own as Steve was away working, bobbing around in the North Sea filming a documentary with Greenpeace, and it was really difficult to get in contact with him.

The next night I raided the freezer and ate six beefburgers in one go. It was obviously time to take a pregnancy test and it was positive. So there I was, a thirty-two-year-old career woman who had never changed a nappy or even held a tiny baby. When I babysat for friends and family the kids were always old enough to tell me they were allowed to eat as many sweets as they liked, didn't have to do homework or clean their teeth, and were duty-bound to stay up watching horror films until 2a.m.

I was completely overwhelmed by the news, but it felt like the right time. Steve and I were settled in our little cottage in Cookham Dean, work had turned a corner and I was enjoying my job again, so I was really happy.

I wasn't able to let Steve know that he was going to be a daddy until he returned from the North Sea, all rough and salty and windswept. I was going to do a big production number, with a table set with candles, and then I would serve up a plate with two hand-knitted baby bootees instead of dinner – I had seen it on an advert and it was lovely – but when Steve walked through the door I couldn't contain myself and blurted out that I was pregnant. He was really chuffed and, being so practical, began crawling round the house on his hands and knees looking for dangerous hazards for his unborn baby to bang into. We decided to keep the news to ourselves at least until after the first scan, just to be sure everything was fine. However, I told my bosses at work, to give them a heads-up, and the news leaked to the papers when I was less than three months pregnant, which was difficult because I hadn't even told most of my friends and family.

Luckily, I had a reasonably straightforward pregnancy and didn't suffer from morning sickness, or my job would have been impossible. It took more than an hour to get into work in the morning and I always worked in the back of the car, either reading scripts or the papers and scribbling down ideas and questions. Then there was the meeting at work before the show and into Makeup. Feeling sick was simply not an option. I never had to excuse myself and throw up over the back of the sofa while I was interviewing the Prime Minister, but I did have days, especially towards the end, when I felt a bit hot and bothered and light-headed. One morning I had to be taken outside on to the roof at LWT during a commercial break to get some fresh air.

Of course, my work ethic kicked in and I never missed a show and never complained about feeling faint or exhausted. I thought that would be letting the side down and soldiered on until I looked as if I was going to burst. Some women have lovely neat little bumps and from the back don't even look as though they are pregnant. Not me. I put weight on everywhere. I swear even my hair got fatter. I was an Easter egg on legs and at least four stone heavier. This was almost entirely due to eating far too much and spending so much time sitting on my bum. Towards the end of my pregnancy, Steve had to help me out of bed. I pretty much went to work, came home (had something to eat), went to sleep, watched a bit of TV (had something to eat), talked to the producer about the next day's show (had something to eat) and went to bed.

GMTV continued to gain viewers as I continued to gain weight, and Eamonn and I were both asked to appear as ourselves on an episode of the late lamented *Brookside*. One of the characters, Penny Crosby (Mary Tamm), was to appear on our sofa and tell all about a sex scandal involving her ex-Tory MP husband who had committed suicide. It was probably a bit too lurid for our show, but it made a brilliant *Brookie* episode. Eamonn and I were a bit nervous because we had to learn lines instead of our usual ad-libbing. But as we were playing ourselves no real acting was required.

Eamonn and I only worked together for about a year, but we did have some laughs. The day we were interviewing the then chancellor of the exchequer, Kenneth Clarke, sticks in my mind.

The next item after the chancellor's grilling was a link to Disneyland, and as we were talking about budgets and shortcomings, through my earpiece I heard our frustrated director shout in despair, 'Will you for Christ's sake tell Mickey Mouse to take a few paces to the right or he'll be out of the effing shot?' This was happening during one of Kenneth's languid and interminable answers, and I just kept thinking about poor Mickey being manhandled thousands of miles away.

One morning we had Daleks on to promote the latest campaign to bring back *Dr Who* (my fellow geeks finally succeeded and it's now one of the most popular shows on TV). During the commercial break, our director was trying to establish how the item would go. Through our earpieces Eamonn and I could hear him saying, 'OK. Coming to the Dalek in twenty seconds. Is the Dalek on talkback? Can the Dalek hear us?' and then the Dalek said, 'Yes, I can hear you', *in a Dalek voice*. Eamonn and I nearly lost it completely. It was hilarious. It was madness. But it was wonderful.

CHAPTER SIX

So That's What It's All About

The one time – so far – that Dundee United won the Scottish Cup, back in 1994, Steve and I weren't able to be there. I was due to give birth at any time and the doctor thought there was no way I'd be able to take the excitement. Also, our pal George, another fanatical United fan, had decided to get married on *the same day as the Cup Final*. All the United supporters who turned up at his wedding in Clitheroe spent the whole ceremony with headphones on listening to the radio. When Craig Brewster scored the winning goal for United the roof of the church nearly came off, at least on the groom's side.

I don't know if George's wife, Janet, has ever forgiven him for beginning his speech by saying that he was the happiest man alive as his beloved team had just lifted the cup, hastily followed by 'Oh, and of course, I got married as well.'

It was probably best that I followed doctor's orders and didn't attend the game as I'm sure I would have given birth on the steps at Hampden, and then I would have had to name our daughter Golac Van de Kamp Cleland Malpas McInally Petric Welsh Bowman Hannah McLaren Brewster Dailly Nixon Kelly Smith, in honour of the manager and our glorious team, rather than simply Rosie.

By the time I was due to go on maternity leave, I had made one of my many hair blunders and gone for a short crop, which made me, as my husband quite rightly pointed out, look like Thelma in *Whatever Happened to the Likely Lads?*. I'd hoped it would be easy to look after with a newborn baby. (Later, another style howler coincided with the Tom Hanks movie *Castaway*. Tom's only friend on his desert island was a 'Wilson' football. He drew a face on the ball and stuck some grass on its head and talked to 'Wilson' all the time. Thanks to my round face and short, tufty hair-cut I was instantly christened 'Wilson' by my cheeky husband.)

With a month to go until my due date, I was ready to quit work and put my feet up. My big plan was to have two weeks running around like a blue-arsed fly, buying all the paraphernalia that comes with a teeny tiny baby, sorting out the nursery and packing my bag for the hospital. Then I was going to watch every single Bette Davis and Joan Crawford movie ever made, which I had bought on video while at the same time eating my bodyweight in mini chocolate Creme Eggs.

Sadly, this was not to be.

I did the two weeks' exhausting marathon shop, cleaned the house from top to bottom and packed my bag for the hospital, but I never did get that fortnight with Bette and Joan. On the night of 7 June 1994, I was on the phone to Eamonn having a catch-up and a gossip about GMTV. As usual we blethered for over an hour and he told me to give him a call when I had any news. Later that night I began to have pains and knew it was time to get to the hospital.

I had decided to go to the nearest NHS maternity unit, which was in High Wycombe, a few miles up the road, close to that dry ski slope where I had made such a twit of myself on *Noel's House Party* nearly nine months before. Steve drove me to the hospital and it was all very calm. I was in the earliest stage of labour and I went into my own little world.

I arrived at 2a.m. and, after a check-up, was told to stay in and get some rest. I was checked in as Mrs Lorraine Smith, which is my married name (this leads to some sniggering when Steve and I check into hotels for a very rare naughty weekend), and was just another apprehensive pregnant woman about to give birth to her first baby. A couple of mums-to-be said they had seen me on TV and wished me well, but I was treated just like everyone else and couldn't have had better care and attention, especially from my midwife, Precious.

For the whole of the next day I was in hell. I used one of those TENS machines, which are supposed to take the edge off the contractions. I thought it wasn't doing any good until I took it off to have a bath. Steve nearly had to scrape me off the ceiling. I can't praise the staff at High Wycombe highly enough. They work stupidly long hours for buttons, but were so supportive to all the women in their care.

I went very quiet, as I always do at times of stress, and as the labour was taking so long, I was given pethidine to dull the pain. This was a horrible experience. I have never taken drugs but I would imagine that this was what a bad trip would be like. There was a cutesy-pie little painting of dormice on the wall and when the pethidine kicked in they changed into snarling monsters with blood on their fangs and giant lethal claws. It was horrific, but thankfully only lasted a little while or I would have been a basket-case.

Having been in labour for more than twenty hours, I was utterly exhausted and in a lot of pain. I was given an epidural, but when a young doctor (who looked about eleven) appeared clutching forceps, he was sent out of the room with a flea in his ear by the experienced midwife who knew I could do it by myself.

My baby girl was born soon afterwards, at just after eleven o'clock at night. It was all very calm, just a little squeak, and then she looked at me with these enormous eyes. For the past few months I had had an image of how my baby would look, and there she was, exactly how I had pictured her. Six and a half pounds of utter gorgeousness, although it was a bit disconcerting that I had put on four stone and she was so tiny. I looked at those massive eyes and that rosebud face and thought, So this is what it's all about. The utterly overwhelming unconditional love takes your breath away. I knew right there and then that I would do *anything* for this little bundle.

I phoned my mum, who was all set to walk down from East Kilbride to see us, and then I phoned my dad, who was in hospital having a minor operation. He skipped back to his bed and the nurses even managed to rustle up a wee glass of whisky for him to wet his granddaughter's head.

Although I was shattered, I simply couldn't sleep. I just stared at this teeny tiny little baby, amazed at how perfect she was. Steve was brilliant, helping me through the labour and taking care of both of us. Like most men he felt a bit helpless, especially in the early stages before the epidural when I was in a lot of pain and he couldn't do much more than hold my hand.

The hospital did fantastic hot buttered toast and Ovaltine, but the rest of the grub was pretty grim. Steve kept me supplied with lovely food from M&S, made all the phone calls to friends and family, and drove back and forth from home to the hospital with clean nighties and baby stuff.

In the morning, after not so much as a wink of sleep, I did a euphoric phone interview live on GMTV with Eamonn, which I'm sure didn't make any sense, then stayed up all day cuddling my baby girl, whom we'd decided to call Rosie because she looked like a little flower.

Joyce was the first visitor through the door with a massive bunch of flowers and a tear in her eye. She sat cuddling Rosie for the whole visit and the two of them have been very close ever since. Joyce is the nearest thing I have to a sister, and since Rosie was born has been known to all our family as 'Aunty' Joyce.

Later that afternoon a mad woman with possibly the silliest job in the world came into the ward waving condoms around and talking about safe sex. As all of us new mums had agreed we were never having sex again, she was greeted with hoots of derision and sent on her way. She was closely followed by a grumpy old doctor who came into the ward when I was staring at Rosie (your own newborn is better than the TV as a source of entertainment) and grabbed both her little legs, then started moving them around in a really rough way. 'We're checking hips today', he bellowed, and I discovered my inner tigress. I gave him a real mouthful about not having the decency to introduce himself to me and for manhandling my precious little girl without so much as a by-your-leave. He was well known for his lack of bedside manner and the midwives gave me a discreet wink and thumbs-up.

I have always been someone who will do anything to avoid confrontation, but when it comes to my daughter I would fight the heavyweight champ of the world and probably knock him on his backside.

Taking your baby home for the first time is very scary. In the hospital you are cocooned and protected. If you have any problems there are experts on hand to help, but once out of the door you feel completely adrift. For the first week I don't think I even washed. I lived in a red tartan dressing-gown and barely moved from the sofa in my living-room.

Steve gave Rosie her very first bath because I was too worried I'd drop her. He is a brilliant dad and from the very start was really hands-on. My mum and dad came down that first week and were a big help, and my mum even managed to bite her tongue and refrain from doling out advice, which was truly admirable. She couldn't get the hang of disposable nappies (she had used terry-towelling 'hippens' with Graham and me) and could never make them stick.

As a new mum, I turned into a big lump of mush. I cried at sentimental soup adverts on the TV and, for the first time in my life, had no interest in what was going on in the news. I was so wrapped up in my little girl, I had no idea that there had been ructions at GMTV and that I was about to get a shocking phone call.

At home, I was walking like John Wayne, getting used to breastfeeding and still so plump people thought I hadn't yet had my baby. (How do those celebrity mums manage to ping back into shape two days after giving birth? They surely must pay for a tummy tuck with their elective Caesarean. It should be against the law as it makes the rest of us feel even frumpier and more undesirable.)

I wasn't even thinking about work, but I knew I was due to go back to GMTV full-time in September. I had been asked to write a weekly column for the Scottish *Sunday Post*, and for a newly launched mother-and-baby magazine called *First Steps*. I had also been approached to do some radio, standing in for Gloria Hunniford, who then had a music and chat show on Radio 2. It was for a couple of weeks in August while she was on holiday.

I knew the writing wouldn't be a problem, but I wasn't sure about doing such a demanding radio show while my head was full of porridge after having a baby, but it would only be for a few hours a day and I thought it would be a good way to ease myself back into work.

I had come back from taking Rosie for a walk when the phone rang.

It was my boss, with the kind of news you need to sit down to hear, even if it still hurt without the rubber ring. I was thanked for all my hard work, but basically told that I was no longer needed at GMTV and my contract, which had run out in July, would not be renewed. They had already hired my replacement, Anthea Turner, and I wasn't to take it personally. They just wanted a change.

I was so shocked. I'd really had no idea it was coming.

I had been very apprehensive about going back to work, but I reckoned that as I was up and away very early and would be able to come straight home after the meeting, I wouldn't be missing out too much on time spent with Rosie. Just the week before I had hired Sian Stewart, from Maidenhead, to look after her while I was at work. That was the first thing I thought of when this bombshell dropped. I just kept thinking, what on earth am I going to tell Sian? She had already handed in her notice to her former employers.

The world of TV can be ruthless but you simply can't take it personally, although it's hard not to. Decisions are made to ditch presenters and contributors because it's the easiest and most obvious way to change any programme and make it look different. Change the cushions and the presenters and it seems fresh and new.

So there I was. I wasn't just overweight, I was seriously fat. My boobs leaked and I had bags under my eyes like a set of Joan Collins' luggage. I was also out of a job. Luckily I still had that offer of two weeks' radio work and the new columns, and I would just have to look for another show. I had done it before, but that was when I was younger and stronger and didn't feel as though my insides were going to fall out if I walked to the shops. Steve was earning a good living as a freelance cameraman and we would manage financially, but I was used to working and I loved my job.

Anthea took over and I stayed at home on 'maternity leave'.

In September, when I would have been going back to my old job, I had another call out of the blue.

Cow & Gate wanted to sponsor a special mother-and-baby slot on GMTV twice a week. It was a big earner for the station but the sponsors would only go ahead if I fronted the programme.

This was my opportunity to get back on air and I didn't even think about turning it down. I was glad of the work and it would be a lovely way to get back in harness. The bosses were also delighted, as it got them out of a hole.

To launch the series I brought Rosie on to the sofa for her first ever TV appearance. This was mainly to say thank you to all the viewers who had knitted her cardigans, little matinée jackets and shawls, and sent cards or other presents. People said it was as though one of their family had had a baby and I was so touched by their generosity and good wishes.

All during that long hot summer I wrote thank-you letters while Rosie slept outside in the shade. Steve drove Rosie and me into the studio. I still looked a bit rotund, but she was *gorgeous*. Sitting on the sofa talking to Eamonn, Penny Smith and Dr Hilary, I didn't feel as though I was on TV. It was just me and some pals having a cup of tea while I showed off my little girl.

Once again, the reaction from the viewers was lovely. There were so many calls saying how much they'd enjoyed seeing me back and having a peep at Rosie. Bosses don't ignore that sort of thing and so after the six-week Cow & Gate stint came to an end, I was offered my very own show at a quarter to nine every morning starting in the New Year. *The Quarter to Nine Show* (do you see what they did there?) meant I would have my own team, my own titles, and the new show would be a mixture of lifestyle, news and human interest. It would be similar to *Top of the Morning*, which I had really enjoyed. Things had come full circle.

CHAPTER SEVEN

Run for Your Life

I have been on a diet for most of my life and must have lost the equivalent of an entire rugby team over the years. There have been times when I simply didn't want to look in the mirror because I felt so fat. It's amazing how you can train yourself to avert your eyes from your body when you're getting dressed, but I'm really cross that I wasted so much time and energy worrying about something so stupid.

I first decided I was a fatty when I was sixteen and joined a slimming club. I virtually stopped eating for a week and lost ten pounds, but I turned into a washed-out rag. My mum was really worried that I was only having an apple and a glass of water for breakfast, nothing for lunch, then pecking at her home-cooked dinner at night. She didn't make a big deal about it, but kept a close eye on me, and it was only years later that she confessed to being worried.

Looking at photographs now, I want to shake some sense into that daft teenager because I was really slim, and looked absolutely fine. I have no idea what was going on in my head to make me think I was fat, and that was in the days before size zero and the appalling cult of thinness that has made so many women hate their bodies and their curves. We live in a bizarre world where young women starve themselves to have the bodies of seven-year-old boys, then have to go out and buy themselves a pair of breasts in order to look like proper women again.

I was lucky that I wasn't the kind of person to succumb to an eating disorder, but I can see how easy it is for young girls to make themselves seriously ill. Working as a reporter meant I had an unhealthy lifestyle and ate a lot of junk food, like fish suppers, takeaway curries and pizzas. If you're out all night covering a story, the only food available is pies and cakes from the local garage. I really was eating an appalling diet, but at least I didn't smoke, and I have always been grateful that I never took up the habit because I would have been on about a hundred fags a day.

My mum and dad used to smoke when they went out for the night, but never in the house because of Graham's asthma. When he was young he suffered really badly. One night when I was babysitting him, he had a really severe attack and started wheezing and struggling. Even I knew it was serious when he started turning blue and couldn't breathe at all. I was really scared and called an ambulance. As always, the paramedics were fantastic, gave him an injection of cortisone and saved his life.

My mum and dad arrived home just as he was being taken to hospital and they felt so guilty I don't think they went out again for years after that.

So I grew up in a smoke-free zone, and I'm very grateful for that because by the time I started work in smoke-filled news-rooms I wasn't interested in taking up the habit. I was delighted when Scotland introduced the smoking ban in 2006 and the rest of the UK followed suit a year later. I despair of young women who smoke because they think it will keep them thin. They don't want to listen when you tell them there's not much fat on a corpse.

They also fail to realise that smoking is incredibly ageing. Your skin is yellow and wrinkled and you end up with a mouth like a cat's bum.

At college I did once buy a small packet of tiny cigars, because I decided they would look grown-up and sophisticated. There was nothing adult and alluring about coughing and spluttering on these horrible little cancer sticks. I almost threw up because I'd inhaled the noxious fumes. I couldn't even finish the first one and threw them away.

When it comes to sizes I am supposed to be a twelve. When I am a size fourteen I look chunky but when I am a size ten, I simply look ill and gaunt. When I went to London to be a presenter, I had such a crazy shift pattern that I barely ate at all. Like so many women, if I'm cooking for the family I'll make a proper dinner, but on my own a plate of beans and toast in front of *Corrie* suits me just fine. Living by myself in London meant I didn't bother to buy any proper food. I became far too thin and it didn't suit me. I looked like one of those Hollywood 'lollipop ladies', with a massive head and tiny body.

Over the years my weight had yo-yoed up and down, with the floating half-stone that has to be addressed just before the summer holidays, and then piles on again when the nights start drawing in, and then the Christmas holidays add even more poundage. It was only after I had Rosie that I developed a real weight problem. I had put on those four stones while I was pregnant, and eighteen months later I still had a good stone and a half to shift. It's a bit disconcerting when people ask you when your baby is due and she's actually walking and talking.

I felt unhealthy and unhappy, and I knew I needed to do something. No one ever said to me at work that I looked like a blob, and I've never been under pressure to lose weight or look a certain way. I have always bought my own clothes, and although I have been getting better over the years, I am no fashionista. Mark Heyes has been a huge help and often grabs me clothes when he's sashaying up and down Oxford Street. I do a lot of shopping in Monsoon and Zara because they happen to be close to Rosie's school, and the Next Directory is invaluable, but I always end up with lots of tops and no bottoms to go with them, and I am forever running out of tights.

When Rosie was a baby I seemed to have nothing in my wardrobe but elasticated waists and loose blousons. I wore some truly vile outfits at work – horrid patterned shirts and maternity trousers. I really did need help. Steve always says I look fine and, like most men, he likes curvy women, but I had gone beyond curves and was on the slippery slope to being plain fat. I knew I had to take action. What worried me more than not being able to get into a size sixteen was that I felt so unhealthy and utterly exhausted.

I carried on yo-yoing for a couple of years and even joined WeightWatchers in my village, managing to lose about a stone and a half. The problem was that when I stopped going to meetings, the weight crept back. Finally, after years of losing and gaining weight, in the summer of 1998 I got a call from my agent

Jimmy O'Reilly, a delightfully gay 'silver fox' who is sadly no longer with us.

Jimmy's death was a real shock. He had booked me to do an awards event on my birthday at the end of November in 2003 and everything had gone really well, but I had the journey from hell getting home. I was stuck in traffic for two hours and then my car was involved in an accident when it was shunted from behind. It wasn't serious and I wasn't driving; but I got a terrible fright. My mum and dad, Steve and Rosie were waiting at home with a birthday cake and presents and I just needed to get back to them, so I jumped on the tube at Queensway and phoned Steve to pick me up from Ealing Broadway, in west London, about an hour away from home. Of course, the train broke down and by the time we got home everyone had gone to bed.

I phoned Jimmy at about nine o'clock from the station that Sunday to tell him about my nightmare trek trying to get home for a piece of birthday cake. As well as having been my agent for the past twelve years, he was also a good mate and as always he made me see the funny side and said it would make a good episode in a sit-com. I spoke to Jimmy every day, and told him I would call him in the morning. He sounded a bit tired but in good spirits, and we planned to meet up later in the week.

The next day, after my Monday show, my mum and I were out shopping when Jimmy's business partner Michael Joyce called and told me that Jimmy had been found dead that morning. Jimmy's boyfriend Jason had said goodbye to him on his way to work. He was a bit worried because Jimmy had seemed exhausted and said he would have a bit of a lie-in. Jason phoned to see how Jimmy was doing, and when the phone rang and rang unanswered, he felt something was wrong and dashed home.

Jimmy had died quietly in his sleep. He had been ill, but no one had expected this to happen, and it was desperately sad. I was glad that I had had such a stupid day as it meant we had had a chance to talk and laugh before he died.

When I got home that day, still in shock, a present of champagne and chocolates was delivered to my door with a lovely card from Jimmy wishing me a happy birthday. It was heart-rending, but very fitting that the last thing I ever received from him was so gorgeous.

Back in 1999 Jimmy, always such a considerate man, wasn't quite sure how to put this to me, but a production company had been in touch wanting me to do an exercise video. They had noticed, obviously, that I was by far the fattest woman on TV and needed help. I didn't know whether to be offended or embrace them as my saviours. This was in the days when fitness videos were still a novelty and not brought out by every soap star and *Big Brother* contestant in what has become a very overcrowded market.

I do remember Joyce and me buying Cher's fitness video back in the eighties and bringing it back to Joyce's flat where we watched it with a glass of wine in our hands, scoffing crisps and hooting at Cher's hair, makeup and teeny-weeny dental-floss outfits, which wasn't the point but a hell of a lot of fun.

If I was going to do this video then it would have to show me puffing, panting and sweating through the routines and there would be no air-brushing or any other tricks. I was teamed with Jenni Rivett, a super-fit South African who had worked with Princess Diana and was one of the few people never to exploit that relationship. While others who had had only a nodding acquaintance with the Princess were making shedloads of money writing about her, Jenni never went public with her memories of

Diana. She only told me that she admired her and that she was a wonderfully sharp, bright and funny woman, and that it was a tragedy she had died so young.

This was my kind of woman – loyal, discreet and utterly trustworthy. I took to her right away. Jenni was tough and no-nonsense but she understood that my level of fitness was non-existent and that I needed encouragement to get back into shape. Her programme, called *Figure It Out*, concentrated on toning up a woman's body and focusing on 'areas of concern', like the tummy, bum, thighs and the tops of the arms. She had a special section called 'Tone Your Woman's Zone', which I was rather afraid would involve lots of pelvic-floor exercises, but it was all about posture and the back, neck and arms being worked out to get rid of bingo wings and those bulges over your bra straps. You can lose about four pounds instantly by straightening up and maintaining good posture, and Jenni wanted women to work on that.

She was enthusiastic and excited until she asked me to do a sit-up while she put her hands on my tummy to assess the muscles. Then her smile faltered. My stomach was a blancmange. I was indeed Kelly of the Jelly Belly, and Jenni realised she had a real challenge on her hands.

The first thing she did was make me realise how much time I spent on my backside. I sat in a car for an hour on the way to work, then a makeup chair, then a sofa, then a desk attending meetings and catching up with mail, and then in a car again on the way home. In the house I sat on my bum watching *Corrie*, and my only real activity was playing with Rosie's Barbie dolls and reading to her, which doesn't exactly get your heart-rate going. I was also eating far too much rubbish. Bacon rolls in the morning, and crisps, chocolates and junk food between meals. I would hoover up Rosie's leftovers. Who knew cold fish-fingers with tomato sauce were so tasty? No wonder I felt tired all the time.

I saw Jenni three times a week and started going for long walks at the weekends. I called it 'walking in a fast way'. It wasn't power-walking but was just hard enough to be doing me some good.

Jenni then created a routine that worked out my whole body. After the first session I could barely walk, but it was amazing how quickly I noticed a difference. By exercising sensibly and ditching the junk food, I felt so much better after just two weeks. Jenni had also given me a healthy-eating plan, with fish and chicken, fruit, vegetables, and lots of water to drink. It wasn't a diet, it was just common sense. We had a six-week plan that would have me shedding about a stone and dropping a couple of dress sizes. Thanks to Jenni's hard work and my determination, we managed to get down to that target in time for the filming schedule in October. I had lost just over a stone and was a size twelve,

I had been doing the exercises in Jenni's front-room and in my own bedroom, but now I had to put on a leotard and show off my figure to a camera crew. Luckily Steve was available to shoot the video, which made it so much easier. It was a bit odd to be doing exercises in a beautifully lit, posh environment, with my hair done and wearing makeup. I was also covered in fake tan and felt like a satsuma, but it looked OK on the screen.

I made a couple of mistakes and wasn't perfectly in time with Jenni, but I told the producers to keep that in because it was real, and I didn't mind looking hot and bothered, because if you're doing the routines properly you get a bit sweaty.

The video was released at the end of December 1998, and Jenni and I did a few interviews with magazines to publicise it, then thought no more about it. She had become a good friend, so I still went to see her. She would make me go for a run in nearby Bushey Park where you could see deer and rabbits and pretend you were deep in the country instead of in Greater London.

At the start of January 1999 we began to realise that our little video was flying out of the shops, and was a major success. A top-ten video chart (no DVDs in those days) shows that *Figure It Out* had reached number three. We were beaten by *The Wedding Singer* and Disney's *Simba's Pride* (the follow-up to *The Lion King*) but we were above *Titanic* and *Good Will Hunting*.

Sadly, we only received a flat fee so didn't share in the mega-profits but I consoled myself with the fact that you can't put a price on feeling fit and looking younger and happier.

Jenni and I went on to do *Figure Happy* together, which wasn't nearly as successful as the first video, but was a respectable seller and, more importantly for someone not sharing in the profits, it also meant I maintained my weight loss.

It was only when Jenni and her family returned to South Africa that I slipped into my old ways, but help was at hand.

In 2002 we did a feature on GMTV about Nina Barough, a remarkable woman who was working as a fashion stylist in New York in 1996 when she had the idea of going on a power-walk with a group of friends to raise money for breast-cancer charities. To make it more fun and to attract attention, she asked everyone to turn up for the walk in brightly coloured decorated bras. That small event raised £25,000 for Breakthrough Breast Cancer.

Two months later Nina found a lump in her breast and it was cancerous. She credits that charity walk with saving her life because she was much more aware of breast cancer and quickly took action. As a busy career woman she would have dismissed the lump as a cyst or simply put it out of her mind, but Nina went for help straight away and her treatment was successful.

When I met her in early 2002, that small charity event in New York had mushroomed into the Moonwalk, a twenty-six-mile walk round London that started at midnight and involved tens of thousands of women. I was bowled over by Nina's enthusiasm, lust for life and commitment, and when she asked me to take part in that year's event, I couldn't say no. My granny had died of breast cancer and two friends were going through treatment so I knew how important it was to raise funds and awareness.

Maggie Peters, wife of Steve's best man Davie, was inspirational in the way she coped after being diagnosed with breast cancer. She fought the disease with a quiet courage and dignity and never let it hold her back. She was lucky. She went to the doctor in Dundee as soon as she felt a lump in her breast and was given quick, competent treatment that saved her life.

My friend Ilaria d'Elia, married to Liam Hamilton, who was a brilliant programme editor at GMTV, was also diagnosed with breast cancer. Ilaria, an Italian-born actress and writer, is a force of nature. She also managed to detect signs early and receive immediate treatment, and continues to deal with her illness in a truly humbling way. Their experiences made me want to help, but I had no idea what I was letting myself in for.

Nina and her gloriously named PR woman, Kate Bosomworth, organised a press conference to launch the Moonwalk, and I had to find a suitable bra to wear and a way to cover up my 'midriff bulge'. Stylist Mark Heyes came to the rescue. He bought a tartan bikini from H&M for £3.99 and sewed heavy black fringing round the bottom of the bra top, which covered up my belly.

Nina and I made the front pages of quite a few tabloids the next morning with our low-cut bras. I had no idea I was showing off so much cleavage and was a bit embarrassed, but it gained some fantastic publicity for the event.

I had to start training, and my pal Joyce, who has always been fitter and more determined than I am, was well up for the challenge of walking twenty-six miles, losing a night's sleep and doing it all in her brassière. Also, as luck would have it, she had moved house and now lived about twenty minutes away from me. This was fantastic because it meant we saw a lot more of her, and it was really good for Rosie to see her 'aunty'.

We had so many fun Friday nights when Steve was off playing football. We would have something to eat, a glass of *vino*, and switch on the TV to music channel VH1 to educate Rosie in some of life's most important cultural experiences, like appreciating seventies disco, Abba, the Cure, the Clash, the Stranglers, Joy Division and Ian Dury and the Blockheads. It was an eclectic education but an important one.

On Saturday morning Joyce and I would both be up early and out pounding the pavements to train for the Moonwalk. Our house was surrounded by steep hills and at first we were puffed out just getting five minutes from the front door. Soon we were walking for miles, along the river to Bourne End or Marlow and through the forest of Burnham Beeches. It was gorgeous in the summer, but miserable when it was cold and rainy.

The most important thing was to time our walks so that we had plenty of loo breaks, something I was becoming more worried about as the day of the event grew nearer and nearer. Where would we be able to go for a wee on the night? Practical Nina had sorted out Portaloos, but with thousands of women liable to want to go at the same time, it was a real concern for all of us. You know what the queues are like for any women's toilet.

Although the training was hard and we spent many hours in all weathers coping with blisters and chafing, I actually enjoyed it. Joyce and I have been friends for years, but inevitably with her high-powered job and my busy life, we didn't see each other nearly as much as we would have liked, and it had been a long, long time since the two of us had had so much time on our own just to catch up. We talked about everything and really got to know each other again. The hours and the miles flew by.

Apart from worrying about pee breaks, we also had to sort out our bras. I knew I couldn't wear that little tartan bikini top that had featured in the papers. It gave absolutely no support whatsoever and my boobs would have been in agony after twenty-six steps, never mind twenty-six miles. I needed a bit more help or I'd be nursing two black eyes.

Once again Mark Heyes came to the rescue and did something very clever with black feathers, sequins and silver chains, which made me look like a dominatrix but helped keep everything in place and was surprisingly comfortable.

Joyce had covered her bra in a riot of butterflies and we both had bum-bags bulging with blister plasters, fresh socks and peppermint foot-cream, flapjacks, money, mobile phones and chocolate. Steve made us a massive pasta dinner at seven o'clock, and then we gathered with our thousands of fellow walkers in a huge tent in Battersea Park. There was a real party atmosphere. With an hour to go, everyone took part in a warm-up and we all wished each other well.

Then Nina took the stage and asked for a minute's silence to remember all the women and men who had died of breast cancer. It was a very emotional moment as we reflected on exactly why we were all standing there hand in hand in our homemade bras, wearing feather boas and covered in glittery makeup.

The Moonwalkers were made up of women going through breast cancer, those who had lost someone they loved and others, like Nina, who had kicked cancer in the arse.

Walking through London at that time of night means you see the city in a completely different way. For the first few hours it's still busy and buzzy, but around 3a.m. you feel as though you're in one of those disaster movies where only women in their bras have survived. The low point for me was after about four hours when the 'half-mooners' split from us and made their way to the finish line. We knew we still had another thirteen miles to go and by then tiredness had set in. I felt as if I was walking under water.

We stopped outside a pub in Chelsea to change our socks, rub some cream into our poor, punished feet and have a quick breather. A caricature of a Hooray Henry poked his large and empty head out of an upstairs window and drunkenly brayed that we were ugly proles clogging up the streets and making him feel ill. I wish I could have come up with a suitably Oscar Wilde-style put-down, but I merely yelled at him to 'go f**k yourself', and was applauded for my succinct riposte.

The last few miles of that first Moonwalk were agony. We were all bent over and trudging to the finish line, like an army of defeated soldiers weary from battle. My feet looked like a couple of pounds of raw mince, and when Joyce and I were being driven home by Steve and Rosie, we vowed never ever ever to put ourselves through such an ordeal again.

Of course, we've been there for the Moonwalk every year since, and in 2006 I even did it twice. I took part in the usual London Moonwalk that May with my friends Joyce, Siobhan

O'Gorman, Joan Grant and Jacqueline Millar. It had now swollen to more than fifteen thousand entrants and raised millions of pounds for breast-cancer charities. Then in June, with my feet barely recovered, I helped to launch the first ever Moonwalk in Scotland.

By this time, demand from women all over Britain, but especially in the north of England and Scotland, who wanted to take part in the event had become overwhelming. Nina decided to take a chance and organise an event in Edinburgh. They had no idea how many would want to take part, and in the end the eight thousand places were snapped up in a couple of days.

I was really excited about the Scottish event – I had done all the training for London – and the gang were fired up too. Joyce couldn't make it due to work commitments, but she stayed up all night texting us encouragement from her conference in the USA. Siobhan had her astonishingly impressive bosom decorated with a shamrock-style bra, and I invested in a special cantilevered tartan corset to hold my boobs in place; Joan and Jacqueline were in matching tartan outfits and my pal Carol, a Moonwalk virgin who was replacing Joyce, was a riot of glitter and colour and excitement. Siobhan's friend, the super-fit Pammie Ballantine from Ulster TV, flew in by helicopter to take part in the event and kept us going with jokes and outrageous stories.

As always, the organisers had pulled out all the stops and a massive pink tent in the middle of the city greeted us all. We had pipers, dancers, and local DJ and presenter Grant Stott kept up the party atmosphere as eight thousand women geared up for the start of the Moonwalk. I was introduced to the crowd and wished them all luck, then stood on the stage with Nina for that minute's silence as we all struggled not to cry.

The Edinburgh Moonwalk was a toughie. The start takes you up Arthur's Seat, which is very a steep hill, but the views of the city, the castle, the River Forth and those famous bridges, were just beautiful in the moonlight. Our route then took us up the Royal Mile, which runs from Holyrood Palace to the castle, just as the pubs were emptying. It was hilarious to see goggle-eyed revellers wondering if they were hallucinating as thousands of busty women strode past them. When they knew why we were out in the drizzle in our bras, with typical Scottish generosity they thrust fivers and tenners upon us and cheered us like crazy. There was such a lot of support for the Scottish Moonwalk with banners and locals giving us tea and coffee, or just clapping and cheering us on.

As always we passed the time talking, laughing and eating the food stored in our bulging bum-bags. Siobhan had the biggest bag I've ever seen and every couple of miles would produce something to eat. I fully expected her to fish out a table, chairs and a three-course meal for all of us from its depths.

The 'bum-bag of happiness' kept us all going, with Siobhan actually hauling out biscuits and cheese at our lowest point around 3a.m., when we were cold, tired and hungry. The food helped and so did the fact that the route took us past the seaside at Portobello and Joppa. The sun coming up over the Forth is a glorious sight and the fresh sea breeze woke us all up.

So far the Moonwalk has raised twenty million pounds for breast-cancer charities. I salute Nina, Kate and her team, all the women and men who have taken part, and all of those who provide back-up throughout the night.

If I'd thought the Moonwalk was tough, there was an even bigger challenge round the corner. As a child, I loved watching the Olympic games, especially the gymnastics, but my real Olympic highlight was the brave marathon runners, some of them staggering over the line like little rubber men and women, gasping like fish out of water and looking as though they were knocking at death's door. It was the ultimate in endurance and bravery.

Although I could never do a triple back salco with grace and elegance like gymnast Nelli Kim or Olga Korbut, I was given the chance to run a marathon like those heroic athletes I so admired. I was asked in 2004 to take part in the London Marathon. As well as helping to promote the Moonwalk, Kate Bosomworth also did the PR for the Flora Marathon and it was she who had the idea that I should take part.

I laughed hysterically at the very notion of subjecting myself to such hell, but the organisers were waving a very, very big carrot. They said that if I completed the course they would donate £40,000 to the charity of my choice. Not only was I being offered a place in the race, which in itself is an achievement as so many runners and fundraisers from all over the world want to compete in the London Marathon, I could also raise a hell of a lot of money. And, with that guaranteed sponsorship from Flora, I didn't have to go round my friends with a begging bowl and a form for them to sign.

I had pretty much exhausted friends and family with all my Moonwalks, so this was an offer I simply couldn't refuse, but the London Marathon is a bloody big mountain to climb. I was assured that I would be given a proper trainer, lots of help and support, and that no one was seriously expecting me to trouble the likes of Paula Radcliffe.

So I said yes. Then instantly regretted it and rang up to say no. And put the phone down without saying anything because they would have thought I was a quitter.

I immediately called Joyce and told her I couldn't possibly do it unless she did it too, and effectively blackmailed her into signing her life away for four months to train for the race. We were raising money for the British Heart Foundation and I was part of a forty-strong team of 'over-forties' who were running with me.

I really hit the jackpot when I was put in touch with top trainer Jane Wake, who entertained no thoughts of failure and told both Joyce and me from the very start that we were absolutely going to complete the race and it was only a matter of how long it took us.

Although by then I had the four Moonwalks under my belt, running is very different from going for a walk, no matter how brisk the pace. At first I couldn't even run for a minute without being out of puff. I had to build up my runs from a virtual standstill. I so wanted to be one of those lithe-limbed sun-kissed girls who could run for miles and simply glow with health and vitality. I also really, really wanted one of those bouncy ponytails that make runners look like thoroughbred racehorses.

Instead I was a wheezing, red-faced fun-runner, with wobbly bits, who sweated buckets and looked like a Shetland pony, but the thing about Shelties is that they are tenacious and stubborn, and it did get a little bit easier as the weeks went by. Once again Joyce and I were out pounding the streets, but this time we were too puffed out to do much talking. All through January, February and March, in the wind, the rain and even, on one occasion, the sleet and the snow, we kept on running. It really was a slog, but we just kept thinking of all the money we would be raising, and that kept us going.

One terrific side-effect was that although I was eating like a piglet, I was losing weight and becoming almost lean. I ate porridge in the mornings and loads of bread, pasta and potatoes, but I was burning it off. I also worked with Jane Wake at the gym two or three times a week. I would come off air, throw on my trainers and tracksuit and head straight for the gym in Chelsea. Just didn't think about wanting to go shopping or for a coffee, or catching up with *Corrie*. Jane would put me through an hour of strength-building exercises and I would go out and run three times a week, and put in some seriously long slogs at weekends.

Steve was lumbered with doing a lot of the dull running of the house, and picking up Rosie from school or her pals' and also cooking tons of pasta for Joyce and me. The marathon took over my whole life, but I was determined to finish the race and not to let myself or the charities down. I had decided to divide the money between the British Heart Foundation, the Scottish Autistic Society, the MS Society and a local heart charity in Dundee called SHARP.

The night before the marathon, Joyce and I shared a room in a hotel near Tower Bridge. Despite our nerves and the fact that we can't stop yakking, we managed a few hours' sleep before our wake-up call from an ITV news crew at 6a.m. They were filming us for the build-up to the marathon and took some footage of us eating a massive breakfast of porridge and toast, then pinning on our numbers and looking very nervous.

Downstairs in the foyer, the real athletes were munching bananas, doing stretches and looking serene, calm and frighten-ingly fit.

We were bussed to Blackheath and had a few hours to fret and stew. I was interviewed by Sue Barker for the BBC alongside Gordon Ramsay, who I have always found enormously funny and hugely attractive because he has the same craggy good looks as my Steve. Gordon is a veteran marathon runner and clocks up impressive times of just over three hours, so he's up there with the elite athletes.

As a so-called 'celebrity' runner, I was given a tracking device so that the BBC could locate me during their coverage of the race.

Waiting at that starting line was really scary. Jane had drummed it into Joyce and me that no matter the temptation we weren't to go running off at full speed but had to take our time and pace ourselves for the first couple of miles. When the gun went off, I knew why she had given us that wise advice. The overwhelming temptation was to run as fast as everyone else around you. I was jostled and elbowed and awash in a sea of testosterone as the blokes, including Gordon, went off like two-bob rockets.

Seeing them all disappear out of sight was dismaying but we kept on telling ourselves that it was indeed a marathon and not a sprint, and that we needed to save our energy for the long, long race. The reason so many people stagger over the line on jelly legs is because they are running on empty and didn't pace themselves properly throughout the twenty-six miles.

As usual, the first five miles were really hard until we got into a rhythm. We weren't exactly going at a fast pace, but we were doing OK. The crowds were brilliant, shouting encouragement and giving us sweeties and ice lollies.

Jane ran with us for a while and I had to give her my tracking device because it kept slipping off. This caused a bit of a hoo-ha, and my dad nearly fell off his chair watching the coverage on TV at home in East Kilbride when it was reported that I had actually gone ahead in front of the entire pack. What happened was that Jane had hopped on the Underground with my device in her pocket, and was waiting for us at the half-way mark, but it looked as if I had run about ten miles in ten minutes. For one brief moment I was in the lead instead of back at the cow's tail.

The worst part of the race was running through Docklands as the crowds had thinned out, we were getting weary and there was still an awful long way to go. News filtered through that the winner, Evans Rutto, had finished the race and was no doubt sitting on his sofa having a cup of tea. As we were less than half-way round, this added to the sense of gloom. We were also desperate for a wee and gatecrashed a pub to use the toilet. The drinkers at the bar gave us a big cheer, which spurred us on for a bit.

Jane met us every few miles to keep our spirits up, but we were still outrun by three Cornish pasties and a man raising money for testicular cancer dressed, inevitably, as a pair of testicles.

A couple of miles from the finishing line I really didn't think I'd make it. Running down the Embankment towards the Houses of Parliament it started to rain. I couldn't believe we were so close yet I just didn't have any energy left. Somehow I kept going but the last mile was interminable.

Then I saw the finishing line and Rosie and Steve waiting for us. That was all I needed to spur me on. I looked round for Joyce so we could cross together but she had noticed the photographers and fled because her hair had gone frizzy in the drizzle. We did give each other a big hug on the other side, along with Jane and Kate and her team, but my biggest hug was for Steve and Rosie, who had been waiting for ages to see us complete the race. I just managed to finish ahead of the oldest competitor, ninety-three-year-old Fauja Singh, in five and a half hours, but I have a feeling that lovely old gentlemen let me beat him.

I went home, collapsed into a bubble bath and was out for the count until the alarm went off at 5a.m. I hirpled into work looking about 102 and unable to walk downstairs. I had to do a bum shuffle instead because my legs refused to work. I vowed that never ever *ever* again would I do something so physically demanding.

As soon as I stopped my training regime, I went up a dress size in about two weeks. I was still eating the same amount of food, but I was doing absolutely no exercise. Not having to train during the week and at weekends was so liberating that I could go out with Rosie for a pizza in Marlow or into Windsor shopping. I could sit on my bum and watch endless TV or go to the movies or have friends round. It was fantastic and I repeatedly told everyone that I would never get back on that hamster wheel.

So where did you find me exactly a year later? You've guessed it. April 2005, and there I was at the starting line again, with my stomach churning, more scared even than I had been the first time round. One good thing, though: Joyce and I had Steve and our pal Craig Millar for moral support. They were both taking part in the London Marathon for the first time, and looked lean, mean and keen. I was worried because I hadn't done as much training as I had the first time and knew I hadn't put in as many miles as I should have. I had done most of my training at weekends in Scotland, but even the gruelling runs from Broughty Ferry, across the Tay Bridge to Tayport and back again weren't really enough.

On the day before the race I came down with a horrible cold and was burning up. We stayed in the same hotel at Tower Bridge and I didn't sleep a wink because I felt so rough and I was so nervous. On the morning of the race a doctor had to give me the go-ahead before I could take part. It was touch and go, but this time I had received an even bigger donation from Flora and I didn't want the charities to lose out on such a lot of money.

I was eventually told I could run, with the proviso that I had to be sensible and if I felt worse I had to seek medical attention. You really shouldn't run a race with a temperature and I was borderline. I honestly don't know how I got round that course – sheer determination and a bit of what is meant by that old Scottish word 'thrawn' (which means so much more than 'stubborn') pulled me through.

We told Steve and Craig to go ahead of us. They had been training for ages and were capable of a really good finishing time. Joyce stayed with me and we were so much slower this time round. The combination of being less fit and feeling so rough meant at times we were virtually walking. Poor Joyce, she could have completed the race hours before me but she stuck with me the whole way round, even when they were taking down the barricades behind us.

More than six hours later we crossed the line and I slumped in a heap. I was a bit dehydrated despite drinking water all the way round, but I was elated to have completed the marathon for a second time.

So that was it. Never ever *ever* EVER again.

Hmmm.

Six months later on a November morning where do you think I was? You've guessed it. At the starting line of yet another gruelling marathon, with Joyce at my side, both of us scared out of our wits. This time we were in New York City and it was the toughest one of all. Again, I had been seduced by the promise of cold, hard cash. Highland Spring were sending a team of runners from the UK to New York, wanted me to be part of their gang and were willing to donate *at least* £100,000 to Breakthrough Breast Cancer. How could I refuse?

I was back on the phone to Joyce to invite her to a weekend in New York City and the promise of exploring Manhattan and all the other neighbourhoods properly. She said yes before I told her that this was not a jaunt round the shops in our high heels, but that we would be climbing back into our sweaty trainers and digging out our running gear from the back of the cupboard. It was back to pounding the streets and putting some more miles in the bank.

The New York marathon is in November so we packed our thermals, hats, gloves, scarves and thickest fleeces. We flew off on the Friday morning, and would have Friday night and all day Saturday in Manhattan before the big event on Sunday. Just before take-off a gorgeous member of the British Airways crew asked Joyce and me to follow her.

As a treat we were to be upgraded to first class and sat in seats 1A and 1B, beyond excited and giggling like schoolgirls.

We toasted ourselves with a glass of bubbly (not part of the recommended pre-marathon training regime, but it would have been impolite to refuse) and happily floated all the way to JFK airport.

On Friday evening we went to a reception at the British Council with Highland Spring's eighty-odd runners. It was a beautiful night and the lights of Manhattan were twinkling away.

It would have been perfect if we hadn't had the big race hanging over us like a black cloud, and could have shopped and gone sight-seeing instead.

On Saturday morning we walked to Times Square in our running gear to have our photos taken beside a huge good-luck message from Highland Spring on that world-famous neon billboard. I think that was when it dawned on us that this wasn't a first-class, champagne-swilling, shoe-buying weekend, but that it was damned serious and an awful lot of money for charity was at stake. We could not afford to fail.

Of course, we should have spent that entire Saturday in bed or doing yoga and meditating, but instead we headed to Saks on Fifth Avenue, bought impossibly glamorous shoes and drank a bloody Mary each (for the iron).

We were both up at 6a.m. on Sunday morning to stand in the crowds waiting to get the bus to the starting line on Staten Island. It was brilliantly well organised with free bagels, bananas, coffee and water for everyone, but I noticed very few people dressed up as pies or sexual organs and an awful lot of serious-looking runners. I turned to Joyce and said, 'I think we're in trouble, and I also think we're about to be found out as impostors and pretendy fun-runners who haven't done nearly enough training.'

A rumour went round that if you didn't finish in under five hours you wouldn't get a medal and your effort wouldn't count. This turned out to be completely false but it haunted us all the way along the route. Even though it was a November morning, it was actually pretty warm and, like most of the runners, we discarded our heavy sweatshirts at the start of the race. These were all bundled up by volunteers and later distributed among the homeless.

The first mile was terrifying. It was uphill over Staten Island Bridge and I just couldn't get my legs to move. I was knackered already, and we'd only been going about ten minutes. It gave me a real fright and I went very quiet and just concentrated on getting to the next landmark.

After five or six miles I felt better as my body warmed up and I settled in for another long, hard race. Much to my delight, Siobhan had flown over from Dublin to cheer us on, and every few miles we would see her and her pals waving a Scottish flag and yelling at the top of their lungs. That sort of support was invaluable, as was all the chocolate she kept throwing at us.

Our old friend 'Mr Testicle' was there, along with some firemen from Wales, who lifted our spirits, and a gang of British squaddies who were running in full uniform. They were cheered and whooped by the Yanks, but they looked utterly exhausted. It was only later I found out that as well as running in their big boots and heavy uniforms they were carrying backpacks that weighed more than I did. That is seriously tough.

I just couldn't believe it was November. The temperature was in the high seventies and we took off everything we could without getting arrested. As well as water, Gatorade, oranges and bananas, the organisers also provided barrels of ice. I ran with an icepack down my boobs for five miles until it melted in my cleavage.

Crossing the bridge into Manhattan was a beautiful sight and the last few miles flew by. At the end Joyce and I felt in remarkably good shape. The sheer thrill of being in Central Park, in the middle of the most exciting city in the world, gave us a sort of natural high, but all I wanted to do was go back to the hotel and soak my poor old feet. My big blisters had baby blisters, but I couldn't go to sleep because I had to do a live link into GMTV and, with the time difference, I would need to be at our studios round the corner from the hotel in Times Square at about 2a.m.

By the time we'd got back to our hotel room and washed our horribly sweaty bodies, wolfed down steak and chips and toasted each other with a cup of tea, all I wanted to do was lay my head down, but I had to pack my little case, put the clammy running gear back on and shuffle off to the studio, looking and feeling like the oldest woman in the world.

Times Square was utterly deserted – so much for the city that never sleeps – but, thankfully, Siobhan was there to help me charm the security guard into letting us in. I hobbled upstairs to the studio where I staggered on to the set, miked myself up and gave the cameraman the thumbs-up to let him know I could hear Kate Garraway in London, and we were off.

I don't believe I made a blind bit of sense to Kate or to anyone else watching that show, and I kept falling asleep during the ad breaks, but I bumbled through it somehow. By then I had been up for almost twenty-four hours, had run more than twenty-six miles in sweltering heat and felt decidedly wabbit.

At the end of the show, Siobhan called a cab and poured me into it. I picked up Joyce and headed straight for the airport for the 8a.m. flight from Newark to London. Due to the time difference, we weren't landing back in Heathrow until later that night and I had to be perched on my sofa, all bright-eyed and bushy-tailed, the very next morning. Luckily I managed to sleep for most of the flight, but there was a comedy moment when Joyce and I tried to get up from our seats. Our legs simply refused to work. I thought we were going to have to be carried off by a gang of big strong baggage-handlers, but by holding on to each other and being carefully shunted down the line of cabin crew, like a game of pass the parcel, we managed to 'deplane' while just about maintaining our dignity.

The truly fantastic news was that our team managed to raise over £200,000 for Breakthrough Breast Cancer, which made all the stiff legs, sore feet, blisters and black toenails worthwhile.

As is usual after any of my marathon runs or walks, I went up a dress size in a matter of weeks because I ate exactly the same amount of food without doing the exercise. I despaired of ever finding a proper balance so that I could eat more or less what I wanted and still be reasonably healthy and stay at a size twelve. Jane Wake came to my rescue and we continued going for long walks and doing deceptively gentle Pilates exercises. We brought out a video together, *Walk Off the Pounds*, which used exercise, healthy eating and, of course, walking to keep fit.

Despite my best efforts, I still tended to yo-yo. In early 2008 I knew I had to do something once and for all to try to make sure I had the right balance of exercise and healthy eating. The *Sun* came to my rescue with their six-week plan and, along with thousands of readers, I greeted the New Year with a new pair of trainers, shopping bags full of fruit and vegetables and the determination to tuck my T-shirt into my jeans.

I think we all know that there's no big secret or instant short-cut to losing weight. You just need to eat less rubbish and get up off your bottom. It's that easy – and that difficult. With Jane's help I started stepping up the walking to a bit of a jog, and she increased the difficulty and intensity of the Pilates moves. I wrote a daily blog for the *Sun*, which focused my mind on what I was eating, and feedback from readers really helped.

It's all about making small changes that are do-able rather than trying to change your life completely. If you are 'on' a diet, you will inevitably have to come 'off' it at some point and you will end up fatter than you were before you started.

I haven't owned scales for twenty years. I don't think it's a good idea to be constantly and neurotically weighing yourself. It's better to have a pair of jeans or a favourite fitted dress that you feel good in, and just aim to get back into it. One of my friends tries on her wedding dress when she feels a bit blobby, then cuts out the junk food for a couple of weeks until she fits back into it. She always remembers feeling her best on her big day, and that's her way of monitoring her weight.

I also don't count calories or fat grams. I think that as a mother, especially of a young daughter, I have a huge responsibility to make sure she doesn't grow up thinking that being on a diet – hopping on and off the scales, obsessively counting and weighing food and bleating about feeling fat – is normal. It's the worst possible example you can set. Your children will grow up to look upon food as the enemy instead of one of the great joys of life.

Women really beat themselves up about not having 'perfect' bodies when, in fact, men don't feel all that comfortable with perfection – and I honestly don't believe they even notice cellulite. I think a little of what you fancy does you good, and that denying yourself food like chocolate and cakes makes you crave them all the more. It's just a matter of cutting down on the junk and getting up off your bum.

CHAPTER EIGHT

Going It Alone

When Rosie was six months old, at the start of 1995, I started my brand-new job, hosting my very own show. It was a fresh start and felt very different because I was now a mum and actually felt 'grown-up' for the first time in my life. I also think having my daughter made me better at my job. I was a lot more understanding, thoughtful and generally a much more contented person. I could empathise more with guests, especially if they were parents and going through tough times.

So, from being in dark despair and thinking I would never work again, I found that everything had turned round. Yet again I realised that you never know what is going to happen next in the wacky world of TV. If I had come back to do the 7a.m. start with Eamonn, I would have had to get up at least two hours earlier in the morning to be at work on time and would have been exhausted. With my new job, I had the best of both worlds.

I was working five days a week but leaving early and coming home right after our de-briefing, so I got to spend lots of time with Rosie.

She was a really good baby and usually slept through the night. I was breastfeeding, so she was in the same room as Steve and me. I also had one of those ghastly industrial-looking breast pumps that I would take to work with me. I would sit in the loo, or in the back of the car with a big shawl over me, pumping away to express milk.

After all the uncertainty it was good to be back with the gang but without all the stress involved in working on the 'main show'. It's always easier when it's 'one singer, one song', even if you get on famously with your co-host. With only yourself to worry about, you can just get on with the job, and you don't need to be involved with any office politics or silly point-scoring. I had my own team and my own experts, and we formed a very tight-knit and happy band.

Anthea Turner was more than welcome to the stress of the 'main show', and there were no hard feelings. On the contrary, I was grateful to her. On my first day back full-time I made a point of wishing her good luck and also telling her I was for ever in her debt: she had saved me having to get up so early. It broke the ice and we never had any problems. We shared a dressing-room and got on very well.

We are both neat and tidy to the point of obsession and our tiny room was always pristine. At the start of 1995, however, it was clear that the partnership between Eamonn and Anthea was simply not working. They are both lovely people, but in those days I wouldn't have invited them to dinner on the same night. It is very tough to throw two individuals together and expect them to click, and to like and respect each other. It worked with Anne Diamond and Nick Owen. It obviously works beautifully with Richard and Judy. Mike Morris and I had a good, solid working relationship – but after a very, very short honeymoon period, Eamonn and Anthea could not bear to be in the same room as each other. It was very tough for everyone around them – although when I came on set to start my show I was greeted like a cross between the Queen Mother and Barbara Windsor. 'Thank God you're here', the crew would cry, as the atmosphere thawed.

The press loved the tension and sadly there are one or two people at GMTV who have made it their business to sell vile and completely inaccurate stories about the station and the presenters to the papers. They have made themselves a small fortune over the years from their tittle-tattle and have caused great harm and upset.

The most ridiculous 'wicked whisper' I ever heard about me was fairly innocuous but complete rubbish. According to the *Daily Mail*, I didn't have a Glaswegian accent and was, in fact, rather posh. They claimed I only put on a Scottish voice to appear to be 'one of the people'. It was so silly and, along with my family and pals, I could only laugh, but it didn't stop me receiving a sackful of letters from people 'disappointed' in me or who had 'always known' I was a 'phoney'. Obviously such a stupid slur wasn't worth making a fuss about, so I pretended to ignore it, but it still hurt and rankled.

Stories about both Eamonn and Anthea were also being leaked to the papers, and although there were some members of management who didn't seem to mind the negative publicity and thought it encouraged viewers to tune in to see if the two of them would actually have a squabble on air (they never did and were utterly professional throughout) it was clear that the situation could not possibly be allowed to continue.

By this time Anthea was flying high. She hosted the live lottery extravaganza every Saturday night, had a raft of TV shows in the pipeline, and was the new Golden Girl. She and Eamonn limped along together but bosses increasingly kept them apart, with Anthea hosting the summer GMTV *Fun in the Sun* programmes from Spain, and Eamonn doing more and more shows with Fiona Phillips, who had been playing a blinder as our Hollywood correspondent.

Anthea eventually left GMTV and she and Eamonn have long since made up. Fiona stepped deftly into the hot seat and has been doing a sterling job there ever since. She is a lovely woman. Totally straight and down-to-earth, and her most important job in life is looking after her two precious boys with her husband GMTV editor Martin Frizzell.

Like all working mums, I try to juggle everything and I can only do my TV job and all my writing because I have a lot of help and support from Steve, my friends, and my mum and dad. When Rosie was at primary school, we had a wonderful girl called Helen Horne, who lived in Maidenhead. She took Rosie to school in the mornings and looked after her if we were both working. Leaving the house at 5.30a.m. every day meant I obviously couldn't take Rosie to school, but the up-side was that I could usually pick her up. Like Sian, who had helped me when Rosie was a baby, Helen was completely reliable, even on those horribly cold early winter mornings, and Rosie adored her.

I never forget how lucky I have been to do a job where I get to spend so much time with my daughter, and although there have been some difficult times on air there have been hilarious moments too. Many of these happened during our annual 'Get Up and Give' week. Every year four 'Cinderella' charities were chosen and we would ask viewers to help them by donating money or volunteering their time. The week was organised by Helen McMurray, who put her heart and soul into the enterprise and who always set presenters a challenge.

One year I was handed a toughie. I was ordered to the London Palladium, poured into a giant crinoline dress and told to perform a song and dance from that year's hit musical, *The King and I*. I thought it would be a bit of a hoot and I could shuffle around for a bit, mime a couple of lines and go off for a cup of tea. No such luck. The producers of the show had been told to put me through my paces. I actually had to learn lines and dance moves and perform 'Shall We Dance?' properly, like a real musical-theatre actress.

My unfortunate co-star in the role made famous in the movie by Yul Brynner was Hawaiian actor Keo Woolford. I was dismayed to see that, when in costume, he had no shoes on. I just knew I would crush his tootsies, but I was even more worried when the musical director asked me what key I sang in. I had no idea what he was talking about. When Rosie and I are listening to Scott Mills on Radio 1 on the way home from school she tells me not to sing along to the Kaiser Chiefs because I sound like a sick frog.

I was in trouble. I can't sing and I can't dance and I was on the London Palladium stage (which, I might add, revolves).

With a lot of help from Josie Lawrence, who was actually playing the Deborah Kerr role of Anna, I sort of got away with it. I didn't stand on Keo's toes and cripple him, and I didn't fall over, but it wasn't the London Palladium's finest hour.

I will always remember one particular moment from 'Get Up and Give' because it sums up the madness and hilarity of breakfast TV. In one corner of the studio, for reasons that escape me, we had a bunch of life-sized dancing bananas. Gareth Gates and his sassy dancers were limbering up to perform after the break; John Stapleton, Andrea McLean, Ross Kelly and I were on air boogieing to a rap track, and among the team manning the phones and taking calls was that morning's star volunteer, Gordon Brown, the then chancellor of the exchequer.

All callers were asked if they were tax-payers. If so, then the charities would be eligible for Gift Aid, which meant they would receive more money. I still wonder what the viewers who got through to the chancellor thought when they heard his distinctive tones asking them, 'Are you a tax-payer?' It would have been rather terrifying even to the most squeaky clean and law-abiding citizen.

'Get Up and Give' was great fun and had huge support from everyone who came on the show.

Indeed most of the celebs and stars who perch on the sofa are on their best behaviour. That's mainly because they have something to sell, whether it's a new movie, DVD, book or TV show, so it's in their best interests to be charming.

I don't think there's much point in doing a job if it makes you miserable, and I can't understand why some celebrities whine so much. They're doing a job they supposedly love, earning fabulous money and being constantly adored. The general rule of thumb is that the bigger the entourage, the bigger the pain in the bum. The likes of Mariah Carey, J-Lo and Britney inevitably turn up with more than twenty people in their wake. I have absolutely no idea what most of these hangers-on actually do and all they achieve is a great big messy fuss around the star. They have to justify their existence, so you get assistants demanding 'special' water for Shakira, when the woman herself – a delight – would be happy to grab a drink from the tap, and you have ludicrous demands for dressing-rooms painted white and lilac, and for them to be scented with expensive and very specific candles.

If a diva's entourage were to demand that her dressing-room at GMTV be refurbished, all we could do would be to clear up the paper plates littered with bits of leftover stale croissants, throw some threadbare towels over the knackered chairs, give the room a spray of Oust and hope for the best. Any daft requests are always greeted with hoots of laughter, because the facilities can only be described as 'basic'.

The exception to the rule about big entourages was actor Jamie Foxx. I think he brought half of New York City with him. We were tripping over big bodyguards and women with powder puffs, but they were all very jolly and he was funny and charming.

Piers Morgan came on the show and was half jokingly girning that his dressing-room was smaller than Simon Cowell's during the run of *America's Got Talent*, so Fiona and I thought we'd make him feel better by showing him our 'facilities'. Piers hooted in derision and thought it was hilarious that we had to share such a dank little hole. He skipped away from the studio extremely pleased with himself.

Fiona, Kate and I share a dressing-room, which is basically a tiny Portakabin affixed to the side of the building. It is boiling in summer and freezing in winter.

To be honest, we don't actually mind hot-seating and getting undressed in front of each other because we're pals and we also know that everyone else is in the same boat. Our bosses are all in tiny offices and our fashion models get changed and made up in the loo. The corridor is littered with the clothes, bags and shoes Mark Heyes buys on the high street. At the end of the show he and his assistant Sarah Tankell have to pack everything up again and take it back to the shops.

Guests perch on the stairs and everyone just gets on with it. It actually gives us all a sense of camaraderie. There's certainly no time or space for anyone to throw their weight about and behave like a spoiled star. They wouldn't last long.

During my long time in breakfast TV, I have been lucky enough to work with some fantastic fellow presenters and reporters. John Stapleton is a TV legend and his partnership with Penny Smith on the *Newshour* every morning is one of the unsung joys of British TV. I was also really sad when Ross Kelly left, because he had a wonderful ability to make even the dullest story sound exciting. I loved it when he was on a live link because I knew I could relax for five minutes as he was always a real pro, never overran and never, ever needed rescuing.

On his last day, we planned a very special surprise for Ross. He *adores* Julie Andrews and I had to interview her that week about *The Princess Diaries*. She was so gracious and lovely that I plucked up courage to ask her a favour. I told her that Ross was a huge admirer and that legend has it he once went to a *Sound of Music* singalong dressed as a brown-paper-package-tied-up-with-string, and would she do a special farewell and good-luck message to him?

Dame Julie was happy to oblige. Ross was beside himself with happiness and it made a wonderful send-off to a really terrific broadcaster. I miss working with Ross. He's one of the good guys.

As I was now doing my own show, it was easier for us to put the sofa under our arms and take the whole thing out on the road. In October 2003 my producer Sophie Hodgkins, Lisa Kelly and the rest of the team took the show to Los Angeles for a week-long special. I hadn't been to La La Land since 1997 when Steve and I attended my friend Pete Morris's fantastic wedding in Beverly Hills.

I have known Pete for ages. We met while we were covering the riots outside Peterhead Prison back in the eighties when he worked for Grampian TV and I was TVam's Scottish correspondent. He also went on to work at TVam and was entertainment editor at GMTV. Pete had moved to Los Angeles with his future wife, Melanie Green, who is a showbiz agent, and I remember him telling me that one of her clients had landed a new role in a sci-fi series that sounded quite interesting. This just so happened to be David Duchovny and the show was the global phenomenon *The X Files*.

I wasn't able to get any time off work, but there was no way I was missing this bash. The clans were gathering and a huge mob of Scots were heading for Hollywood. Steve and I flew out after my show on the Friday morning. We had that night in LA, went to the wedding on Saturday and flew back on Sunday. It was impossibly showbiz and hugely glamorous, except for the cheap economy flight, which was all we could afford.

David Duchovny was at the wedding alongside Hollywood A-listers like Michelle Pfeiffer, looking even more beautiful in real life, and we all did a very unconvincing job of trying to look nonchalant and not pinching each other and giggling in sheer excitement.

Pete's daughter Rebecca was a beautiful bridesmaid and her mum Julie was there with her partner. She and Pete have always remained good pals and a great example of a civilised separation.

We had a couple of hours' free time on Saturday morning before the wedding and I headed for the nearest mall. I had realised that although my dress had looked OK in the shop in London it just wasn't glam enough for this event, and I managed to buy a sassy little lacy number for about fifty quid, which I have never had the nerve to wear again but made me feel very Rita Hayworth.

The wedding was simply perfect and, as befitting LA, it was exactly like something out of the movies. The venue was a glorious Dynasty-style mansion and the ceremony itself took place outside on an immaculate lawn with beautiful gilt chairs lined up in front of the flower-covered altar.

Melanie came down the aisle to the strains of a Scottish piper on the balcony. All the men were in kilts, which greatly tickled the women of Hollywood, especially when they did a *Braveheart* bare-bum salute later that night. The glorious Julia Fordham sang for Pete and Melanie and dedicated her hit 'Happy Ever After' to the newly-weds and it was just the most fantastic day. As we sipped champagne and breathed the same air as Hollywood stars Pete and I reminded each other that this was just a bit different from sitting in the car outside a prison on a freezing winter night eating pie and chips, while the horizontal rain battered on the windscreen, and you knew you would be there until the wee small hours.

As it was LA everything had to finish early. At midnight the plug was pulled and we went back to our hotel in West Hollywood. Along with pals Tony Fitzpatrick, Jason Pollock and Mark Hagen, who produces *TOTP 2*, Steve and I watched the sun come up from our rooftop pool and decided that life was pretty damned terrific.

In 2007 Steve, Rosie and I went back to LA and spent New Year with Pete and Melanie and their wee boy McKenzie. The family live in Ginger Rogers' old house and have built themselves a terrific life. Pete works as a producer and his first movie *Trust Me* was released earlier that year. Pete and Melanie celebrate New Year at four o'clock in the afternoon in LA when it is midnight in Scotland.

LA is a village. Also at the party was Ross King, one of the stars of Pete's movie. He also does a regular slot with me on *LK Today*. On New Year's Day we went to see him at his house in the Hollywood Hills and he is also living the American dream. If you stand on his balcony you have the actual Hollywood sign right behind you.

Ross had a very successful career in the UK, hosting shows like *Pebble Mill at One*, but went to LA six years ago to try his luck at breaking into the big-time over there. For a bit of a laugh he entered a competition to find a weather presenter for KTLA, the local TV station, and out of thousands of entries he walked away with the prize. He is now their top entertainment anchor and has won three prestigious Emmys.

He has his own radio studio in his house and still does his shows for Radio Clyde and Radio Forth. He does a brilliant showbiz slot with me every Tuesday and, along with Tina Baker's soap news, and any time I can persuade our bosses to let me do a film review, it's – as Harry Hill would say – my 'TV Highlight of the Week'.

Ross feels that life in LA is like being in a movie and when we did our week-long special that was exactly how we all felt. We did an entire programme from Hugh Hefner's Playboy Mansion. I had a right good look around, including a peek at the infamous grotto, just off the swimming-pool, where piles of fluffy white towels and bottles of baby oil gave me a bit of a clue as to what happens in there.

Many a showbiz A-lister has taken advantage of Hugh Hefner's hospitality, and when I interviewed the old goat, he was utterly charming. We also ran into Jack Osbourne playing pool in the house and a gaggle of disconcertingly similar blonde, busty women with names like Bambi, Cherry and Brandy, who were all tooth-achingly 'nice' and utterly thrilled to be living with Hugh and his money.

We interviewed Sharon Osbourne on the roof of our hotel, and she was most impressed when her two tetchy dogs made a beeline for my Steve and sat happily in his lap. They usually snap at strangers, but they both were drawn to him, proving animals are always the best judge of character.

Another impossibly glamorous assignment was to interview Elton John at his villa in Nice. Steve was coincidentally booked as the cameraman, which meant we needed to find a babysitter for Rosie, but Elton's 'people' said she could come too. The villa was utterly sumptuous, on top of a hill looking out over the sea. It was a sort of homage to Gianni Versace, the late fashion designer, who had been a great friend of Elton's. Versace was murdered in Miami in July 1997, and Elton had attended the funeral with Princess Diana.

Of course Diana herself was killed just weeks later. I believe she was a victim of nothing more than being driven by a drunk and not wearing a seatbelt. I suppose it is hard to accept that such a 'mundane' accident could have killed her, but I have always discounted the outlandish conspiracy theories. On the night before her funeral, from about midnight right through to the morning, I was broadcasting from Whitehall, just across from Downing Street, amongst the crowds that lined the funeral route. As I talked to people who were camping out with their Thermos flasks and homemade sandwiches, there was actually quite a jolly atmosphere, but when it became light, the mood changed dramatically.

People began to cry, moan and keen. It was very disturbing and almost medieval as they threw flowers at the coffin, wept and howled. After our broadcast I went home to watch the service on TV and, alongside the card with 'Mummy' written on it attached to the flowers on Diana's coffin, Elton's performance of 'Candle in the Wind' was the most moving moment.

I hadn't met Elton before, but had been warned he could be 'difficult'. I just wish every star I interviewed was as difficult as Elton. He was a dream to talk to, and his home was simply stunning, stuffed with expensive modern art, beautiful furniture, and a good, happy vibe. The famous Versace Medusa head logo was everywhere in the villa, emblazoned on soap dishes in the bathrooms and woven into the towels round the pool.

Elton was upstairs getting ready for the interview, but his partner David Furnish made us very welcome and told us to set up on the balcony. While Steve and his soundman, Ian Birch, set up the lights, Rosie did a drawing for Elton, which he happily admired. He really was so kind to her. She was a bit shy at first, but he chatted away and obviously is one of the few adults who can talk to children properly. No wonder so many celebrities, like Victoria Beckham and Liz Hurley, have asked him to be godfather to their children. I know the presents must be terrific, but Elton and David take a real interest in those children, and spend time with them, and that's worth a lot more than money.

CHAPTER NINE

Beyond Belief

S ome events are so shocking that you simply cannot believe they have actually happened, and the day pure evil visited Dunblane was one of them.

On 13 March 1996 I was on the way home after my show when I heard on the radio that there had been a shooting at a school in Dunblane. I immediately thought this tragedy had happened somewhere in the USA, in a place that happened to share the same name as the peaceful town in Scotland half-way between Glasgow and Dundee.

Like the rest of the country, I was utterly shocked that something so horrific could have happened in our own back-yard.

Sixteen children and their teacher at Dunblane Primary School were senselessly murdered and at least a dozen more shot and injured. It was unimaginable that such an atrocity could happen there. It felt completely unreal and impossible to comprehend.

I know Dunblane very well. It's a beautiful town and a favourite stopping-off place for travellers coming backwards and forwards from Glasgow to Dundee, Perth or Aberdeen. They can break their journey, stretch their legs and have a cup of tea. It's the kind of place parents are keen to move to from the city because it's quieter, friendlier and a safer place to bring up a family. You could never contemplate such violence and horror being unleashed on a place like Dunblane.

When I got home I called GMTV. They wanted to do the whole show live from Dunblane the next day. I packed a bag and headed for the airport and a flight to Scotland. Arriving at Dunblane later that afternoon, I found the whole town in a state of profound shock. Flowers were piling up outside the primary school and the streets were thick with reporters and camera crews. When there is a tragedy, even one as grim as Piper Alpha or Lockerbie, there are always black jokes and sick comments from the hardened press corps. Not this time.

Some of the self-styled toughest newspaper men and women were white-faced and tearful, while experienced police officers had clearly been weeping. A school photograph of the children was released to the media. They were all from Primary One, which meant they were five or six years old. The cowardly bastard had slaughtered defenceless kids and their teacher.

That night at a press conference a police officer read out the names of those who had been murdered. There were so many that I thought he would never finish this litany of dead children. That was when the enormity of what had happened that morning really sank in. So many little children were dead, and so many families torn apart.

There was Primary One teacher, Gwen Mayor, her pupils Victoria Clydesdale, Emma Crozier, Melissa Currie, Charlotte Dunn, Kevin Hasell, Ross Irvine, David Kerr, Mhairi McBeath, Brett McKinnon, Abigail McLennan, Emily Morton, Sophie North, John Petrie, Joanna Ross, Hannah Scott and Megan Turner.

Their killer had fired a few shots in the empty assembly hall just after nine o'clock, then burst into the gym, full of little children having fun and playing games, where he opened fire on them. He had hunted down those frightened little kids and pumped bullets into their bodies. His killing spree lasted for less than four minutes before he shot himself dead.

Some children were killed instantly. In a room awash with blood distraught medical staff battled to save the lives of those who had been shot and were badly injured. It was eerily quiet because the children who had survived were too traumatised to cry.

After the press conference I went back to the hotel in Dunblane and wrote my weekly column for the *Sunday Post*. In one of those horrible ironies, the first Sunday after the massacre was Mothers' Day.

It took me hours to write a piece about how the mothers of those dead children would never again be handed a precious homemade card or a bunch of daffodils. Of course, no matter how much we sympathised and shuddered at the thought of losing our own children, we had no idea of the depth of the pain and suffering of those grieving families. How could we possibly know?

I didn't sleep at all that night. I couldn't even begin to imagine how I would feel if a madman had burst into my daughter's nursery school and started firing bullets at the little ones as they played innocently.

The next morning, I was up much earlier than usual and at around 4a.m. Eamonn and I stood outside the cathedral on that bleak, cold morning with just a few notes in our hands and two and a half hours to fill. It was a tough show to do. I just wanted to be by myself to weep, but this was no time to be self-indulgent. Our viewers needed to know what was happening, have a chance to make their views known, and to express their sympathy for the bereaved.

It was clear there was a real anxiety among parents all over the country that this might happen in their own children's school, as well as a growing anger that a maniac was able to get his hands on such dangerous weapons and carry out this savage act.

On a show like GMTV, presenters are allowed to express opinions and emotions in a way that isn't possible on a straight-forward news programme. I think this is one of the strengths of GMTV, but it is a big responsibility as well as a privilege. That day, without being mawkish, we tried to echo how everyone in the country felt. We were all shocked, bewildered and desperately sorry for the parents and families of those who had lost their children. The murders made us want to hold our own children closer and it also made us realise that nowhere can ever be completely safe.

We did the Friday show live from Dunblane too, but I felt strongly that we should now leave and not impose on the people of the town any longer. None of the families wanted to talk to the media, which was completely understandable.

What I wasn't aware of at the time was that many of the bereaved families, and the parents of those children who had been severely injured, were watching the show. I'm glad I didn't know as it would have made it almost impossible to do my job.

As it was, I had barely been able to hold myself together.

When I arrived back home in Cookham after the flight south, the first thing I did was give my two-year-old daughter a massive hug and hold her tight. Later, I cried buckets and, like everyone else, felt utterly helpless but desperately wished there was something I could do for the parents and families of the children killed in Dunblane.

I was to be given that chance.

Steve told me the police in Dunblane had been on the phone and I was to call them back immediately. I spoke to Ian Hamilton, the police officer who had been assigned to the Ross family. Joanna Ross, who was just five years old, had been one of those murdered. Her mum, Pam, had been touched by our coverage. She also read my column in the *Sunday Post* every week and she wondered if she could talk to me privately.

I had no idea what possible use I could be, but if Pam thought I could help in some way then I obviously wanted to see her. Ian told me that Pam had a baby girl, and Rosie gave me her favourite teddy bear to give to four-month-old Alison. I grabbed some photos of Rosie and headed once more to the airport.

On the journey back up to Scotland it dawned on me that I wasn't a trained grief counsellor or social worker, and I had no idea what I would say to a woman who had suffered the worst possible bereavement.

I was picked up by Ian Hamilton and taken back to Dunblane. We arrived there around 5p.m. He was a lovely man and it was clear he was being a real rock to Pam and her family, but even this big, tough policeman was finding it difficult to come to terms with what had happened.

I began to get very nervous as we reached Pam's house. I was really concerned about whether I would be of any help or comfort at all. As soon as I walked through the door, I knew it would be all right. We both hugged, burst into tears, and I knew we would be friends. We just clicked.

Pam's daughter had been killed just two days before and she was clearly still in shock, but she was putting on the bravest of faces. She said she just wanted to curl up into a ball and howl out her grief and rage, but her baby needed to be fed and changed and somehow that kept her going. Little Alison gave Pam and her husband, Kenny, a reason to keep functioning and brought some normality to those dark days.

The house was full of family, neighbours and friends who just wanted to say how sorry they were. No one could really grasp the enormity of what had happened. Pam's mum made endless cups of tea, and Joanna was remembered with love and a sense of bewilderment.

Pam and I talked and talked and talked on that Friday night. She told me that on the last morning of her life Joanna had walked to school hand in hand with her grandpa, Jimmy. Pam was still on maternity leave after giving birth to Alison. Later that morning she had a phone call from her worried brother, telling her there had been some kind of shooting incident at Joanna's school. No one knew very much about what had happened, but Pam left Alison with her mother-in-law and drove the short distance to the school. She couldn't get through as the roads were blocked off so she abandoned the car and ran the rest of the way.

Just picture that frantic mother racing to the school and hearing rumours from shocked groups of parents that there had been a disaster, that Primary One pupils were involved and it had happened in the gym.

Joanna was in Primary One and she had gym that day.

It was chaos at the school. When Pam told the policeman at the gate that she had a daughter in Primary One, she was taken away from all the other anxious parents to a house next to the school where there were other parents and family with children in Gwen Mayor's class. It was clear something was very wrong.

Kenny came to join her, and they had to wait for hours to find out what had happened to their Joanna. I know Pam still finds that very hard to take. Those in charge were drafting statements for the press while she and Kenny waited to hear whether their daughter was alive or dead. The authorities were obviously under pressure, but the parents should have been their number-one priority.

That night, Pam showed me photos of her daughter taken during the five short years of her life. Joanna was a beautiful little girl with blonde hair, blue eyes and a heartbreakingly happy face. She was also a cheeky monkey with a stubborn streak and loads of character. We cried and we even laughed as Pam remembered funny things Joanna had said or done.

Eventually Kenny said that as we had been talking about his daughter, would I like to see her?

I had no idea that Joanna was upstairs in her room. I felt honoured that they both wanted me to see their beloved child.

She was on the bed, in an open white coffin, wearing her favourite Pocahontas nightie. She looked as though she was asleep and would wake up at any minute. Her little face showed no sign of the bullets that had killed her.

I didn't think I had any tears left, but I cried so hard with grief and with a deep, deep anger that this little girl and all the others had been robbed of their future by an evil, deranged killer.

Kenny is a typical working-class Scottish man who doesn't easily show his emotions, but he was heartbroken. Standing at the foot of his daughter's bed, his voice shook as he said, 'Look what this monster has done.' He told me to keep watch over my own daughter and to realise how lucky I was to still have her.

I will never forget seeing Joanna's fingerprints on the window of her room. Can you imagine how heartbreaking it would be to want never to clean the windows because you would erase that trace of your dead child?

It was after midnight when I left to stay with my mum overnight. We both sat and talked into the wee small hours.

Pam had asked me if I would come to Joanna's funeral on the Monday morning. I was deeply touched to be asked and I called my boss, Peter McHugh, to let him know I wouldn't be coming into work that morning. To his eternal credit, he not only said it was fine, but when I told him that this, of course, was completely private and not something GMTV could cover, and that I also would not talk about it on air, he understood and completely agreed.

Not once did anyone from GMTV put pressure on me either to secure an 'exclusive' interview with the families or to talk about Joanna and her mum and dad. If they had done, I would have obviously refused, but I was never put in that position.

Other news organisations might criticise Peter and me and claim we should have used my bond with Pam to secure access to the funeral and an exclusive interview. I think it is more important to be a decent human being than to go after a story at any cost. It never occurred to me to exploit my friendship with Pam. It would have been not only inappropriate but also a real betrayal.

Now that over ten years have passed, we both feel it is time to talk about what happened.

Joanna had a joint funeral with her friend Emma Crozier in Lecropt Church at Bridge of Allan. The two little girls had been christened together on the same day, 5 August 1990, in that church. Their small white coffins were side by side, and it was just so desperately sad. Everyone was thinking what a waste it was of their young lives, their hopes and dreams for the future.

In the midst of their grief the families could not have been more welcoming to me, and even thanked me for coming to the service. Their dignity was very humbling.

The media kept their promise and stayed away. Even the most hardened snappers and snoopers knew this was a line that was not to be crossed. There wasn't a photographer, reporter or camera crew in sight. Joanna and Emma's families were able to lay their girls to rest in peace and quiet.

Pam remembers police outriders escorting the funeral cortège from the church to Dunblane cemetery and how traffic stopped on the main road and people stood by their cars bowing their heads; builders stepped down from scaffolding and took off their hard hats. There was an overwhelming wave of sympathy and respect, and a sea of flowers.

How Pam managed to keep herself together for the funeral and the reception afterwards I will never know. She is one of the bravest women I have ever met. I know that afterwards she went home and cried and grieved, but that day she was incredibly strong, saying she owed it to her daughter not to break down.

Just before I left, she looked at me and told me she felt so guilty because she was supposed to protect her daughter and she hadn't been there when she'd needed her. She was so worried that Joanna had been frightened and calling for her mummy and she hadn't been there to save her. Pam looked so hurt, bewildered and bereft. It broke my heart.

I flew back that night as I had to go to work the next day. It felt very odd to be doing a 'normal' show that Tuesday, and I made sure that I opened the programme by telling everyone in Dunblane that we were all thinking of them.

Sadly, even in those early days, there was a very small minority of people in Dunblane who felt resentment towards the parents and simply wanted to forget about the murders. The insensitivity and selfishness of those few sour individuals were staggering and, sadly, they made a lot of noise. They wanted the parents of the bereaved and injured to 'move on' and basically shut up. They didn't want their town to be associated only with the horror of the murders. Thankfully, the vast majority of people were fiercely protective of the bereaved families, and the families of the children who had been injured, and wanted to do everything in their power to help them.

Pam and I phoned each other regularly and blethered for hours on end. We talked about the growing Snowdrop Campaign to ban handguns, so named because snowdrops were the only flowers in bloom on the day of the murders. We talked a lot about Joanna and how everyone was coping, but also about a million other things.

Pam was doing remarkably well but, like all the other parents, she had good days and bad days. A few months later she asked if I would come to one of the regular meetings the parents held in the town. It was their way of helping and supporting each other, and of discussing practicalities like a memorial for Gwen and the children. Once again I was struck by the strength and bravery of these men and women, who had been brought together under the most appalling circumstances.

They decided to hold a service for their children and for their teacher, Gwen, and asked if I would read out a poem, and also read out the name of each child while their parents lit a candle in their memory. The service would be called 'Out of Darkness and into Light', and would be a celebration of those lives lost. I was deeply touched by their request.

The memorial service was to be held in the massive Dunblane Cathedral and broadcast live by the BBC. Prince Charles would be there, representing the Queen, and the pews would be full of dignitaries. None of that mattered to me. I just wanted to make sure I didn't let the families down by stumbling over my words or becoming upset.

There was a rehearsal the night before the service, and as I climbed up into the pulpit I knew I was in trouble. My throat closed and I couldn't speak. I stood there with the poem in my shaking hands and tears running down my cheeks, unable to utter a single word. I was led away in despair. What if I did this tomorrow? The families were relying on me to read out the very special poem they had chosen and that meant so much to them.

I simply had to pull myself together. I stayed with Pam and her family that night but didn't get much sleep. The next morning I asked Pam if it would be all right to go into Joanna's room and read out the poem as though I were talking directly to her. She said I could so I went in, sat down on the bed, read it through out loud and immediately felt so much better.

We reached the cathedral about an hour before the service was due to begin. It was a solemn occasion but it was also an uplifting one. On the altar stood seventeen white candles. Each had a name etched on to it, one for Gwen and one for each child, They looked so beautiful, and as I read out each name, the parents stepped forward to light the candle for their child.

I stood there with my fingernails digging into my palms to stop myself crying, and full of admiration as the parents managed to make this deeply moving tribute to their children. The lighting of the candles was to symbolise hope, and especially the hope that the whole community would now take its first steps out of darkness and into light. The poem chosen by the families was 'Little Child Lost' by Eugene G. Merryman Jnr. This is the version I read out in Dunblane Cathedral that morning.

Shall we ever find anything other than a child that can be such a paradox in our lives?
A little person that can generate such a conflict of anger and love.
One that causes so much sorrow when they have been hurt, only to cause so much happiness with their laughter.
One who can cause so much fear for their safety and well being, and then so much comfort and serenity when they are asleep in your arms.
This little person has the ability to pull at each and every emotion known to us, and some that we weren't even aware we had.
When the loss of a child happens, no matter how, what do we do then?
Will we ever escape the sound of their voice?
Will we never stop catching a glimpse of them out of the corner of our eye?
The answer is that you do see and you do hear, just as you continue to love, for that child was part of your soul.
Although you may not always hear them, as they move upon the wings of the wind, nor may you always see them as they go past on a ray of sunlight, be assured they are with you.

Though we many never be able to explain your loss, or console you, I wish
to thank you, for without your child and other children who have gone
before us, there would be no children in Heaven.
Playing where they never tire, your child is safe and happy.

I honestly don't think I would have been able to read out the
poem in the cathedral without breaking down if I hadn't had that
rehearsal in Joanna's room. After I had sat down, legs shaking,
Mick North, whose daughter Sophie had been murdered, gave
me a hug. I couldn't return it because if I had I would have
started sobbing uncontrollably. I sat there on the pew trying not
to cry and asking myself how I could possibly be so weak and
self-indulgent when the parents and families were being so stoic
and dignified in their grief.

After the ceremony we went through to a back room to have
tea with Prince Charles. He valiantly made small-talk but I
couldn't help thinking how much more at ease Diana would
have been in this situation. She would have sat beside parents and
asked them about their children, held their hands and
understood their suffering.

That first Christmas, I was sent a present from all the families,
a specially made silver pin shaped like a snowdrop as a thank you.
It is one of my most precious possessions.

There is a heartbreaking corner of the cemetery in Dunblane
where the children and their teacher are buried. Gwen Mayor
would have been looking forward to retiring now, and the
children who were murdered would have been sixteen and
seventeen years old. I hope that the monster who killed them is
suffering all the torments of hell.

CHAPTER TEN

Talking the Talk

I love radio. It's intimate, instant, exciting and, best of all, you don't have to have your hair done or wear any makeup when you're presenting. You can sit there in your tracksuit, dipping HobNobs into your tea and no one will ever know.

1997 kicked off with a new job, and a new challenge when I was asked to present a late-morning show on Talk Radio. It meant rushing almost straight from GMTV after our post-programme meeting, and making the short ten-minute journey to the station headquarters in Oxford Street, where I had to be on air by eleven o'clock. It was hectic, but terrific fun. It gave me the chance to tackle some of the biggest news stories of the day and to analyse and discuss them with our listeners.

Talk Radio was a revelation. In among the usual gripes about local government's failure to empty the bins and tirades against traffic wardens, we launched a section called 'A

Beginner's Guide to . . .' This was the brainchild of producer Dixi Stewart, a terrifyingly intelligent young woman who had bright ideas tumbling out of every pore. Subjects we tackled ranged from the works of Albert Camus to the postmodernism of Jean Baudrillard, which I remember introducing to the listeners thus: 'We want you to decide whether Baudrillard is a cure for the vertigo of contemporary culture or one of its symptoms.'

We discussed Freud, the Devil, Thatcherism, Einstein and Buddha. I really loved doing my homework for these items, reading tons of books and having lively discussions with Dixi and the team. It sometimes made the inside of my brain go white hot, but it was so exciting and exhilarating. The listeners enjoyed being stretched and so did I.

Dixi Stewart was eventually poached by Radio 4, and my new producer, Jez Wright, brought a bit of edginess to the show. My signature tune was changed to the Verve's haunting 'Bitter Sweet Symphony' and we had a lot more music in the show, as well as all the usual discussions. It was always challenging and we had some fantastic guests.

Within the team of Amy, Emily, Jez and myself, we had a competition to see how long I could spend not asking a guest obvious questions about what they were best known for. This meant that Morse's creator Colin Dexter wasn't actually asked about his most famous detective until half-way through the interview and only after we had exhausted his favourite subject, which was crosswords.

Once when a guest was late we played all of 'Bohemian Rhapsody', which is more than six minutes long, while she ran down Oxford Street and arrived puffing and panting just as the divine Freddie was whispering the last words of the song and bashing out that final chord.

I did have one major clash with Talk Radio, which almost led to me being sacked. We sent Rosie to the local nursery, which was a five-minute walk down a leafy lane and part of Herries Primary School, where she would be going in a couple of years. As she was an only child, I wanted her to have the chance to play with other children and she went there for two mornings a week. Just before Christmas I was told that my three-year-old had been chosen to play Mary in the nativity play.

This was *huge*, but the play kicked off at twelve noon, right in the middle of my radio show. As this was the biggest event of that or any other year, as far as I was concerned, there was no way I was going to miss seeing Rosie holding the baby Jesus upside-down and waving at me from the stage. Those are the precious moments you remember until the day you die.

I'm afraid that when I was told there was no way I was being given the time off, for once I stuck to my guns. Of course, this was another occasion when I should have used the old 'food-poisoning' excuse, but I never have and I never will. I wanted to be honest and laid it on the line that I would have to leave the station if I didn't get the time off. After a Mexican stand-off and the threat that I'd be fired, finally, with great reluctance, and because I managed to find a replacement, I was allowed to miss that one show. It was the first time I had ever not turned up for work. Through sickness, one hangover from hell and while heavily pregnant, I was always there.

I couldn't possibly tell you what radio or TV shows I did that week in December 1997, or what I wrote in my column, but I can remember every single nano-second of that nativity play. It was just beautiful. Joseph waved at his mum, the angel had a hissy-fit, the innkeeper forgot his words, and my little girl looked so adorable in her blue robe and little white headscarf pinned on with black Kirby Grips. She did indeed hold Jesus the wrong way up, and giggled and waved at me.

There is nothing on this earth more moving and uplifting than a bunch of three-year-olds singing 'Away in a Manger', especially if it's out of tune and they all finish at different times. I blubbed through the whole ten-minute production and could have watched it all day. It was well worth putting my job on the line for.

I have always loved Christmas, and when Rosie was little it was even more magical. That year, we did the usual looking to the skies on Christmas Eve to see if Santa was flying by. As we lived under the Heathrow flight path there were always lights in the sky, so we just found the biggest one and said that was him.

When Rosie went to bed, I poured a massive dram of Highland Park whisky for Santa (his favourite) to wash down his mince pie, and of course there was a big orange carrot for Rudolph. I also put a torn piece of red velvet on the fireplace for Rosie to find in the morning, and a letter to her from Santa that I had written in glitter pen. When she woke up she was so excited to find that Santa had been, had drunk all his whisky, eaten his mince pie and even left a piece of his cloak behind.

We had some brilliant Christmases in Cookham Dean. On Boxing Day the bleary-eyed, turkey-stuffed locals would gather on the village green for the traditional games. There was mulled wine to top up the booze from the day before, and teams competed with one another for the coveted wooden toilet-seat trophy. Games included tug o' war, egg-throwing, wheelbarrow races and a truly evil obstacle race. You had to crawl over hay bales, dive under a net in the freezing mud, then bob for a tangerine in an icy barrel of water. No one really cared who won. The whole point was to get muddy, have a laugh and end up in the local pub for a pint.

Our team was mostly made up of the Cookham Wanderers, a football team Steve and a bunch of his pals had started when we first moved to the village. Our friend Timmy Mallett, who worked on *Wacaday* at TVam, was one of the stalwarts. They all played five-a-side in the village hall on Friday nights until the membership grew so much that they had to train and play in proper sports centres.

It was a brilliant social club as well as a footie team, and the Cookham Wanderers' Christmas parties were legendary. The boys also play in Europe and for a while were probably the only British side to have won in Spain, Germany and Portugal.

In May 2000 Rosie was drawn out of the hat to be team mascot for Dundee United's last home game of the season against Motherwell. To make it a really special weekend the Cookham Wanderers came up to Dundee and played in a charity match against the Dundee All Stars. This gave my husband the chance to play opposite one of his all-time heroes, the legendary Davey Narey, and to score a goal against Hamish McAlpine, one of Scottish football's real characters. I think Davey let him get past and Hamish definitely looked the other way so he could score. Steve has only mentioned it about three and a half thousand times since.

The event was organised by former United player John Holt. The sun shone, the crowd went wild and the boys raised hundreds of pounds for local charities.

The next day we piled into Tannadice to watch Rosie being a mascot. She was given her own tangerine-and-black strip with her name on the back. We had to wait just outside the shower room before going on to the pitch, and I had to clasp my hands over her young eyes because every time the door swung open we were assailed by the sight of manly chests, thighs and taut, naked buttocks as the team put on their strips. No wonder I looked so pink-cheeked as I led her out of the tunnel and watched her join the team.

I don't think I have ever seen my husband so proud as when his daughter ran on to the pitch and the whole 'shed' burst into a chant of 'Rosie! Rosie!' She went out hand in hand with the then United captain Jason de Vos and had her photo taken with the team. It was a magical day.

We were up and down to Scotland all the time to watch United and to visit friends and family, and at the same time we had some brilliant times in Cookham Dean. We lived close to Rolf Harris, who is an adorable man and who also throws some fantastic parties. Rolf stands at the door with his accordion and plays an appropriate off-the-cuff tune for his guests as they arrive. We were treated to a spirited version of 'Bonnie Dundee'.

Rolf also gave Steve some master classes in painting. Steve left school at sixteen to be an apprentice electrician but he is a very talented painter and should really have gone to art college. He has painted some fantastic works for our house, including a series depicting friends and family raising a toast to the world at large, which now adorns our dining-room. The one of my dad quaffing a glass of beer is my favourite, but they all capture the essence of each person so well.

For my forty-fifth birthday, and sticking with the penguin

My gorgeous daughter aged 13.

You're under arrest! Me as a New York cop to promote our week of programmes in the Big Apple.

With Siobhan and Rosie at the RAF Leuchars Battle of Britain Ball in 2007.

Being 'dragged' around Dundee pubs before being installed as University rector.

Rosie as Dundee United mascot, 2000.

With Siobhan after the London Moonwalk.

My first London Marathon, 2004.

Playtex Moonwalk 2005

With Joyce after finishing the New York Marathon in 2005.

With Rosie and Steve after my first London Marathon.

The start of the first Scottish Moonwalk: Carol, Joan, Jacqueline and me.

With Rosie and Elton John at his home in the South of France.

Steve, Rosie and me with Dundee's most famous superstar Brian Cox, at his wedding by the banks of the Tay.

Me and Sharon Osbourne during our GMTV interview.

A rare shot of Dec without Ant – and Rosie!

Rosie and the legend that is Billy Conno

In the hot seat hosting *HIGNFY*.

With The Biggins, Graham Norton, Russell Brand and Barbara Windsor – it doesn't get any more camp.

Dr Kelly with Mum and Dad after being awarded an honorary degree from Dundee University in June 2008

On Concorde as a fortieth birthday celebration.

Beware the pussycat – with Rosie in Namibia, 2006.

With my pals in Spain – Jacqueline Millar, Hugh Grant, Craig Millar, Joan Grant.

Steve getting rabbit ears on Christmas Day in Sydney.

Sundowners at the famous Fish Eagle Bar in Botswana, 2007.

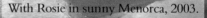
With Rosie in sunny Menorca, 2003.

In Malaysia with Graham and Rosie, 2004.

At the Trevi Fountain in Rome.

theme that had worked so well in the past, Steve painted me a beautiful picture of two emperor penguins and their fluffy chick. He has painted glorious vivid scenes of Africa and Scotland. There's something very gratifying about having your walls adorned with your husband's work when it all means so much. I just wish he had time to paint even more.

During most of the time we lived in Cookham Dean Ulrika Jonsson was our next-door neighbour. I know it sounds a bit like a TV presenters' ghetto, but it wasn't like that at all. Cookham is just really close to London, but still feels as though you are deep in the countryside, and it was a happy coincidence that we became neighbours.

I have known Ulrika for years, ever since she was a weather-girl at TVam. My dad is a huge fan because she can drink whisky like a bloke and swear like a trooper. Rosie is a couple of months older than Ulrika's son Cameron, and the two of them played together when they were little kids, coming and going between the two houses through a gap in the fence. He was a cheeky, funny, delightful little boy and has grown into a splendid young man.

Ulrika's colourful love life is well documented, but she is a terrific mum. Thanks to her various romances, she had paparazzi at the bottom of her garden on a regular basis, but most especially in 1998 when she was attacked by her then boyfriend Stan Collymore in a pub in Paris during the early stages of the World Cup. Back home the next day, Ulrika called me to ask if it was still OK to come over and watch the Scotland versus Brazil game at our house as planned, along with her ex-husband John Turnbull, with whom she has always remained friends.

We had a houseful of overexcited Scotland fans and had all

dressed up suitably for this momentous occasion, which was really our equivalent of the World Cup Final. They were wearing kilts, Scotland strips and Braveheart-style face paint. The house was bedecked with flags and banners, and we were all set for another glorious defeat.

When Ulrika came up our path, I opened the door looking like William Wallace's mad-eyed mother-in-law. It was just like that scene from *Notting Hill* where Rhys Ifans is blinded by flashbulbs as he's mistaken for Julia Roberts's lover. The paparazzi pack had followed Ulrika to our house, snapping away the whole time. Luckily they didn't recognise me, but it was a very odd experience to be under siege from the assembled media. Every time someone went to the kitchen for a beer – and this was often – they would be taking photos on their long lenses through my window.

The paparazzi were out in force again when Ulrika had her perplexing fling with Sven-Göran Eriksson, who was then the England manager, and when she fell in love with and married Lance Wright while hosting a show to find him a girlfriend. I always found Ulrika good company and very honest about her mistakes when it came to men. She went through hell when her daughter Bo was born with a heart condition, and as any parent knows, when your child is sick and in pain it is the most frightening, earth-shattering experience.

I will never forget my sheer terror when Rosie suffered a febrile convulsion when she was just eighteen months old. She had a very bad fever and wasn't getting any better when she suddenly started having a fit. I was absolutely hysterical and, as always, it was Steve who saved the day. He put us both in the back of the car and drove to the local health centre in Cookham, where she was given medication. An ambulance took us to High Wycombe hospital, where she had to stay overnight. I was with her all the time, couldn't sleep a wink, and just kept looking at my fragile baby girl and hoping she would be OK. In the end, Rosie's convulsions were an isolated incident and she was fine, but at the time I feared the worst.

When you are a working mum and anything happens to your child, especially if you aren't there to kiss it better, the guilt is almost unbearable. I was on air when Rosie was bitten in the face by a dog. I wasn't told until the end of the programme, but in my imagination she'd been horribly injured, and I cried and sweated during that long journey home.

I burst into the house at the same time as she came back from the doctor with Helen. It had been more of a nip than a bite and the skin wasn't even broken, but I felt like the worst of all mothers.

It is hard not to overcompensate for the time you spend away from your children, and over the years I've had to stop myself lavishing 'stuff' on Rosie when I've felt that work has been taking over and she hasn't been getting enough attention. I really don't think there's any answer to it. If you work and you're a mother you must reconcile yourself to the fact that you will always feel guilty and inadequate. After finally managing more or less successfully to juggle being a mum, presenting on GMTV and doing my radio show, things changed again overnight.

Former *Sun* editor Kelvin MacKenzie took over Talk Radio and wanted to turn it into Talk Sport, so I knew my days were numbered. There would be no place for Beginner's Guides to Quantum Physics and the Universe, but I reckon we could have made an interesting programme about the Offside Rule.

So, at the end of 1998, I breezed into Kelvin's new office, gave him a welcoming bottle of whisky and told him I'd be off, then. I'm sure he still thinks he sacked me, but I resigned about one and a half seconds before he was able to utter, 'You're fired.'

We did our show as usual, although my team were white-faced and trembling. Apparently, Kelvin's first rousing speech to his troops had consisted of informing them that the station was useless and they were all c★★★s.

You just know when it's time to pack up your tent and move on, and that certainly was a sign for me to put away my headphones for the time being, but I'd love to do more radio in the future.

CHAPTER ELEVEN

All Human Life

I have been lucky enough to inherit my mother's good skin and high cheekbones and, despite all my worrying and the stress of being a working mum, I still feel young inside. I spend a lot of my time on air testing anti-ageing products and giving the low-down on plastic surgery, but I actually do very little to combat the ageing process. I sometimes buy some of those lotions and potions, but I never have time to use them. I suppose I think that by simply possessing a concoction that promises to erase wrinkles and give you the neck of a ten year old it will somehow work by osmosis, even though I never take it out of the packaging.

I am also not a fan of plastic surgery, probably because I have seen so many examples on the show of when it all goes horribly wrong. I've had to interview women who looked like Klingons. I also have this Calvinistic outlook that you don't go under the knife unless something is wrong with you and it's life-threatening.

The best beauty tip I ever got was from my aunty Carol. She is ten years older than me but she looks like my twin. Her big beauty secret is Vaseline. She has plastered it on her face all her life, especially at night, and it has really worked. It is also reassuringly inexpensive.

So, as far as growing older is concerned, I really didn't look upon turning forty as a huge milestone in my life and I don't look ahead to being fifty as anything to worry about. To me age is just a number, but that doesn't mean you shouldn't have a bit of a celebration to mark those milestones. I treated myself to a very frivolous pink leather tight-fitting jacket from Karen Millen, and wore it on the show on the morning of my fortieth birthday. It comes and goes out of fashion, but I can't bear to put it on to the pile of clothes I regularly give to charity during one of my ruthless clear-outs.

Steve bought me my gorgeous new diamond wedding ring, and the show on my fortieth birthday included many surprises, all courtesy of my pal Siobhan who was also my producer back then. She arranged for Julie Hesmondhalgh, who plays Hayley Cropper in *Coronation Street*, to record a special birthday hello for me from the actual set of my favourite soap. I thought it was just another clip for our weekly soap round-up, which, thanks to the effervescent Tina Baker, is one of my favourite bits of the show.

Tina did say that Hayley had something very special up her sleeve, and I was genuinely touched that Julie took the time and trouble to record that greeting just for me. Along with Eileen (Sue Cleaver), Hayley has long been my favourite.

There was also a piper, a hunky Scottish model in a kilt carrying a massive bunch of flowers, and a huge chocolate cake and champagne from the production team.

By far my best fortieth birthday present was being hired as columnist on the *Sun*. To this day it remains the job I am most proud of and the one that gives me the greatest satisfaction. It's the hardest thing I do all week, but such a privilege to be able to unleash my anger and frustration over issues or individuals who have incensed me, or to give praise to those who deserve it.

I have been threatened with legal action by Britney Spears and deeply offended many public figures who take themselves way too seriously.

Sun readers take the trouble to write with their support or, sometimes, their rage at my opinions. I have filed copy from all over the world, and there is nothing better than being on the train or the bus or in a café and seeing people holding the *Sun* in their hands and reading my page.

I work on the column all the time. My handbag is stuffed with articles torn out of newspapers and magazines that might spark off an idea, and I have a notepad where I jot down any random thoughts. I keep this by the side of my bed on top of my pile of books. It's amazing how often a good idea comes to you in the middle of the night and slips away in the cold light of day.

The team at the *Sun* are fantastic. They simply let me get on with it, and I just try to put into words what has made me angry, sad, happy or tearful during the week. I like to think that if something has touched me or made me livid, the chances are, it will have done the same to you. Knowing what it is like to be the subject of criticism, I always try to be fair and not simply to take cheap shots at someone. If I have to have a pop, I like to think it's because they deserve it.

I sit in front of the blank computer screen and type out bullet points on the stories I'm going to cover. The strongest one will be my lead. I have the two thousand words sent over to the paper by early evening on a Thursday, and if something breaks overnight or changes I have until Friday night to do any updates.

I write the *Sunday Post* piece on Fridays and usually concentrate on Scottish stories. I've been doing the column since Rosie was two weeks old, and many readers still remember her birthday, which is really touching. I also enjoy my role as an agony aunt. In many ways it's a job I've been doing for years, as a lot of the letters I received at TVam, GMTV, the *Sun* and the *Sunday Post* were and are from people needing help with their problems. Going through my postbag for *Best* magazine is one of the most fascinating and sometimes upsetting jobs of the week. All human life is here and some of the letters really are heart-breaking, from women and men leading lives of desperation. Many are about relationships, but I've found many problems can be solved just by talking, which sounds so simplistic but is nonetheless true.

I do wonder what would ever happen if my computer was broken and had to be repaired, and the engineer had a look at the search engines I use. For research, and for helpline numbers, I have had to visit all kinds of sites, including those dealing with incest, abuse, and some very bizarre fetishes indeed. It's all part of life's colourful tapestry and I reckon I'm now unshockable.

My friend and producer, Siobhan ended up working in New York and I had some fantastic weekends staying with her in her Manhattan apartment. I would fly out to see her after the show, with my clothes stuffed into a tiny cabin bag so that I didn't have to check in any luggage. That meant I was through Customs quicker, saving precious minutes for shopping. My body clock might have thought it was 2a.m. but in New York it was just time to get ready for dinner and a night out. We saw Elvis Costello perform in Central Park, had manicures and pedicures, window-shopped up and down Fifth Avenue and pretended we were extras in an episode of *Sex and the City*.

I actually always thought Siobhan would end up in New York. A couple of years before, in May 2001, we both took my show to Manhattan for a week and she was in her element. Before we left, I had to have some photos taken for the TV listings magazines, and Nikki Johnceline, GMTV's head of press, suggested I dress up as a New York cop, and hired me a genuine outfit.

I have always been partial to wearing a uniform, and as soon as I put this one on, complete with handcuffs, baton and badge, I felt very powerful indeed. For a laugh I thought I'd go up to our boss Peter's office in character and tell him he was under arrest. I channelled the spirits of the mighty Cagney and Lacey, burst into his office and told him, in my best Brooklyn accent, to assume the position and that he was taking a trip downtown.

What I didn't know was that he was in the middle of a very important meeting with our brand-new managing director, Paul Corley. Everyone had been very keen to make a good impression on the new big cheese, and clearly he was never going to forget his first encounter with me. I mumbled at them to have a nice day and beat a hasty retreat.

During my week-long *LK in the USA* stint, I interviewed Joan Rivers in a deli that sold sandwiches as big as your head, took a helicopter trip around Manhattan, interviewed top movers and shakers, and even did one whole show from the very top of one of the Twin Towers. We filmed the journey up in the lift to the 106th floor, which made our ears pop and our stomachs lurch, then recovered with a meal at the famous Windows on the World restaurant atop the North Tower.

We filmed an interview there with makeup artist Bobbi Brown. The weather closed in and the howling wind made the whole structure quiver. Looking out of the window and watching Manhattan disappear under a black cloud was a very eerie experience. As a sufferer of vertigo, I was in a state of mild panic during that whole shoot, and I remember asking one of the security chiefs about their strategy if there was ever a serious fire, or another terror attack. In 1993 a car bomb had exploded under the Twin Towers complex, killing six people and injuring more than a thousand. The terrorists had made the chilling promise that they would be back and that next time they would succeed in destroying the Towers and killing as many people as possible.

As I stood at the top of the world with the relaxed and upbeat safety officer, who assured me that the Towers and all the people who worked there were safe, there was no inkling of the horror that would be unleashed just four months later.

Over the years I have shared my highs and lows with many viewers and readers, and been overwhelmed by their generosity and kindness. Their understanding was to give me such strength and comfort during one of the toughest times of my life.

In May 2001 I discovered I was pregnant, but right from the start this pregnancy was completely different from my first one. I'd sailed through first time with no morning sickness at all and, apart from raging heartburn, I'd had little to worry or complain about. I just got fatter and waddled when I walked, but I was really healthy and happy.

This time Steve and I decided not to tell anyone until I was at least past the three months stage. I felt it would be safer, and although you never think anything bad will happen, I knew how upsetting it would be for me and for everyone else if it went wrong. I also didn't want to risk my pregnancy being leaked to the papers again before I'd had the chance to tell my family and friends.

Almost as soon as I had done the test and realised I was pregnant, I began to feel really sick. Although it is called morning sickness, I actually felt worse in the afternoon. Some mornings, though, while I was on the way to work, I thought I'd have to stop and throw up, and I felt really clammy and queasy. I found that drinking hot ginger tea as soon as I woke up helped, but I felt really tired and drained all the time. However, I was forty-one, and just put it down to being older.

I was reasonably fit and healthy and I try to eat wisely and well, but as soon as I knew I was pregnant I cut out all booze. I don't drink that much anyway these days, but I don't think you should risk even the odd glass of wine when you're expecting. I followed all the rules, everything properly cooked, no soft cheese and plenty of rest. But I just didn't have any energy at all, the exact opposite of my first pregnancy when I couldn't sit still and was always on the go.

My granda Kelly died just before I found out I was pregnant and things had been really hectic at work, so I was looking forward to a relaxing week's holiday with Steve and Rosie in Scotland. It meant I would see my mum and dad and could tell them the good news face to face. I didn't get that chance.

It was on the first day of our holiday at the beginning of June that things began to go wrong. We were travelling up to Oban when I got a stabbing pain in my right side which was horribly uncomfortable. I tried not to be too worried but I needed advice and some reassurance. As no one but Steve and I knew I was pregnant, I needed to talk to someone I could trust.

I called my friend Jacqueline Millar, who had trained as a nurse and is one of the most trustworthy and sensible people I know. She told me not to worry too much and to take things easy, but that if something was going to happen, there wasn't really anything I could do to prevent it, but not to dwell on that. Jacqueline, who has three grown-up daughters, understood, and talking to her made me feel a lot better.

We decided to continue with the holiday and that night I stopped feeling so awful and took that to be a really good sign. We were staying in a lovely cosy little hotel in Port Appin when I woke up around 4a.m. feeling utterly ghastly and completely drained. I was bleeding quite a bit and it was clear that something was wrong.

Steve called the local GP who was the kind of gentle country doctor I thought only existed in stories like *Dr Finlay's Casebook*. He came right away and said it looked as if I had lost the baby but I should go to hospital for a scan to make absolutely certain.

Luckily Rosie, who was seven years old at the time, slept through all of this and had no idea what was going on.

He made an appointment with Ninewells Hospital in Dundee, which was hundreds of miles away but it made sense as we have lots of friends and family there. At that time we also had a little holiday home across from Dundee in Tayport.

It was a long, hard drive, but because I had to keep Rosie

amused by playing games and reading to her, and also because I didn't want her to realise anything was wrong, I had to carry on as though nothing had happened. This actually helped me, because I couldn't get too tearful or panicky as it would have upset my little daughter.

We dropped her off at a friend's and went on to the hospital, where I was taken for a scan. All the staff were very understanding but it was so hard to adjust to the fact that I was no longer pregnant.

The scan seemed to be taking a long time, and the nurse looked puzzled, staring hard at the picture on her screen and trying to get a better view. Finally she said, 'There's something here. I think there's a heartbeat.'

I thought I'd misheard her. There I was, thinking my baby was dead, and she was telling me there was a chance I could still be pregnant. Tears rolled down my cheeks. I'd been feeling that my whole world had tumbled down around my ears, but now it seemed there was hope.

I was told that lots of women can bleed quite badly yet still go on to have a healthy pregnancy and a safe delivery. Having prepared myself for the worst, now I was about to believe that things might be all right after all.

It was getting late, so we picked up Rosie and went back to Tayport with strict instructions that I should put my feet up and rest. I felt totally exhausted so I went to bed, but a couple of hours later I woke up in severe pain, almost like the first stages of labour. I crept out of bed, went downstairs and lay on the sofa. Throughout that night I continued to lose a lot of blood. Every half-hour I would have a pain, which was followed by a surge of blood. I knew, of course, that this was a really bad sign, but part of me refused to acknowledge that I was losing the baby. I clung to the hope that everything would be OK. That was why I didn't wake Steve, because if I told him what was happening I'd need to face up to it and then it would be real. But in the early morning I knew I needed help. Steve took one look at me and phoned for an ambulance.

I was so weak I couldn't even walk. I was worried about Rosie being scared. She saw me sitting at the bottom of the stairs and said that I looked as 'white as a sheep'. I couldn't believe that my little girl could still make me smile at such a horrible and traumatic time. Again, knowing that I didn't want her to see me upset and anxious stopped me from breaking down.

I had to be given oxygen, put on a drip, then expertly lifted on to a stretcher and taken to the hospital by the paramedics. These men and women are incredible. To them, it's all in a day's work, but when you're scared and feeling vulnerable, their calmness and professionalism are so reassuring. I felt light-headed and woozy when I arrived back at Ninewells Hospital. I had left there full of hope, but I knew now that I had miscarried. I had to have an operation that morning and there was nothing more to be done.

I lay on that hospital bed and tortured myself afterwards trying to work out why this had happened. When I had been at my granda's funeral, before I knew I was pregnant, I had toasted his memory with a whisky. Could that have had an effect? What about the kind of food I'd been eating before I knew? I remembered having a Brie sandwich. You aren't supposed to eat soft cheeses. I hadn't known I was pregnant then, but could it have made a difference? I'd also had a dental check-up before I knew. Was I pregnant then and could the X-rays have made any difference? Then, earlier that month, I'd been sent to Cannes for two days to report on the film festival. It was a very last-minute trip and I'd had to have my passport delivered to me at the airport as I didn't have it with me at work. Normally, thanks to my days as a reporter, I usually have a passport, a clean pair of knickers and a mini-toothbrush and toothpaste in my handbag at all times, just in case.

Helen, who looked after Rosie while I was at work, met me at the check-in desk with about five minutes to spare before it closed. I was stressed to the limit because I thought I'd miss the plane and be too late to do the next day's show. On and on, round and round in my head. I thought about all of these things, because I needed to know why this had happened to me. You think that if you can find a reason, then maybe you can stop it happening again.

Of course, as I now know, there are often no reasons, and I've lost count of the number of people who told me 'it was for the best' and also how common the problem is, with one in three women miscarrying at some point in their lives. I assume this was said to make me feel better, but it had the opposite effect. It just made me realise how many women go through the same pain and misery.

You make plans, build up your expectations and look forward to your new arrival. My baby would have been due around New Year, so we'd planned a very quiet Christmas and Hogmanay and were looking forward to welcoming in 2001 with a brother or sister for Rosie. I had written all those dates in my diary. I had to cross them out later and that upset me as it was so final.

Sadly, my mum heard the news when a journalist phoned her at home. Someone at the hospital had called the papers so the journalist contacted her while I was under anaesthetic and before Steve had had a chance to ring her. At the time when we had planned to tell my mum and dad they were going to be grandparents again, a reporter was asking for her reaction to the fact that I had lost my baby.

My family were brilliant. My mum and dad came to stay and friends rallied round. I was overwhelmed with flowers and cards, and what really comforted me were the letters I received from women who had gone through the same thing. They opened their hearts, shared their experiences and I appreciated it so much.

Steve was wonderful throughout, and I felt like hugging the friends and family who remembered to ask him how *he* felt. So often all the attention is given to us women, but people often don't remember that husbands and partners suffer too. They are sometimes not allowed to show their feelings and they get forgotten.

I think I went back to work a bit too early, and I don't think I really grieved enough. I put on this front of being 'fine', and even managed to convince myself I was coping, but for almost a year after it happened the smallest things would make me cry. I would be watching a soap about a baby being born, or even see a cute baby in its pram looking adorable, and a wave of grief would hit me hard.

Of course, I had to keep telling myself that it could have been so much worse. I miscarried at just over two months, which was bad enough. It must be unbearable in the later stages of pregnancy.

Later that year, three of my friends had babies. It was a little bittersweet buying them presents and giving them cuddles, but my overwhelming feeling was one of happiness that my friends had had safe pregnancies and healthy babies.

Steve and I didn't manage to have another baby, but I think I'm blessed because I have been lucky enough to give birth to a healthy baby girl who has grown up into a gorgeous, funny, cheeky teenager. Over the years I have had to interview so many women who haven't been able to have a child of their own, and many who have gone through multiple miscarriages. They suffer every day from an unimaginable sense of loss. I consider myself very lucky to have my daughter.

CHAPTER TWELVE

Reach for the Sky

I n September 2001 I was asked to do my own show for Sky – called *Lorraine*. I was really flattered to be headhunted to front the whole morning's programming for the up-and-coming channel. Thankfully the show was being produced by my pal Siobhan O'Gorman, who is always bursting with energy, enthusiasm and good ideas. With her on my side, I knew we had a really good chance of pulling it off, but it wasn't going to be easy as there was so much air time to fill.

I was worried that we had such scant resources and very little time to set up the show, but everyone worked incredibly hard. The show went out from nine thirty until noon every weekday, with a break in the middle for episodes of *ER* and *Friends*. You might think this would be impossible as I was actually live on air with GMTV until 9.25 every morning – but we had a cunning plan.

In the five minutes I had to spare before I went from being on GMTV to appearing on Sky, I changed my cardigan and walked a few feet across the studio to the sofa that was still warm from the bottoms of Fiona and Eamonn. We changed the cushions and brought down a massive red-and-black blind emblazoned with my face and the set then looked completely different. I have to confess that big blind worried me greatly. It was rather Stalinesque, the kind of thing you would see flown outside the Kremlin in the bad old days. Our skilled technos did something clever with a switch and, hey presto, at 9.30 in the morning the new titles were rolling and we were on Sky TV.

Most new TV shows have months to get the format just right and do a series of 'pilots', a sort of dress rehearsal in which mistakes can be ironed out and new contributors given a chance to get some experience on camera. We did all of that on the air. It was what we were used to.

Usually live shows rehearse their items or at least have a run-through, but we can't do that at GMTV. The studio is in use from 6a.m. onwards, so there is no way we can rehearse my show unless we come in at two in the morning. We rely on the goodwill and experience of our crew to get through items with lots of props and complicated moves, and because we've all been doing it for so long, it usually works and if it doesn't, we hold our hands up, laugh it off, and move on.

Our directors and camera operators have a chance to rehearse the pop bands and singers, but only during short commercial breaks throughout the morning. The performers rush in from makeup, often with their curlers still in and only half a face done, do a really quick sound check and mark through the dance moves, then have to shut up or are cut off so we can go to the news or weather. Even with all those TV flying hours under my belt, I still get caught out now and again.

You would have thought I'd have learned my lesson when Noel Edmonds tricked me with that 'Gotcha', but nearly ten years later I was caught out again when Ant and Dec tucked me up like a kipper on live TV. At our planning meeting, one of the producers, Stephen Hanley, told us he had a cracking story about two old blokes who had found love through a lonely-hearts advert. They were rich and single and very specific about wanting to meet young nubile women, and had put an advert in their local paper stating: 'We are wealthy and happy to spend, spend, spend on the right girls. We want two broad-minded women between eighteen and twenty-one years, looking for romance and possibly marriage.'

Both chose a couple of applicants, but the fifty-year age gap meant that the girls were being called gold-diggers. It was an intriguing human-interest story. Stephen told us that we had them booked on a live link from their home in Southend-on-Sea and their girlfriends would be on the sofa with me.

I thought it was a bit odd, but everyone was very enthusiastic, and Stephen even said they were all brilliant talkers and very excited about being on the show. The next morning when I got to work I just couldn't help feeling that something was a bit 'off' with the story and asked Stephen to double-check everything. He should be awarded an Oscar for his performance in talking up the story, saying it was going to be terrific, and that the girls were more than happy to talk about the accusations that they were only in it for the money and to discuss their sex lives. So I was won over.

I had no idea it was all an elaborate set-up. Half-way through the item, I introduced the two 'old men' and up they popped 'live from Southend-on-Sea'. What I didn't know was that the two seventy-somethings were in fact the twenty-seven-year-olds Ant and Dec, who had come into the studio at three in the morning to be made up to look aged and frail.

They were nowhere near Southend, but in a different studio just a few flights of stairs below where I was sitting. The crew were so clever. They put the monitors quite far away from me so that I couldn't see the boys in great detail, and they were both utterly convincing as silly old men.

I asked the two girls (both actresses in real life) if they weren't just taking advantage of the besotted old men and were nothing more than gold-diggers. They defended themselves, but I wasn't convinced and felt that the two poor deluded old blokes were being used and abused.

Here's some of the interview:

LK: Did the inclusion of the world 'rich' in the advert make it more attractive?

'*Suzanne*': It did at first but when we met them they were such lovely blokes.

LK: I can understand them looking for companionship, but isn't there a danger that you're just taking advantage of two old guys?

S: They enjoy our company and we enjoy theirs. It's not like we're trying to abuse them or anything – we just like having fun.

LK: What do your friends and family think of it?

S: I suppose they're not too happy.

LK: How many dates have you been on?

S: Three.

LK: And do you all go out as a foursome because apparently the two of them live together, just like Morecambe and Wise?

S: Yes.

LK: OK, let's meet the boyfriends. Seventy-year-old George Botham and seventy-two-year-old Kenny Burton joining us live from their house in Southend-on-Sea. Good to see you.

Dec [a.k.a. George, in a gruff wheezy voice]: Morning!

Ant [a.k.a. Kenny]: Morning.

LK: Now, I understand what you're getting out of this – you're going out with nice young girls – but what do you ultimately want? Is it marriage?

Dec: A bit of fun. The girls are having fun.

LK: Now Kenny has no children but, George, you have a son. So when you eventually die, where will the money go? To the girls?

Dec: Probably, yeah. My son Terry took his family to Canada and he's not part of my life any more.

LK: Now, I'm not being unkind, but these are two lovely young women. Why do you think they would be going out with you? Surely they're just after your money.

Dec: Not really. They like our company and we like their company. They're a lovely pair of girls. Everybody's happy.

Ant: You can't take it with you.

LK: No, you can't, but don't you think they're just at it?

Dec: At it?

LK: Well, I was going to ask as delicately as possible about how serious the relationship is. Is there a sexual element?

Dec: Yes, of course.

LK: Was that part of the deal?

Ant: Well, there's no deal, really.

At this point there was a bit of a pause while Dec produced two rings and started to get down, very slowly, on one knee. The signal 'broke up' and we lost transmission.

I looked horrified at the prospect of an on-air proposal and linked quickly to a break. After the commercials for Toilet Duck and stool-softener, I said, 'Welcome back, and let's see if we can contact George and Kenny now', but when the shot of the house in Southend came up George and Kenny had gone and only their wee dog remained.

This was when Ant and Dec entered my studio and I realised I'd been well and truly stitched up. Dec said he wanted to propose to me instead, and I shrieked that they were monkeys and that this was what they'd both look like when they were old!

It was a brilliant set-up, and I had to go on their Saturday night show to watch the tape and be given a real roasting. Apparently the boys were keen to tuck me up after I'd written in my *Sun* column about a similar prank they had played on Simon Cowell. The two of them entered *American Idol* dressed as rastas and fooled Simon into thinking they were fame-hungry US singers. I wrote in my column that I'd loved the show but couldn't believe Simon hadn't seen though their 'ludicrous' disguises.

Of course I'd failed to spot that the old fogeys were indeed Ant and Dec, thanks to a fabulous makeup job and their acting ability. It remains one of my fondest and funniest memories of working on TV.

★

Back on the Sky show, Siobhan and the team were coming up with ideas to get viewers' attention. Our cheeky 'homage' to the smash ITV Saturday night show *Pop Idol* became a cookery-talent search Siobhan inevitably named 'Pot Idol'. It was one of our big early successes. One of our contestants, Craig Wilson, 'The Kilted Chef', has gone on to open his own restaurant, 'Eat on the Green' in Ellon, near Aberdeen, and is doing really well.

The Sky show was great fun but completely exhausting for all of us. I was on air almost continuously from eight thirty until midday and needed to keep my energy levels up. Sadly, I did that by eating far too many bacon rolls and spending too much time sitting on my backside. The weight piled on again.

I was also suffering from wearing contact lenses in a dry, overheated studio, and by lunchtime my eyes were like Dracula's, all red and raw-looking. I normally just had them in for the hour I was on air with GMTV, but having to keep them in for hours on end was really painful. I decided to have a laser operation, and went to the Moorfields Eye Hospital in London. You sit in a dentist's chair and have drops popped in to anaesthetise your eyes. Then you're zapped for a couple of seconds and you can see again. It's so clever and easy.

I had a couple of hours that night feeling as though I had an eyelash or a bit of grit in my eye but the next day I was fine. I had to put in drops three times a day, but otherwise it was no trouble except that I couldn't wear makeup for a week. I did look a bit odd on TV with no mascara, but I just shoved on some glasses and it was fine. No one expects us to look like glamour-pusses, and I just told the viewers I'd had my eyes lasered.

That's the joy of GMTV. If I get stuck in traffic and don't have time to put on full makeup and do my hair, which has happened to me more than once, I simply go on air and explain to the viewers why I'm looking windswept and interesting.

Our first big signing for Sky made the front page of the *Sun*. It's hard to believe now, but the fact that daffy Helen Adams from *Big Brother* had landed her first TV job was a big deal back then. Helen appeared on *Big Brother* before the show became nasty and repellent, and was an instant hit, thanks to her sweet nature and truly dippy comments – 'I love blinking, I do' – and for her romance with Paul Clarke.

We also took a chance on a new, raw fashion graduate. The one and only Mark Heyes has since become an influential commentator on fashion and one of my very special friends. He is a sweet-natured, funny and extremely talented man who has saved me from many a fashion *faux pas*.

Boyzone star Keith Duffy had a regular slot on the show with his 'Blaggers Guides', Tracey Cox was our sexpert, we had Steve McKenna reviewing movies, and Ben Shephard covered showbiz. We got off to a cracking start on 3 September, with Victoria Beckham as our guest, launching her new solo single.

Now, I've given the Spice Girl a bit of a hard time over the years for her seeming inability to smile, her over-styled fashion sense and teeny tiny frame, but when she came on the show she was really sweet and funny. We did a shoot with her visiting her favourite designer shops: she took me to D&G, Gina, for shoes, and Gucci. In return I showed her New Look and Dot Perkins.

We were constantly followed by the paparazzi, who yelled at Victoria to attract her attention. The whirring of their cameras was as irritating as a swarm of very irritating mosquitoes. I honestly could not bear to lead that sort of life. I would hate to have the level of fame that means you can't go shopping to buy loo paper or pick up your child from school without a hullabaloo. I know people like Victoria have probably become so used to the attention, and possibly even thrive on it, that it becomes their norm. Frankly, I don't think there is enough money in the world to make up for that level of scrutiny, and for not being able to throw on a tracksuit and have a coffee with your mates.

I know I'm on TV almost every day, and have been since the eighties, but because of the kind of no-nonsense, down-to-earth programme I do, there is, thankfully, no danger of snappers chasing me down the road at home or following me when I go on holiday to get a shot of me looking bad in my swimsuit. I don't go to posh eateries unless it's a special occasion and I'm taking my mum out for a treat, and I'd much rather go to my local cinema to see a movie than attend a première. You need to get all dressed up like a dog's dinner, fight your way through the traffic in London to get to Leicester Square, then stand like a lemon while you have your photo taken, in the full and certain knowledge that you'll wind up in *Heat* magazine in 'What Were They Thinking?', or with your funny toes highlighted in the 'Circle of Shame'.

The celebs who moan about press intrusion should stop drinking in posh bars and clubs and just go down to their local instead, and they should stop whining about being 'pestered' by the public. What a cheek! I always find people are lovely to me when they bump into me in the supermarket or out shopping. They just want to chat for a couple of minutes, and it's good to know that they watch the show and enjoy it so much. It's great to get the feedback and it's only a few minutes of my time. I do feel a bit of an ecjit carrying around those cards with my picture on them to sign for people (especially as I'm usually out and about with no makeup on and my hair tied back, and the picture looks like my far-better-looking younger sister), but if I leave them at home I have to scrawl my name on the back of a fag packet, which is even dafter.

When Rosie was about four she couldn't work out why total strangers would greet me like their long-lost mum/daughter/aunt and ask for my autograph. With a wee perplexed face, she asked me, 'Why do you scribble on bits of paper for people, Mummy?' When you put it like that, it is indeed madness.

I've often had to play 'myself' over the years. As well as that appearance in *Brookside* with Eamonn back in 1994, I have been in a number of TV shows and was once even in a movie. I played a news reporter in *The James Gang*, and am very proud to have shared my tiny scene with Oscar nominee Toni Collette.

Toni starred in the magnificent *Muriel's Wedding* and went on to appear with Bruce Willis in *The Sixth Sense* and with Cameron Diaz in *In Her Shoes*, as well as in the massive indie hit *Little Miss Sunshine*. But on a cold day in Cardiff in 1996, Toni was standing with me in the grey drizzle outside a burgled jeweller's pretending to be a police detective hunting down a gang of thieves while I played a TV reporter. The cast included John Hannah, as the feckless Spendlove James, and James Nesbitt in one of his first movie roles. It was a crime comedy romp, and as it was a British movie it was made on a shoestring. I was thrilled to be asked to take part and was up all night learning my lines.

On the day of filming we huddled in the caravan, drinking watery tea out of paper cups, and I was getting more and more nervous about my 'big' scene. I'd shared a car with Toni to the location, but she was busy learning her lines and I was too shy to strike up a conversation.

I was becoming more and more nervous about getting my lines out without making a mistake. I had them off by heart and had made Steve pretend to be Toni Collette over and over again until I was word-perfect.

On the set, the clapperboard clapped and it was 'Take One'. Somehow, I managed to get all my words out in the right order, but with the conviction and skill of a forest of redwood trees. It was certainly not award-winning stuff.

I could have kissed Toni when she miffed her first line and we had to start again for Take Two. I relaxed and pretended this was a run-of-the-mill news story, and we had it in the can on the second try.

It was a blink-and-you'll-miss-it appearance, but I have the DVD and I am on the cast list, and no one can take that away from me.

I was also asked to appear on *One Foot in the Grave* by its writer and creator David Renwick, who is an utter genius. It remains one of my all-time favourite comedy shows and, in common with all the seriously successful TV programmes, gave us a character we could really relate to. Victor's exasperated rage at traffic wardens, council officials and bureaucracy resonated with all of us, as did his catchphrase.

We all know what we mean when we call someone a Victor Meldrew: it's become shorthand for 'grumpy old git', and if we utter, 'I don't belieeeeeve it', it means we're close to meltdown. I was given the part of a breakfast-TV presenter (big stretch there) who had to interview a doctor on TV about irritable-bowel syndrome in an episode entitled 'The Executioner's Song'.

Victor watches the spoof programme on a giant TV screen, convinced that the doctor is talking directly to him and that his own bowels are in turmoil.

Annette Crosbie, who played Victor's long-suffering wife Margaret, is a devoted dog-lover and campaigns on behalf of abandoned greyhounds. She was not at all happy with David Renwick over a scene where a little dog pops out of a hat-box because she thought the animal was getting bored. I can't imagine she was overly thrilled by that classic scene in which Victor picks up a puppy and holds it to his ear instead of the phone, but it's up there with Del Boy falling backwards into the pub cellar as a comedy gem.

In 2003 I had to draw on all my acting experience when I was asked to play a Scottish breakfast-TV presenter called Lorraine (are you seeing a pattern here?). I had to interview Sun Hill police officer Cathy Bradford (Connie Hyde) whom no one knew had framed her colleague for murder.

Again, I had a script to learn, but it was so well written and Connie was so convincing that I actually found myself believing she really was a police officer. As it was recorded in my own studio and I was sitting on my own sofa, it even felt like a real interview. This was a massive storyline at the time for *The Bill* and led to the departure of the unstable Cathy, who was sectioned and carted off. It was very odd to watch me being myself in a drama like *The Bill*, but it worked.

In 2006 I was asked to take part in Scottish soap *River City*. Since the axing of *Take the High Road*, this is the top soap in Scotland and has built up a huge following since it was launched in 2002. *River City* is set in the fictional Glasgow area of Shieldinch and has a colourful line-up of social cripples and psychos, sprinkled with a few decent people. My favourites include shellsuit Bob, his mammy Scarlett, and lovely Gina who owns the Oyster café. I (thankfully) played myself again and was introduced to the good people of Sheildinch as a friend of Billy Davies, played by gorgeous Gray O'Brien, who owned the Moda Vida hair salon in Shieldinch. I came into the salon to visit Billy, and bumped into Scarlett, a big fan of GMTV, who invited me to Gina's wedding. Poor Gina was marrying Archie Buchanan, a nasty piece of work and one of the baddest of soap baddies. I felt as if I had crawled into my TV set.

Scotland has always had a wealth of comic talent, from Chick Murray to Billy Connolly and from Stanley Baxter to Rab C. Nesbitt's Gregor Fisher. Two present-day comic geniuses are Ford Kiernan and Greg Hemphill, who starred in the sketch show *Chewin' the Fat* and went on to make *Still Game*, a sit-com that can be raunchy and bawdy but also bittersweet and tender. It follows the antics of two old codgers, Jack and Victor, who live in Craiglang in Glasgow. I was deeply honoured to be asked to take part in the series. Once again I was to play myself (clearly the word was out that this was really the only role worth offering me).

The boys own the independent production company that makes the show for BBC Scotland, and in my experience this always makes for a far happier ship. The atmosphere was relaxed, the catering truck was stacked with the best of grub, with bacon and sausage rolls constantly on tap. The cast had a comfy Winnebago, and both Ford and Greg were happily playing a computer game involving life-sized plastic guitars. There were also dishes of home-made tablet, bowls of Maltesers and real tea and coffee, instead of the usual greyish sludge you get out of the

BBC machines. The boys could not have been more welcoming and were full of energy and enthusiasm.

My cameo role was to interview two of the characters, miserable tight-fisted old Tam (Mark Cox) and his downtrodden wife Frances (Kate Kennedy), who becomes pregnant at the age of sixty-two. They are hailed as the UK's oldest parents and it's the kind of story that we absolutely would cover on GMTV.

In the studios just outside Glasgow, the clever crew had re-created my set. To be honest, it was actually much better than the original. The sofa was comfy, the cushions were plumper, the vases and ornaments far more expensive. Mark and Kate are young actors and they needed to be transformed into sixty-somethings with expertly applied makeup.

Once they were in character it was really easy to interview them, especially as Frances was cuddling a real-life baby who behaved like an angel throughout. The scene was all about tight-fisted Tam suddenly realising he can get lots of free nappies, clothes and toys for his newborn and being led off the premises shouting his address for companies to send the goodies.

When the episode was screened, Victor and Jack were shown watching the interview in the pub and I'm very proud that Jack announced I was more 'pumpable' than Judy Finnegan.

As well as being asked to take part in some iconic shows, I have also had a name-check on one of the best-loved programmes ever to be screened on British TV. I was sitting in my dressing-gown with a cup of tea and nearly choked on my KitKat when Deirdre on *Coronation Street* was buying new specs and asked the optician to give her some like 'Lorraine Kelly from GMTV'. This was in the days before my laser operation and when I wore some truly outlandish face furniture. My phone immediately went nuts with my hysterical friends screeching down the phone that I had been mentioned by the mighty Anne Kirkbride. I was really chuffed.

In 2007 the feckless Cilla, who abandoned the *Street* and little Chesney to go and work in Las Vegas, revealed that she watched *LK Today* for the cheap fashion. It was hilarious and, again, for weeks it was all anyone wanted to talk to me about.

For my finest TV moment I didn't have to do anything at all. I am a huge fan of John Simm and the two of us bonded while we were waiting to go on *Friday Night with Jonathan Ross*. We were both terrified and more than a little intimidated by the other two guests – Halle Berry and Hugh Jackman. I was wearing my lucky black dress, and Helen Hand, who is a cracking makeup artist at GMTV, had done my hair and makeup so I felt pretty confident – but there's nothing more certain to make you feel like a lumbering cart-horse than sitting beside Halle Berry. She shimmers with utter gorgeousness and is also a genuinely sweet-natured woman.

Hugh Jackman is equally good-looking, but even he doesn't have the charisma, likeability and sheer awesome talent of our own John Simm. I've been a huge fan since I saw him as Raskolnikov in *Crime and Punishment* and also in other classy productions such as *The Lakes* and *State of Play*. He was also a very chilling Master in *Dr Who*.

John was on the show to talk about the second series of the utterly sublime *Life on Mars*, one of the best things ever to have been transmitted on British TV. I get very excited about top-quality television and *Life on Mars* is up there with *Deadwood, Rome, I Claudius, The Naked Civil Servant, Frasier, The West Wing* and *Studio 60 on the Sunset Strip*, as far as I'm concerned.

Life on Mars is all about Sam Taylor, a detective, who is

knocked down by a car in the present day and wakes up in the seventies. 'Am I mad, in a coma or back in time?' Watching the culture clash between Sam and his superior officer Gene 'The Sweeney' Hunt (Philip Glenister) is brilliant. Sam is kept in touch with his 'real' life with messages from the test-card girl on his old-fashioned TV. He is flicking through the channels (by hand – no remote controls in those days) when he comes across one of those old Open University professors with a mullet haircut, a brown kipper tie and a Paisley pattern shirt. He says, 'I don't know what you're looking so smug about, mate. One day you will be replaced by the lovely Lorraine Kelly.' I was genuinely lost for words and that bit of the DVD is almost worn away.

Working on the Sky show every day, as well as GMTV, was completely crazy, utterly exhausting but really stimulating. It was sassier, cheekier and saucier than the GMTV show. It was also responsible for one of the most surreal experiences of my life.

Shortly after the show launched, I was in a studio with Helen Adams, shooting an advert to promote using your Sky box to do Internet browsing and shopping. It featured a giddy Helen buying lots of new shoes and makeup while I explained the technical bits. We were half-way through the shoot when news broke that a plane had crashed into one of the World Trade Center's Twin Towers in New York. We all huddled round the TV to watch the horror unfold, but had to keep going back to talk about digital shopping and Helen's hair.

God love her, the scale of this human tragedy didn't seem to have dawned on Helen, although I'm sure many people that day thought they were watching a Hollywood movie and couldn't believe their eyes. Luckily we didn't have much more to do, and

I was able to get home and start preparing for the next day's show. Obviously there would be only one item on the agenda. Those were dark days.

It is hard to explain to your child that this isn't one of those sci-fi Hollywood blockbusters in which the White House is blown up and Manhattan reduced to rubble. This was horribly real and the world changed for ever. It was so difficult for everyone to try to talk to their children about what had happened without frightening them, and it's easy to forget the shock, sorrow and rage we felt at the time for those who were murdered and their grieving families.

The only reason the Sky show lasted as long as it did was because of the hard-working production team headed up by Siobhan, and our crew who worked overtime, but there was no way we could keep up the pace and after eight months both GMTV and Sky called it a day. It was a shame because it had been a very enjoyable TV experiment, but there was an increasing realisation that we were all stretched far too thinly.

As one door closes a window often opens, and after the Sky show folded, I was approached by producers at *This Morning* to see if I would be interested in presenting the show on a regular basis. Fern Britton wanted to cut back her appearances to three days a week and they needed someone to present on Mondays and Fridays. I was more than happy to give it a go. I had appeared as a guest on the show and was always struck by the fun-filled atmosphere and the friendliness of the whole team. I also knew Phillip Schofield would be a joy to work with.

Every Monday after my show was finished, and after a quick debrief with my gang on *LK Today*, I raced downstairs to the secret passage between the two studios (my fastest time was five minutes and thirty-two seconds), did a quick change of outfit, an update with Phillip and the producers and was on air by 10a.m. to do a quick trail (just to let everyone know what was coming up in the show).

Then we would talk through the show, rehearse any complicated items, and we were on air for two hours from 10.30 to 12.30. There was a news break in the middle when we would have tea and toast and talk to our guests.

It was always a really good atmosphere and I loved working on *This Morning*. It was one of the few jobs in which I haven't fretted or worried. There was no pressure on me as I was the 'stand-in', and everything was made incredibly easy and comfortable. I remember the first time I was shown into Fern's massive dressing-room: I acted all cool in front of the researcher, but when she had shut the door I immediately called all the girls at GMTV and shrieked down the phone – Fern had her own loo, a shower and scented candles. There was also a thick fluffy carpet, a TV that worked and even fresh flowers. It was seriously impressive.

I will always have a huge affection for *This Morning*. I was treated like a princess. It was stress-free, good fun and Phillip is indeed one of the nicest men on TV. He has a wicked sense of humour, and does a wonderful impersonation of Catherine Tate's foul-mouthed old Nan. He made me very welcome and part of the team from that very first show. Phillip is one of the very few people in the wacky world of TV Land for whom no one has a bad word. He is a true professional who treats everyone with old-fashioned courtesy, a hugely underrated quality.

Not all presenters, especially the men, are as generous as he is, but Phillip isn't riddled with self-doubt and insecurity. He has nothing to prove and does the job because he loves it.

We went though a phase of doing mad trails for the show. We raided the dressing-up box and re-created the opening credits of *Dallas* and *Emmerdale* – I even got to do a Joan Collins impression when we did a take-off of *Dynasty*.

One Friday when I was coming down from Scotland, I turned up on set twenty minutes late and still wearing a crash helmet after a mad motorbike ride from London City airport. I was mortified to be so late as I am usually early for work but the 6.50a.m. flight from Dundee to London had been delayed by fog and then we had to circle round London for about forty-five minutes. I could actually see the *This Morning* studios from the plane window and was almost crying with frustration. I would gladly have bailed out with a parachute strapped to my back and taken my chances.

When we landed at 10.30, the show had already started, so I jumped on one of those hair-raising Virgin courier bikes. My leather-clad driver asked if I wanted a gentle ride or the 'Full Alton Towers Experience', and with the clock ticking I went for the latter. If I hadn't been so stressed about being late for work, I would have enjoyed the thrilling ride. My helmet was wired up with a microphone and the driver gave me a guided tour of the landmarks on the way to the studio, but the Dome, London Bridge, the Tower of London and the London Eye were nothing more than a blur.

When I got to the studios, I ran on to the set, red-faced from the wind lashing, to reveal the worst case of helmet hair ever seen on British TV. Phillip dissolved into giggles at the sight of me, and during the first commercial break Lyn from hair and makeup and David from Wardrobe did a sterling job of trying to make me look half human.

On my second Christmas with the show we decamped to an amazing country house in West Wycombe and did a whole week living the life of country ladies and gentlemen. As it was *This Morning*, nothing was done by halves. I had the use of Fern's Winnebago on the days she wasn't there, and once again I was on the phone to the girls at GMTV to shriek this time that I had a *heated toilet seat*.

It was a glorious setting: the great hall had a massive Christmas tree and all the rooms were bedecked in festive decorations. There were roaring fires, carol singers and even a figgy pudding or two. Of course, as this was TV, a lot of it was sham: with thirty seconds to go before we were on air, I reached over to the sumptuous-looking chocolates to sneak 'just one' and nearly choked. It was made of very convincing painted wood. I furtively put it back on the plate, with toothmarks in one corner, and tried do the opening link with Phillip though our chortles.

I did many bizarre interviews on *This Morning* but I reckon one of the strangest was with the poor bloke who drank his own wee because he said it cured his epilepsy. He sat for the whole interview clutching a full pint of his own freshly squeezed urine, which bubbled and festered under the hot lights. At the end of the interview he downed the lot in one go, which was both repellent and impressive at the same time. He confessed that he didn't have many friends and had real bother finding a girlfriend, but didn't seem to realise that guzzling your own wee might be a bit of a handicap.

It was one of the few occasions when I have been simply lost for words.

CHAPTER THIRTEEN

Dragged Through the Mud

One of the most fun jobs I've had was helping to present the BBC's Eurovision coverage in May 2003. I also broadcast to the biggest audience I will ever have when I gave out the UK's scores. I can't remember being so nervous for years but I really didn't want to cock it up in front of an estimated worldwide audience of 600 million.

Lots of the deranged and desperate presenters who announce the votes from around Europe are bedazzled by the absurdly massive viewing figures, seeing it as some kind of audition for global fame, and trying to joke with the host and hostess to beef up their role.

This is always a big mistake and makes for some toe-curling television. Sitting in front of a backdrop of the proudly gay watering-hole that is Old Compton Street in Soho, I just gave the results, smiled sweetly and raised a glass to our contestants

Jemini. As you may remember, my good-luck wish bombed horribly. The duo, Gemma Abbey and Chris Cromby, scored the first ever '*nul points*' for the UK after a performance that had dogs jumping off high buildings. They were completely off-key but, to be fair, they did sing 'Cry Baby' in tune every other time they performed it, just not when it really mattered.

My pal Siobhan watched me on the Internet in New York during her Eurovision party and, at the same time, so did my brother in Singapore, which was astounding.

Over the years I have been asked to take part in lots of different TV programmes, but I never thought that one show would bring me to the brink of quitting TV altogether and see me accused of a heinous crime. That was what happened in 2004 when I was asked to take part in a strange current affairs/reality show hybrid.

I suppose it was only a matter of time before the whole *X Factor* phenomenon ventured into the world of politics. After all, politics is often referred to as the really dull bit of the entertainment industry, so when I was asked to take part in *Vote for Me*, I was intrigued as it was completely different from anything I had ever done before. The idea was that producers wanted to give members of the public who would never get a chance to be part of the political process a chance to have their voices heard.

Now, I am of the Billy Connolly school of thought, and believe that anyone who actually *wants* to be a politician should be barred from ever holding office, but the idea of this show appealed to me.

The applicants were whittled down to just sixty and I was on the judging panel alongside ex-*Sun* editor Kelvin MacKenzie and hugely respected political journalist John Sergeant. Kelvin was obviously cast as the Simon Cowell of the show, which made me Sharon Osbourne and John a most unlikely Louis Walsh.

There was the usual collection of fruit-loops, show-offs and attention-seekers among genuine people who were sick and tired of no one listening to their point of view. A real sense of anger and frustration came through from a lot of the applicants, who felt disenfranchised, alongside people dressed as clowns and harmless eccentrics happy to have a fun day out.

We turned up for filming in October 2004 in Birmingham. First of all, each candidate had to stand in front of us and spout their manifesto, which they had to make very short and sweet. Among those who put forward intelligent and entertaining points were Dominic Carman, son of the late George Carman, a famous 'celebrity' barrister, and Kevin Donnellon, a twenty-nine-year-old college lecturer from Liverpool, who whooshed into the room on his electric wheelchair and gave a really passionate speech about disability rights.

He had the same chance as King Arthur Uther Pendragon, a long grey-haired Druid in flowing robes, and a rather earnest man who wanted a bank holiday in honour of the legend that is Bruce Forsyth. Then there was Zafar Khan, who turned up with a home-made rubber head of Tony Blair under his arm. His manifesto consisted of wanting Blair kicked out of Downing Street. His party trick was to kick the rubber head in our direction. It whizzed past John and almost took his ear off. John, who had been handbagged by Mrs Thatcher, looked genuinely disconcerted to have narrowly missed being clobbered by another prime minister.

All human life was there, and it was our job to slash the sixty down to just eight finalists. They would then be tutored in all the dark arts of the politician, including speechifying, communication skills and debating. Then the public would vote for their favourite. It all seemed straightforward enough, and during the two days' filming in Birmingham the contestants were set challenges to make our decision easier.

One of the first was for them to force their opinions on us during an informal meeting. They had to battle for our attention and it all became rather heated and rabble-like. I found myself surrounded by would-be politicians all trying to get my attention, bellowing their ideas and shouting each other down. I'm sure it made for entertaining TV but I found it extremely intimidating.

I was well aware I was being filmed so I put a brave face on it and tried to talk to as many of the candidates as possible. One of them had a novel way of attracting attention: she took her top off and came over to our group in her bra, which exposed most of her breasts. I was a bit flustered and tried to cover everyone's embarrassment by making a joke about it in a sort of mild 'Trinny and Susannah'-like fashion.

I made contact with her boobs for about a nano-second. It was obviously all caught on camera and I thought no more about it.

Kelvin, John and I then went to a darkened room to debate on who would go through to the final eight. Viewers would vote, then the winner would have the chance to stand as an Independent in the general election, with the advantage of exposure on national TV. I was gravely concerned about one of the candidates, who was slightly to the right of Genghis Khan and proudly stated that his was the 'cabbies' manifesto'. Rodney Hilton Potts seemed to have only one theme: a torrent of bile against all immigrants to the UK. He put forward his views in a florid and highly offensive way. I am quite sure most taxi drivers would have been appalled. We were to clash many times on the show, but I had a sinking feeling that he might go all the way and win.

He was the candidate I was most worried about, but I had no idea that when the show went to air in January 2006, it would be another attention-seeker who would cause me real pain and months of distress and unease. Unbeknown to me, the woman who had been happy to show off her impressive cleavage had decided that I had assaulted her during the filming in Birmingham, and made a formal complaint to the police there. Astonishingly, they took her seriously, even though the 'incident' had actually been broadcast on TV, and no one had said anything to me at the time.

My agent Michael Joyce called me to tell me that a complaint had been made about me and I was being accused of 'sexual assault'. Of course I knew it was ludicrous, but I had a complete sense of humour failure. I know some thick-skinned individuals would have been able to laugh it off as a lot of silly nonsense, but not me. I'm a real worrier and took it all to heart.

I was horrified to be accused of something so utterly vile, and outraged that someone could make such an accusation against me. I didn't sleep a wink all night and drove Steve mad by going over and over it. I didn't want to heap embarrassment on him, my daughter or my friends and family, however innocently, and I was mortified that such an accusation had been made against me. It made me realise how vulnerable you are when you're in the public eye. There have been countless examples of celebrities or well-known people being accused of all sorts of heinous crimes, only later to be cleared of any wrong-doing.

Matthew Kelly was ludicrously accused of child abuse, Michael Flatley was devastated when falsely accused of rape, and Paul Weller had to endure an entirely made-up accusation of sexual abuse. Their names were dragged through the mud even though no charges were ever brought to court.

I was told not to worry about it, and that it would all blow over, but a week later, a grim Michael called to say that two police officers from Birmingham were coming to interview me and that we needed to hire a lawyer. I have never seen him so angry. He knew how ridiculous the whole thing was, and also realised all too well that this would put me into a complete tail-spin. I cannot tell you how horrified I was. I had never had any contact with the police before, other than appearing as myself on *The Bill*.

It was another week of sleepless nights and up in the wee small hours making tea and fretting about what would happen in the worst-case scenario, if somehow this false accusation ever came to court. In the cold light of day I would be more optimistic and think that the police and the justice system have far better things to do than to accuse a happily married mum-of-one of sexual assault when taking part in a TV show, but the horrible niggling little voice in the back of my mind kept saying that the law is an ass and I was in trouble.

Because they had not shown the woman the door and had embarked on a lengthy and costly investigation, I am afraid I rather lost faith in those who enforce the law.

Michael and I turned up to see the lawyer in his swish rooms in the City of London, and met with the two police officers, who were very professional and correct. When they switched on their tape-recorder, I realised that neither Noel Edmonds nor Ant and Dec was going to burst in and giggle that it was all a set-up and hadn't I been a good sport? This was real. I just burst into tears and cried for the whole hour as they questioned me about a ten-second incident that had already been on TV. It was bonkers. I felt like Alice going through the looking-glass.

The tape-recorder didn't work so I had to make my statement very slowly as the police officer painstakingly took it down by hand.

It was a nightmare and I went out of that room feeling really shaky, jittery and queasy. My lawyer tried to reassure me, but when he said, 'If it does come to court I'm afraid you have already lost, because your reputation will be trashed', I was in despair. He said all we could do was wait for the Crown Prosecution Service to look at the evidence supplied by the police. They would make the decision as to whether or not there would be a trial.

As I have said, the 'evidence' had appeared on the first episode of *Vote for Me*, a blink-and-you'll-miss-it completely innocent encounter that had turned into this total waste of time and money, and heaped stress and torment upon my head. I went home and phoned my friend Siobhan, who had moved back to Ireland from New York to launch the *Afternoon Show* over there. We had been calling each other every day and she had listened to all my woes.

When I told her what had happened, she told me not to worry, but when she put the phone down, she immediately booked a flight from Dublin to London. She was so concerned about me that she came all the way to Cookham Dean to give me a cuddle, talk things through and try to cheer me up. She is a wonderful friend and really helped me through a very dark time. I know I was overreacting, but I was deeply wounded that anyone could accuse me of such a crime, and angry and frustrated that it had gone so far.

A couple of days later I was getting into the car and reading the papers as usual when, to my utter shock and horror, I saw the banner headline 'Lorraine Kelly Accused of Sexual Assault' on the front page of the *Daily Mirror*. I couldn't believe that this had been leaked to the press and I was shattered. I knew it was a load of old rubbish, but I was devastated to think my family and friends and everyone I cared about would see it and that people who watched GMTV might think there was an iota of truth in it.

In fact, I was so upset my driver Ali had to stop the car at Buckingham Palace so I could throw up into a plastic bag. I was in a terrible state. I felt ghastly but was determined not to slink home. I decided to go to work as usual.

When I arrived, I noticed that all copies of the *Daily Mirror* were suspiciously absent from the green room, makeup room and the studio. Everyone was extra nice to me, but no one addressed the elephant in the room. I could feel myself getting upset, and although there was nothing left to throw up, I went to the loo to try to stop myself crying. As always, it was full of models putting on their makeup and nervous guests waiting for their five-minute 'ordeal' on the sofa. I went outside on to the roof for a blast of fresh air and told myself not to let this thing get to me, and to do a good show as though nothing had happened.

I phoned Steve and, as always, he talked me down and told me not to be so daft and that I was worrying way too much about something that would be at the bottom of the budgie's cage the next day. After talking to him I did feel a lot better, and having a live show to do always means there's no room for worries or woes. You need to concentrate completely on the job at hand.

After GMTV I just wanted to go home and disappear under the duvet, but I had to run out of the studio, jump into a car and be whisked to *This Morning* where we were doing the show live from the Ideal Home Exhibition. Apart from Steve, Phillip was the first person that day to mention the story instead of ignoring it. He gave me a hug, told me not to worry and that everyone who knew me would realise it was a heap of rubbish. I got lots of calls and texts and emails from friends and people I have worked with over the years, all outraged on my behalf, which was exactly what I needed.

No other newspaper followed up the *Mirror* story and even they didn't run any sort of follow-up, but that single front-page story gave me nightmares. The lack of sleep, not eating and constant fretting made me look like a raddled old hag. Poor Helen and Simon had their work cut out in makeup trying to make me look half alive in the mornings. I went to work every day, and after the show I phoned Michael to see if we had any news from the CPS. Obviously they had a hell of a lot more important cases to deal with, but it was more than two months before I heard that there was no case to answer. That was forty-two days of stress and worry.

At times I could forget about it and get on with my life, but it was always there, like a big black cloud over my head. It reinforced the fact that if you don't have peace of mind then your life is utterly miserable. We take peace of mind for granted until we lose it, a bit like good health, but having something forever gnawing away at you is so soul-destroying and destructive.

I didn't feel elated when I finally received the news that this ludicrous charge was not going to be pursued, just enormously relieved that I could put the whole thing behind me and angry for all the pointless tears and anguish. I had gone through hell and had made everyone around me really worried. I still don't know why the woman took such extreme action against me, but I will never forgive her for putting me through such a hideous time.

CHAPTER FOURTEEN

Homeward Bound

A year before the ill-fated *Vote for Me* I had actually gone through a far happier election process. I'd received a call from a group of students at the end of 2003 asking if I would be willing to stand for election as rector of Dundee University. As previous rectors had included the likes of Peter Ustinov and Stephen Fry, I was a bit daunted, but thought that as they had been good enough to ask me to stand, I really should give it a go.

I was up against the broadcaster Lesley Riddoch, an extremely intelligent and feisty woman with her own show on BBC Scotland and a long list of award-winning TV and radio shows under her belt. The other candidate was MI5 whistleblower David Shayler, who was jailed in 2002 after being convicted of breaching the Official Secrets Act.

The campaign opened in January 2004. My fantastic election team, led by student Maurice Golden, sprang into action with leaflets, T-shirts and huge enthusiasm. I did tours of the students' union to meet as many potential voters as possible and had to appear at the hustings, where all the candidates need to make their pitch for votes.

As the hustings were held midweek, I flew up from London right after the show, then back on the last flight as I was on air the next day. Lesley told me later that she knew she had a fight on her hands when I turned up in a mini kilt, told stories about George Clooney and promised not to put the price of beer up in the students' union bar.

On election day it was freezing and snowing, but we all canvassed outside the main university buildings. It was a serious contest, and I'm afraid I caused my team to wince and groan when I merrily told all the students that the most important thing was to cast their vote, even if they weren't supporting me. I also annoyed the opposition by giving everyone a cuddle when they came outside after voting. One of them sniffed that he didn't think cuddles were an essential part of the democratic voting process.

My pal Craig Millar's daughter Louise, who was a student at Dundee University, made me a brilliant red T-shirt with 'Vote Lorraine' on the back and 'Lorraine Loves You' on the front, which went down a storm.

I honestly didn't think I had any chance of winning. Unlike the other two candidates, I hadn't gone to university – but I hadn't counted on the number of students who loved to watch breakfast TV, either when they got back from a particularly heavy night out or as they were getting ready for the first lectures of the day.

Later that night I was called into the counting-room and told the good news that I had won. I don't think Tony Blair was more elated when he was swept to power in 1997, and we all thought – wrongly – that the world had changed for ever. My team had worked so hard against formidable opposition and I will always be very grateful to them.

The day of my installation was just fantastic. I flew up to Dundee with a team from GMTV, including my producer Sophie Hodgkins and director Michael Metcalfe, who were filming the whole proceedings. I was lucky with the weather and the sun shone. Thanks to Sir Peter Ustinov, who was the first rector of the university alongside the Queen Mother as chancellor, there is a delightful tradition whereby the newly elected rector is put into a coach and 'dragged' round Dundee by members of the university rugby club, taken to pubs in the city centre and made to have a drink in every one.

As I was the first woman to be elected rector, I was honoured to be 'dragged' around in my Cinderella coach by the university's ladies' rugby club and there was much chortling about them 'pulling' me. I had to wear my blue-and-red rector's robes and stop off at various hostelries that had put up special banners in my honour.

I didn't get to choose the drinks I had to quaff, hence the queasy mix of absinthe, a pint of heavy and a mixture of Glayva and Drambuie. There were some brilliant photos of me drinking a pint in a one-er and leaning on the bar with my head in my hands. It was all for the cameras, although it was a miracle that I got through my inauguration speech without a hiccup.

Siobhan flew over from New York to see me installed and my mum and dad came through from East Kilbride, and, of course, Steve and Rosie were there along with some close friends, including the wonderful Hugh Grant.

The first time I'd met Hugh, he was wearing a crash helmet and running at full speed towards his old kitchen units. This was his way of taking a fairly mundane domestic job and turning it into a party. He threw a barbecue at his house to celebrate the arrival of his new kitchen, and everyone was invited to put on crash helmets and play their part in destroying what was left of the old one. The idea was that two people held the old cupboard door and the person wearing the crash helmet took a fast run at it. Maximum points were gained if they put their head right through it and smashed it to bits. Luckily no one was hurt in the process, and it was certainly one way to break the ice. We hit it off right away, which was just as well as we were off to his place in Spain a couple of weeks later.

I do enjoy telling everyone that I'm off to Hugh Grant's apartment near Marbella, before I add that my Hugh Grant is a large, black-bearded Scottish man who lives by the banks of the Tay, can drink a bottle of Viña Sol in one massive glug, and is a hell of a lot more fun than the floppy-haired actor who shares his name. Hugh and his wife Joan, who is also a fellow Moonwalker, have become really good pals and are the kind of people you can completely relax with. The fact that they are both accountants explodes the myth that this is a profession for the grey and the dull.

Hugh and Joan live their lives in bright, brilliant Technicolor. He did once get extremely cross with me that first time we went to Spain, when Steve and I, Craig and Jacqueline Millar, he and Joan all went to play golf. Hugh is a brilliant golfer, but I had never played before in my life. With my first ever drive, I somehow managed to hit the ball to within two feet of the hole. I remarked that this golf lark was easier than it looked, which didn't go down well, but it was when I yelled at Hugh 'Which one is the putter?', as I honestly didn't have a clue, that I heard him groan in utter despair. Of course it was a fluke and I went on to do tons of fresh-air swings and more than my share of 'moosie crawlers', which is where the ball trickles along for a few inches like a little mouse.

On the day of my installation as rector, Hugh and Joan, Steve, Rosie, Siobhan and my mum and dad were joined in Dundee by my friends from work, Sophie, Michael and Mark Heyes, and it was good to see so many friendly faces.

I was eventually 'dragged' in my coach to the City Chambers and, on a balcony above the City Square, I waved to the crowds of students and Dundonians who had gathered to wish me well. I felt a bit like Evita up there. It was heady stuff, and you can see why politicians get addicted to even tiny little slivers of adulation. I enjoyed that wonderful day, but as a one-off only. I know that if I ever started to exhibit the slightest hint of diva-like behaviour, Steve and my mum and dad, as well as all my pals, would soon be giving me a reality check, but thankfully they haven't had to.

I was very nervous at making my rector's address to the academics, professors and students, so it was good to see my family and friends in the audience. They all came to a wonderful dinner at the principal, Sir Alan Langland's house. It was one of those days you just want to wrap up in a box and tie with a red velvet ribbon, then unwrap any time you feel a bit blue.

The next morning we were all up stupidly early because we were doing my entire GMTV show live from Dundee. There would have been no way to get back to London in time to go on air and it was a terrific opportunity to celebrate the city and the university. We set up in the University Tower Café, with beautiful views of the city and the Tay Bridge. The sun was still shining and, as luck would have it, Dundee's most famous citizen, Hollywood superstar Brian Cox, was in Scotland performing on stage in Edinburgh.

He had just completed filming *Troy*, acting pretty-boy Brad Pitt and hunk Eric Bana off the screen, and was also heavily involved in supporting Dundee University's research into diabetes. He was the perfect guest and I was so pleased that such a big star had agreed to get up at an unearthly hour to come on the show. We had also filmed the joys and attractions of Dundee, and Mark Heyes had teamed up with some of the design students to do a special fashion item. It was also a chance to highlight some of the world-renowned and groundbreaking work being carried out by the university, and it remains one of my favourite shows ever.

The university team, led by Joan Concannon, gave us lots of help that morning, and gave me so much support during my term of office. As rector, it was my job to represent the students and to help them in any way I could. Everyone who holds the post has their own idea of what they should be doing, and I was a sort of 'agony aunt'. I had lots of emails from students who wanted help with organising events, and for me to attend fundraising functions, but there were also students who had problems with their course work, or were finding it hard to settle in and make friends.

Difficulties with accommodation, money worries and even boyfriend troubles were common. The university has a terrific support system in place and a lot of help is available, so I was able to point them in the right directions. I am a very organised person and I really had to be even more of a 'Monica' than usual during those three years. At times I would be answering emails and other correspondence when Rosie was in bed, and often didn't get finished until after midnight.

Part of the job entailed attending the University Court, which I couldn't do as often as I would have liked because it was held on a Monday when I did my stint on GMTV and *This Morning*. I did fly up and down in a day to be there when I could, and I had the student presidents keeping me in touch with any major events.

The highlights for me were the graduation ceremonies in the summer. I had to arrive at Dundee City Council's imposing chambers early in the morning and go straight to the 'robing room' where all the university's deans and dignitaries gathered. Everyone was donning their colourful robes. Mine had been specially made for Stephen Fry. He is a big lad so I looked like a little kid wearing her dad's overcoat. I had to keep lifting it up so I wouldn't fall over, especially as I always wore a pair of really sassy shiny high heels that just peeped out from beneath it.

We were helped into our official gear by splendid gentlemen in livery and lined up for the chancellor's procession. I was directly behind the Lord Provost, John Letford, and the bearer of the city mace, a wonderfully ornate and grand object that bestowed even more dignity on our procession, as did the chancellor, the principal and the university mace-bearer.

We had to walk from the council chambers across the city square, which is partly cobbled so I had to concentrate very hard on walking with dignity and not wobbling on my high heels. We entered the Caird Hall to the strains of 'Gaudeamus' and went through the crowds and up on to the platform. All the while I willed myself not to trip on my oversize robes. The atmosphere was electric and very emotional.

Each year, around 3,500 students from Dundee University graduate, and their proud parents and families, who have often made big sacrifices to ensure their children get the best possible start in life, come to see them. As the students came on stage to be 'capped', which means they are tapped on the head by the chancellor with a posh Dundee bunnet, you could see the relief and joy in their faces.

I loved it.

The second graduation ceremony I attended was especially moving, as we had a very special honorary degree to bestow on one of the bravest women I have ever met. Jane Tomlinson, who died in 2007 after a long battle with cancer, was a true inspiration. I interviewed her many times over the years and was astounded by her spirit and determination. Jane was diagnosed with breast cancer in 1991 and thought she had beaten the disease, but it came back seven years later and in 2000 she was told that it was terminal. Jane's way of dealing with her illness was to set herself challenges and at the same time raise money for her charity in order to help others. She ran marathons, did long-distance bike rides and pushed her poor, sick body to the very limit. She was a modest woman, and no saint, but she was a truly remarkable human being.

When she received her honorary degree the entire audience gave her a spontaneous standing ovation. She was overwhelmed and shed a tear, as did most of the students and their families. Jane was a very special person and I am so glad the university gave her the honour. I know it meant a great deal to her.

During my three years as rector it was a joy to see all

those bright young men and women with the whole world at their feet. All too often the media focuses on the feral young thugs who commit crimes, and forgets that there are some young people who work hard and play hard and give us all hope for the future.

I also really enjoyed the start of any university year, with the welcome to all the freshers, and I caused a bit of a stushie when I told them all to study diligently for their degree but also to enjoy their time in Dundee. I said it was all right to have a drink now and again and to have sex, but they needed to make sure they used protection and had safe sex. I thought it was better to get the message of sensible boozing and safe sex across without being too heavy-handed, but I was lambasted. One particular man of the cloth took huge exception to my comments and I was accused of promoting drunkenness and fornication.

It would have been funny if it wasn't so out of touch. I was actually telling students not to waste their time binge-drinking and sleeping around, but in language I hoped they could relate to. There's no point in thundering from the pulpit and expecting abstinence and chastity in this day and age. What you need to ensure is that students value themselves enough not to have sex as casually as they would a pint, and to respect their health by not binge-drinking every single night. I honestly believe that achieving your degree is only part of a university experience. It's also about making friends for life, taking advantage of all the opportunities you can grab hold of, and finding your place in the world.

In June 2008 I was asked back to Dundee University to receive an honorary degree in law. Finally, after three decades, my mum has a picture of me as a graduate with my scroll and robes. I will always be grateful to the students at Dundee University for electing me as their rector for three years. It was a real honour and privilege, and something I will never forget. It also means I have letters after my name and if anyone shouts 'Is there a doctor in the house?', I can legitimately put my hand up.

Steve and I always knew that one day we would go home to Scotland. Even when we lived down south, we went back as often as possible to our little holiday home in Tayport.

Believe it or not, on occasion I could get back to Scotland in less time than it took to travel the mere twenty-six miles to Cookham Dean from the studio. I would drive from GMTV on the banks of the Thames to London City airport, hop aboard the plane to Dundee, cross the bridge to Tayport and be standing outside in the garden, watching dolphins bobbing around in the water, faster than I could get home through the murderous London traffic on the dreaded M40.

One particular journey to Chalkpit Cottage took me a knuckle-chewing three hours, and I worked out that I was spending at least twenty hours a week stuck on my backside in the car. Even leaving so early in the morning, commuting was horribly stressful.

Although I loved Cookham, my little house and all the friends we had made, both of us were homesick and Steve especially was very keen to move back. With Rosie due to start secondary school, we knew that if we were going to return to Scotland, it had to be sooner rather than later. I wouldn't have wanted to pull her out of secondary school half-way though her education. I remember when I had to change schools when we moved to East Kilbride when I was thirteen, and at that age it's really daunting to turn up at the school gates and not know a soul.

Another strong reason for going home was to be nearer Steve's sister Margaret, who had been diagnosed with multiple sclerosis not long after our wedding. This is one of the cruellest diseases imaginable. It attacks the central nervous system and can cause loss of balance, depression, spasms, memory loss and difficulty with speech and swallowing. Your body just gradually shuts down. It is a creeping and insidious illness, and Margaret is now virtually bedridden.

She was so beautiful at my wedding, golden-haired, laughing and dancing all night, and in a few short years MS had robbed her of so much. We bought our holiday home in Tayport mainly because it was right across from Margaret's flat. It meant we could keep an eye on her and visit her as often as possible. It was clear she was becoming less independent and needed her family around her.

As is always the case, when Steve decides he's going to do something it gets sorted at a head-swivelling pace. If I have a vague idea of maybe thinking that perhaps one day the living-room will need painting, he has the colour charts whipped out and the work done before I have a chance to put it off. The same with holidays, weekends away and buying new furniture. It's researched, sorted and completed.

I know that when you buy a house you should check on so many things, like the council tax, how close the shops and schools are and how much it will cost to heat, but I always go on instinct. If I step into a house and get the feeling that it's a happy place, it smells 'right' and I feel comfortable, that's all I really care about. Just so long as it's affordable and not in need of a new roof, I always think any other problems can be sorted out.

When we went to see the very first house we looked at in Perthshire, I knew right away that we had found the perfect home. It was near a river, quiet and a bit quirky, with lots of curves and interesting nooks and crannies. It had been built with reclaimed stone and there were even a few ancient pieces where you could still make out weathered carvings. It was a 'happy house' and we both loved it. It also ticked all the practical boxes and we knew it was just right for us.

Another plus was that our dog Rocky, a three-year-old Border terrier, was in his element. Until we got Rocky, I could never understand people who claimed their dogs were part of the family, but now I totally get it. We never had cats or dogs when I was growing up, but we did have goldfish, hamsters and Graham's sneaky-looking white mice. He also had a baby lizard, but when I picked it up one day it went round and round in frantic circles in the palm of my hand, fell flat on its back and died. I put it back in its cage and never said a word – until now.

Graham also rescued a baby sparrow with a broken wing when he was about seven years old. He was a really kind-hearted wee boy. He wrapped it in cotton wool, called it Bod and kept the poor thing alive for a couple of days. We were all really sad when Bod cheeped his last.

When I met Steve I inherited Jimmy the Cat, who had been bought from a cat shelter for 50p. He was a cat that looked and acted like a dog. He never killed or stalked anything, but used to fetch sticks and bring them back. When he died of old age at our house in Cookham we rescued another cat and called him Maurice Malpas, after the legendary Dundee United player, and gave him to Margaret to keep her company in Tayport along with her beloved cat Daisy.

When she was ten, Rosie decided that she really wanted a dog and that it would be called Rocky. Steve had been filming *Vets in Practice* and all the vets told him that a Border terrier was one of the best family dogs to have because of their energy and personality. He had to go to Bristol to find Rocky and bring him home. He was the cutest little thing I've ever seen.

I'm sure it goes against all the experts' advice, but for Rocky's first two nights with us, I ended up sleeping on the couch with him 'just in case he's frightened'. He settled in really quickly and has been the fourth member of our family ever since. Even my mum, who isn't all that keen on pets, adores him, and he loves it when she and Dad come to look after him because they walk for miles and miles.

Since we moved home my parents have been brilliant. They look after the house and take care of Rocky when we go on holiday, and help out by picking up Rosie from school when Steve and I are working. I couldn't do without them.

Of course, there was no way I could continue working on a live daily TV show in London if I lived up in Scotland, so I needed to hatch a cunning plan. I didn't want to leave my job and, thankfully, they didn't want me to go.

My idea was to do the show live on Monday and Tuesday, then record Wednesday's and Thursday's shows. That way I could spend the majority of the week at home in Scotland. Lots of other programmes do this, and as my show is about lifestyle and entertainment rather than news-based, it would make perfect sense. Initially the bosses at GMTV weren't all that keen on the idea and I was asked to come up with some other solutions.

My producer, Sophie Hodgkins, and I drew up a complicated plan that involved me doing some weeks live and some pre-recorded, and even 'special' shows that I would top and tail, a bit like Sir Trevor McDonald, who comes on at the beginning and end of his current affairs programme. It took us ages and we were flushed with triumph when we showed our master plan to the boss.

Peter McHugh had a look, hemmed and hawed a bit, then beamed at us and said he wanted to go back to plan A. We'd give the two days live and two days pre-recorded a go and see what happened. We told him he was a genius and started making plans right away.

I really am hugely indebted to GMTV for so many things, but especially because they have bent over backwards to allow me to continue to present the show I love. The knowledge that I still had a job was a huge boost and swept away any niggling doubts I had about heading back north, but it was still a wrench to leave our home in Cookham. It was where we had brought Rosie as a two-day-old little scrap, and we'd spent a fortune and long hours turning it into a real home. I was very sad to leave, but also excited to sort out our new place in Scotland.

Thanks to those regular flights from Dundee to London City airport, I can do the journey from door to door in just under three hours. Over the past three years I have settled into a well-oiled routine. I come to London on Sunday evenings, leaving the house around 5.15, and reaching Dundee airport in plenty of time for the flight at 6.35, unless I get stuck behind a tractor. The airport car park is right outside the little terminal. It's free of charge and I leave my car there to pick up when I return on Tuesday evening. I walk a few steps to the check-in, where there's rarely more than one person in front of me.

It can be a bumpy flight in that little plane and there are

times when white-knuckled grown men whimper on their way down south, but we regulars try to look nonchalant. I get picked up at London City around 8p.m. on Sunday. Scripts and briefs for Monday's show are in the back of the car and I read through them during the short journey to my wee bolthole in London.

When I get in, the first thing I do is phone home to let Steve know I have arrived safely, and then I make a final call to my producers and do my homework for the next day. I try to go to bed as early as possible, but it depends what's on TV and how much work I have to do.

The next morning I'm up around 5.30 and in the studio an hour later. I look though the papers and talk through any changes with Pauline Haase and Katherine Quinn, who head up the production team, and with Chris Ward and Laura Wilson, my producers. A lot of my team have been with GMTV since they were teenagers working as runners, basically underpaid dogs-bodies at everyone's beck and call.

This means they have a real inside knowledge of the show as well as a fierce loyalty to and pride in what they do. They often have to fight for stories as there is a real rivalry between my part of the show, *LK Today*, and *GMTV Today*. Pauline and my team are like terriers and always fight their corner.

Our biggest frustration is when an item we are doing is 'nicked' and aired earlier in the morning, or if we lose out on a guest altogether. It can work both ways, and the GMTV producers find that some guests won't want to get up so early and are far happier to do my pre-recorded shows. I've had the chance recently to interview Sarah Jessica Parker, Cameron Diaz, Russell Brand and Ashton Kutcher because of the later start.

On the morning of any show there are usually at least a few

things to juggle, especially if news has broken overnight or if a guest has failed to turn up. I'm lucky enough to have my hair and makeup done by Helen or Simon. I can go through the papers or make changes to the script while they work round me.

I wish we could broadcast what goes on in the makeup room. Our TV critic Richard Arnold bursts into the room just after seven o'clock like a whirlwind. Dr Hilary Jones conducts an impromptu medical service, with everyone queuing up to tell him their aches and pains, and he and Penny Smith try to outdo each other with daft jokes and funny stories. Hilary has a fantastic sense of humour, which makes it easy to talk to him about anything, whether it happens to be on or off screen.

I don't know how we have managed to get away with some of the subjects we've tackled so early in the morning, but there isn't a single part of the human body that we haven't poked, prodded or discussed in eye-watering detail.

Our weather women Andrea and Claire Nasir pop in to touch up their makeup between their broadcasts, and it's our only chance to have a catch-up.

Sue Jameson often comes in to dry off after standing outside in the rain doing one of her crisp, authoritative reports. I am a huge admirer of Sue. She has a brilliant turn of phrase and is always utterly reliable and professional. You can throw anything at her, from politics to panto – sometimes the two can be so easily confused – and she will deliver an enlightening insight.

She also makes the most amazing cakes, and just before Christmas she is inundated with orders from all of us for her delicious, personalised designs. I have tried to pass off her triumphant chocolate cake as my own, but no one believed me as it was just too ridiculously good.

I go into the studio at around 8a.m. to do a quick trail of what is coming up in the show that morning; and then I try to make sure I have a chat with my guests to put them at ease and make sure they don't have any worries. I go back in at about eight thirty, cross my fingers and pray that *GMTV Today* isn't overrunning.

If they come to me late then we might have to cut some items altogether and shorten others as we go along.

After Monday's show, we have our usual post-mortem meeting, then a big discussion about the next day, when we have to do those three shows. I have a lot of homework as there are sometimes more than fifteen separate interviews, but to me it isn't really work. The variety in what I do means that every single day is different.

I might be talking to a bereaved mother, a distraught victim of a crime, discussing fashion trends with Mark Heyes or soap plots with Tina Baker. A big delight is when live bands perform, and even better if it's an artist I greatly admire. I was beside myself when kd lang agreed to perform on the show.

Madonna once said of kd that 'Elvis is alive and she is beautiful', which is a brilliant description of this talented and charismatic performer. Her single 'Constant Craving' is my all-time favourite and she has the kind of voice that gives you goose-bumps. She came on set wearing a suit, barefoot, and, with just a piano for accompaniment, sang Neil Young's 'Helpless'. It was so astoundingly beautiful that I forgot I was on TV and became totally lost in her performance. It was like a private concert just for me and the crew, and it was so incredibly moving that I could feel myself starting to cry on live TV.

I pulled myself together because I had to interview her right after the song and I would have looked a right twonk snuffling my way through it. She really was something special, so comfortable in her own skin.

Often on a Monday I will go and see a screening of a movie that hasn't been released yet so that I can talk to the star afterwards. This is one of the best perks of the job. I am a real movie buff and there is nothing better than sitting in a cinema where you don't have any adverts and where no one is laughing, talking, munching or crunching and you can just enjoy the film.

Of course, it's always a worry when the movie is rubbish, because I know I have to interview the actors. In these cases I refrain from telling them what I thought of the film, and swiftly move on to other areas of their lives, but it's tricky.

The pre-recorded interviews with big A-listers promoting their films are rather strange. You are ushered into a suite in a very posh London hotel with lots of PR people rushing around. There will be two chairs and two cameras. One chair is always beautifully lit. That's for the star. The PR people usually place a giant poster or logo right behind it, with the name of the movie in big letters. This is very annoying as it means all the interviews will look exactly the same, whether they are on MTV, *Blue Peter* or *LK Today*.

The star is sometimes sitting there already, and you are ushered into their presence, but usually they are wheeled into the room by their 'people'. It's a totally artificial, rather intimidating and generally frustrating experience because you are only ever allotted about eight minutes' 'face time' and it's virtually impossible to strike up any sort of rapport or ask any meaningful questions.

There are exceptions to this rule. When I interviewed George Clooney I was only supposed to have six minutes, but we started talking about golf in Scotland, of all things, and he became very interested and animated. This is not necessarily because he has a huge interest in the subject, but because he is utterly charming and works very hard at making sure everyone has a good interview. I talked to him for ages about all kinds of things, including his pet Vietnamese pot-bellied pig, sadly now deceased, and how George manages to keep a low profile. He told me he often just puts on a black beanie hat and an old jacket, keeps his head down and wanders around cities like London on his own. He says sometimes people look at him and think, 'That scruffy bloke's a lot like George Clooncy, he really should smarten himself up a bit' and they leave him alone. It shows that even a mega-star can have some sort of privacy if he so chooses.

Will Smith was another brilliant interviewee. Of course, it helped that I enjoyed *I Am Legend*, the movie he was promoting, but I have never seen Will in a bad film. At that time rumours were sweeping the US that he was thinking of standing for President. Will found this hilarious, but I reckon he would be the coolest president ever. When we finished the interview I told him I wished all big stars were as easy to talk to. He looked directly at me and said, 'But it's my job.'

I could have kissed him. I'm sure there are plenty more things George Clooney and Will Smith would rather be doing than talking about a movie they finished shooting months ago. They both, however, realise that promotion is a big part of their job. By doing all of these interviews, and being asked the same dumb questions over and over again in hotels around the globe, they will encourage people to spend their money and go and see their film. So they make a real effort to bond with the interviewer and disarm them.

Russell Brand has the same attitude and when I interviewed him for *Forgetting Sarah Marshall* he was a joy. He was sassy, flirty and just the right side of naughty for breakfast TV. People like George, Will and Russell make my job a whole lot easier and I just wish others would follow their example.

Harrison Ford clearly hates being interviewed and was grumpy and monosyllabic. As a massive fan of *Bladerunner*, I haven't really been able to look at that masterpiece of a movie in quite the same way since I met him. Bruce Willis was very pleasant, but so introspective and keen to sound highly intelligent that his answers didn't make sense, and I almost had to be prodded with a sharp stick to stay awake.

I felt very sorry for Sandra Bullock and Keanu Reeves, who were promoting their film *The Lake House* in 2006. I walked into the room and they looked shell-shocked. A print journalist from a magazine in Scandinavia had ripped into them about how he had disliked the movie. In the UK we hacks are generally very polite. Their movie was no classic, but just an inoffensive romantic comedy.

I don't think they were used to being so heavily criticised, but their experience made it an interesting interview for me because we were able to talk about their lives as stars rather than just the plot of the film and its release date.

With the notable exceptions I have already mentioned, I don't think press junkets ever really work. It's far better to have the star in the studio live and unleashed, interacting with other guests and commenting on the day's happenings. It also gives the whole studio a real buzz. When George Michael came in live, I wasn't alone in being utterly star-struck. In fact, I couldn't even go into the makeup room to say hello to him because I was so in awe. I broke out in that embarrassing prickly red flush you get on your neck when you're all nervous.

Poor George must have thought I was a right eejit, but this was the man whose music I had grown up with and, along with the Scissor Sisters' utterly sublime 'Don't Feel Like Dancing', I always play 'Club Tropicana' to lift my spirits if I'm stressed or a bit miserable.

So, the perks are many and I still feel very naughty coming out into the daylight after watching a movie on a Monday morning. It's rather decadent when everyone else is doing a proper job. It's strange, though, to think that when I was at primary school and we were asked to fill out a careers form I didn't put 'Journalist' or 'TV Presenter' but wrote that I wanted to be a fighter pilot. In those days it was impossible for a woman to have been considered for such a career, and I'm certain I wouldn't have made the grade anyway. Times have changed dramatically. Women make fantastic pilots, and through my job I have been lucky enough to experience the thrill of flying in a jet.

In September 2006 I was asked to help launch the world-renowned RAF Leuchars air show, which takes place every September as a tribute to those who fought in the Battle of Britain. The airbase commander wondered if I would agree to go up in a Tornado jet as part of a diamond formation. *Would I?* It was my dream come true.

In the skies above our house in Perthshire, we are visited sometimes two or three times a day by pilots at RAF Leuchars on training missions. I know some people hate the noise, and it can be scary if you're half-way up a hill and one of those beauties comes roaring out of the sky, but I just find them astonishingly beautiful and rather reassuring.

I had to be given a full medical to assess whether I was fit enough to be in the back of this multimillion-pound jet. Then I was kitted out with my G-suit and helmet, and talked through the whole process. Not once did I feel scared or worried. I was in the hands of true professionals, and even after I'd been told about what would happen if we had a malfunction and I had to eject, I had no qualms about climbing aboard. My pilot was the esteemed Squadron Leader Pete Brombley. He was the ultimate idea of a dashing pilot, square-jawed, flinty-eyed and cooler than a cucumber in a deep freeze at the South Pole.

Pete inspired confidence even when he handed me my sick bag. He showed me how to operate my oxygen slide and told me if I felt queasy I could have an extra blast. In the highly unlikely event of him collapsing in a heap, I was shown his ejector button as well as my own. I was beyond excitement as we took off and climbed up into the clouds.

We were rehearsing a tricky diamond formation involving nine jets that would be one of the highlights of the air show that weekend. Pete and I were in the 'whip' jet at the back, which makes sure that everyone is in the right place at the right time. I was so close to the other jets I could see the whites of the pilots' eyes. We flew at 700 miles an hour, at times upside-down, and went supersonic over the North Sea. We pulled over four and a half Gs – that's four and a half times the force of gravity. This is where your G-suit comes into its own. When you're travelling at that sort of speed, the blood drains from your head and you would pass out if the G-suit didn't squeeze it all back up to where it came from. It's a bit like being cuddled by a gorilla, but I found it exhilarating.

Going up in formation and seeing those beautiful machines close enough to touch, and realising how magnificently the pilots flew them, was incredibly moving. It was a bright sunny day, the scenery in Fife and around Dundee was dazzling, and I felt close to tears to have experienced something so utterly perfect. I can't thank the team at RAF Leuchars enough for helping me fulfil a long-held childhood ambition.

The next year the runway at RAF Leuchars was being re-laid and, instead of the air show, the organiser Alison McKenzie and her team put on a Battle of Britain ball. Dress-code for the night was 1940s uniforms or Second World War style, and it was all in aid of the RAF benevolent fund, the Royal Air Forces Association and CLIC Sargent, a cancer charity for children.

The event kicked off with a 'Salute to the Few' fly-past from a Second World War Dakota as the guests sipped cocktails outside in the sunshine. With a lot of hard work, one of the massive aircraft hangars had been transformed into a glamorous ballroom, and the evening began with an air-raid warning and Churchill's splendidly rousing Battle of Britain speech over black-and-white newsreels from the forties. As I was hosting the ball, I had a WW2 RAF uniform made, which must have horrified purists as I wore it with impossibly high black heels.

Siobhan came over from Ireland and looked utterly splendid in her costume. Steve, Rosie, Hugh and Joan, Steve's cousin Bob and his wife Carol all came along. Our guest of honour was Hugh's mum Margo, who had actually served during the Second World War as a WAAF, and it was a very special evening with music from the RAF Squadronaires and dancing from the Fly Right Dance Company. The insignia on my 'uniform' meant that

I out-ranked almost everyone there and spent the evening being saluted by gorgeous pilots.

It was simply magical.

My Mondays are jam-packed. I do try to have a bit of down-time, but it isn't always possible as there is always so much to do for the show. I try really hard to see my pal Jane Wake and go for a run or do a Pilates session. Inevitably I have to let her down because I need to do an interview, but she doesn't mind being stood up for the likes of Brad Pitt or the cast of *Sex and the City*.

Mondays are when I try to catch up with letters from viewers and readers. I had it drummed into me from an early age that I must always reply to correspondence and *never* forget to send thank-you letters and I really appreciate the feedback. My brother and I were brought up to say 'please' and 'thank you', and to have very good manners. Sadly, it's something that seems to be considered old-fashioned these days, when in fact it's common courtesy. I weed out the letters that need a swift reply and handwrite as many as I can, but I also have standard letters for people who need information on the items we have featured on the show.

I try to cram in as much as I can on a Monday, maybe catching up with Joyce or Sophie, or going to the movies or just walking around London. The busier I am, the less likely it is that I miss home. I know I am only away from late Sunday until Tuesday tea-time, and that I am incredibly lucky that GMTV has agreed to such a set-up, but it is still hard to be away from Steve and Rosie – and Rocky. I don't think you ever get over that working-mother guilt and the feeling that you aren't doing either job particularly well.

Monday nights are usually pyjamas, beans on toast, double *Corrie* and doing my homework, reading scripts and briefs and looking for extra information on the Internet for the three shows I need to do the next day.

Tuesday really is a crazy day and one of the most difficult tasks is choosing three outfits to wear, one for the live show, one for Wednesday and another for Thursday. I always seem to have left the right shoes for my outfit at home in Scotland and *never* have the right colour tights.

When I come off air after Tuesday morning's live show, we have a quick meeting, then go through any changes for the pre-records. There's only an hour to sort everything out, but as I have done all my research the night before it gives us enough time to have a good run-through before it's eleven o'clock and in our heads it's Wednesday. We do the show 'as live', which means that we stop for nothing unless a guest swears or keels over.

The crew, who have been up since four o'clock and have already worked on three and a half hours of live TV, make it all possible. I bribe them shamelessly with chocolate and Krispy Kreme doughnuts to keep their energy levels up, and they really do pull out all the stops. At times it's like watching a DVD on fast forward as they dart round the studio bringing on guests and changing the set.

Once Wednesday's show is over I do a very quick change and just after midday we are all in a Thursday mindset. We've usually finished by one thirty, when we have a really good post-mortem meeting and throw some ideas around for the following week. Then I need to dash to London City and the flight home.

On Wednesdays I write my *Best* agony aunt column;

Thursdays I do my *Sun* column and on Fridays it's the *Sunday Post*.

There are times when I sit in front of that blank computer screen and wonder where the ideas will come from, but there's always an issue that makes me seethe, or some silly celebrity making a buffoon of themselves to give me plenty of fodder.

It's a very busy week, and at times I do get overwhelmed, but somehow I manage to get everything done, even if I'm still writing columns and articles at midnight. Keeping afloat and on top of everything isn't just down to my work ethic, but also because Steve does such a lot to help me. He has his own freelance career, but also deals with all the baffling and truly enormous amount of paperwork that goes with the two of us being self-employed; he will do the big supermarket run (and bring back all the right shopping), put out the bins, mow the lawn (which I cannot do) and generally much more than his fair share.

It's a real partnership, but I do think you have to work at a relationship and not take each other for granted. We still go on 'dates' whenever we can, get dressed up and go for a meal or to the movies.

I believe I have one of the best jobs in TV, but in 2007 all the GMTV presenters were asked to choose the job of their dreams and be filmed doing it for the show. I promptly opted for assistant manager of Dundee United. I gatecrashed the players' training day in Dundee, channelled my inner wee Jim McLean, barked orders and bossed them around.

Our manager, Craig Levien, one of the most intelligent and effective managers in Scotland, made sure I didn't get too carried away and, as always, the backroom staff at United were warm, friendly and welcoming. They were all really good sports and bought me a special jacket with my initials on and a strip signed by all the team. Sadly, even though I had brought my little rubber duck, I didn't get to join the boys in the showers, but they did have an unbroken run of impressive wins after my visit, and I put it down to my punishing training schedule.

Under Craig Levien, United have recaptured some of the classy play that made them so watchable in the eighties, and this has brought them the respect of other sides in the Scottish Premier League. In 2008 they reached the finals of the CIS League Cup. As any true fan knows, in the build-up to a big game you feel like a cat on a hot tin roof. I was asked to be on Eamonn's Radio 5 Live sports show on the Saturday morning to review the game on Sunday.

I was on with those two doyens of footie Colin McAllister and Justin Ryan, who know as much about the Scottish Premier League as I do about interior design. It was a very funny show – and the production team had even dusted down my very favourite Dundee United moment so I was able to relive that Kevin Gallagher goal against Barcelona in the UEFA Cup in 1987.

I was also invited to be on BBC Scotland's *Sportscene* as a pundit, alongside ex-Scotland and Chelsea star Pat Nevin and presenter Stuart Cosgrove. I know I was on to talk about football, but the first thing I did was make sure I had black trousers and a tangerine cardigan to wear. Once I had my team colours sorted, I did my homework and made sure I wouldn't let my side down by not being able to talk footie with the big boys.

One of my favourite United players is the Irishman Noel Hunt. He is the sort of player who runs his heart out and always gives 110 per cent. When he scores Hunty always does an impressive forward somersault, and I was hoping he'd be doing a lot of tumbling that day. I actually had a really good feeling about that final. There was a lot of emotion in the air; Craig and his boys were desperate to win for chairman Eddie Thompson, who, as I write this, is battling cancer.

The seventeen thousand United fans who travelled to Glasgow were also completely behind their chairman. Many were wearing tangerine T-shirts emblazoned with 'There's Only One Eddie Thompson', and this chant rang around the stadium before the game. Looking at that sea of tangerine and black gave me goosebumps. It was going to be our day and when Noel Hunt scored that opening goal, and did his somersault, we went berserk. Then Rangers equalised with just minutes to go and we were into extra time.

Mark de Vries, a player we had all been whining about during the whole game for being too slow, slotted in a cracking goal and all of a sudden we did a 360-degree turn and he was a hero. Rangers equalised, it went to penalties and the unbelievable happened.

It wasn't in the script, but we lost.

At the airport that night, as I waited for the flight from Glasgow to Gatwick, I saw a few other slumped figures wearing tangerine-and-black scarves. We grunted ruefully at one another in a sombre salute of fellow-suffering. The journey south was long and weary, but it would have flashed by in an instant if we had won.

At work on Monday morning, there was none of the usual joshing about how my team had done from our cameramen and props boys. Those true footie fans knew I was heartbroken, and my tea was placed before me in my usual Dundee United mug with a consoling choccie biccie beside it.

Although we have huge fun on *LK Today*, there's only so much you can get away with at nine o'clock in the morning, and on later shows you can be more sassy, cheeky and even a bit rude. Although still in the best possible taste, of course. I have been a guest on the BBC's *Have I Got News For You* twice and both times was paired with Paul Merton, who might look languid and laid back but whose wit is razor sharp as well as hysterically funny. He and Ian Hislop are both fantastic on the show and very generous, as long as you don't make the mistake of trying to take them on.

Too many deluded smart-arses have turned up on set hoping to be funnier and wittier than the team captains and that is just never going to happen. As a guest you are given a very rough idea of what's likely to be in the show and you are shown the 'odd one out' photos about an hour beforehand and a few of the newspaper headlines, but that's it. Sitting there in the dark waiting for the lights to come up and hearing the theme tune is exciting and bloody scary. Both times, I went with the flow, laughed my head off and had a great time.

I was flattered to be asked back as a guest host after Angus Deayton was given the boot by the BBC for taking drugs and womanising. I actually found being Paul's partner much more daunting than being in the hot seat. As the presenter you have all your jokes on autocue and you always get the last word. I absolutely loved being in that chair and in charge of the naughty schoolboys.

Hosting *The Friday Night Project* was completely different and gave me the chance to really let my hair down. Alan Carr and Justin Lee Collins have to be the most unlikely combination since Paul McCartney and Heather Mills, but they work really well together. The boys came into GMTV a couple of days beforehand to do some pre-recording for their show.

One of the things I love about our production team and crew is how relaxed they are about having presenters from other shows popping in to do a quick sketch or interview. Alan and Justin rampaged through the studio like an enthusiastic hairy sheepdog and a nippy Yorkshire terrier.

While I was in makeup they went off to rifle through my wardrobe to find an outfit for me to wear on that morning's show. The low-cut see-through black top and zebra-print mini-skirt complete with fishnet stockings and stilettos was absolutely perfect – if I had been a hooker. I still don't know where they found them.

Their show is recorded at LWT, just downstairs from GMTV. It was where they used to do *Blind Date* and where they still record all the big variety shows. I'm not used to working in front of a live audience, but I absolutely loved it. As the host, you deliver an opening monologue, and for once I understood why someone might want to be a stand-up comic. Despite the terrifying prospect of a whole audience sitting with their arms folded and daring you to make them laugh, when they actually do guffaw at one of your jokes it's quite simply the best of all possible highs.

I had already filmed some sketches for the show, including a spoof charity appeal called 'Bras for Africa'. Basically I had to ask women shopping in a busy London store if they would take off their bras there and then and give them to their less fortunate sisters in Africa, who needed their 'support'. To add to the sense of occasion we had red-headed Liverpudlian poppet Sonya singing a special anthem, which had a rousing chorus of 'Braaaaaaas for Africaaaaaaaa', to be sung at lung-bursting level.

Astonishingly, I managed to collect dozens and dozens of bras of all shapes and sizes. Some could have been used as hammocks and others would have been too small for Barbie, but all the women who whipped them off thought they were helping a very good cause, and were real sports when told it was just for a daft TV show.

I also did a sketch dressed as *Celebrity Big Brother* winner Chantelle, complete with a monstrous blonde wig and a too-tight pink terry-towelling tracksuit, which gave a whole new meaning to 'camel toe'. Justin was US basketball star Dennis Rodman and Alan was a scarily convincing Rula Lenska, who opened the sketch shaving off a false beard. I had an absolute hoot. The boys were adorable and I would love to do something similar again.

My very favourite programme to guest host is *The Paul O'Grady Show*. When I've been standing in for Paul, I've danced a cancan, been attacked by giant bats and even managed to achieve a genuine *Guinness Book of Records* award for putting on the most kilts in under a minute. It's not really up there with running the fastest 100 metres or eating the most baked beans, but I have the certificate to prove that I'm a record-breaker. The show is such good fun because Paul and his team have created a really warm, friendly environment where you can get away with just about anything. Paul's witty but sometimes acerbic humour stops everything being too sugary-sweet, but this is a programme with real heart. That's why it's so successful, and why guests clamour to appear with him.

The scariest programme I have ever appeared on was *Question*

Time where I was one of the panel. Unlike many other 'ready-eyed' TV shows, *Question Time* never, ever, bends the rules. You aren't given any kind of clue or heads-up on what sort of questions will be lobbed from the audience. There are no retakes if you make an arse of yourself. You need to think on your feet and try to sound intelligent and reasonably well informed. I'm a bit of a news junkie anyway, but the week before the show. I swotted up on every possible news-story or current hot topic that might possibly come up. I have to know what's going on, not just for *LK Today* but for my columns in the *Sun* and the *Sunday Post*.

Once again I was sitting in a darkened studio, waiting for the opening titles and the famous *Question Time* music, trying to stop my legs shaking and my throat going bone dry. The utterly charming and twinkly David Dimbleby must have noticed how nervous I was because he made sure I was allowed to answer the opening question before the eager politicians.

'Man in the green shirt' from the audience asked why Prime Minister Tony Blair hadn't sacked a particular 'off-message' minister. I replied that perhaps he had pictures of the PM and his wife Cherie naked, which made everyone laugh and I relaxed a bit. As a 'civilian', you can speak your mind honestly and you're also cut a lot of slack.

I actually felt a bit sorry for the politicians, who had to toe the party line no matter what their own private beliefs. Inevitably, it means that at times they come across as insincere and unconvincing. *Question Time* is recorded about an hour before transmission and goes out 'as live'. There's no time for major edits, so all your gaffes, stammers and inane blunderings are there for the world to see.

After the show, everyone went for a civilised meal and the politicians, who had spent the past hour jousting, sniping and desperately point-scoring, got along like bosom buddies. I think I just about got away with my appearance on the show, but it was far too scary for me to want to do a repeat performance, and I cannot imagine why anyone would ever want to be a politician these days. It's like being the manager of the England football team. You're on a hiding to nothing, with people queuing up to give you a right good verbal kicking. I could never cope with that level of criticism and attack, and I wouldn't put my family through it either.

I would also find it impossible to keep my mouth shut and parrot the party line and would end up being constantly told off.

When he was still chancellor of the exchequer, Gordon Brown invited Steve, Rosie and me to lunch at his house in Scotland. It was a lovely afternoon, really relaxed and friendly, and it was good to see a politician who is a real hands-on dad and family man. He kept looking at his watch throughout the meal and I thought he was waiting for an important phone call from Tony Blair or maybe from President George Bush, but he turned to Steve and said, 'If we hurry up we might just make the Raith Rovers game against Forfar.' I wasn't tempted even by such a glamour tie and stayed to talk to Sarah, while Gordon took Steve to the match and paid for him to go in.

Like all politicians, Gordon Brown might have made some gaffes, but he was spot-on in his choice of wife. Sarah Brown's a thoroughly decent woman. She does tireless work for the charity she set up in the name of her tiny baby daughter Jennifer, who died when she was just ten days old. Being Sarah, it's all done in a quiet, non-showy way, but the money raised and the research being carried out into many projects, including premature birth and death, is making a real difference to the lives of women and children all over Britain.

Gordon Brown happened to wonder if I had ever thought about going into politics, and we had a really interesting conversation. My experience on *Question Time* had convinced me that I'm not a political animal and would never shine in that sort of environment. (Just think of the extra issues I'd have to fret over that would keep me awake at night!) I try to do as much as I can to help with various organisations and charities, especially the smaller ones that don't have the clout or the cash to make a lot of noise. Being able to do that is one of the real benefits of having your fat face on the telly.

Breakfast TV has been very good to me and, as long as people still enjoy watching, I'm happy to stick to the job I have loved for more than twenty years. There's lots more that I plan to do in the future – more TV shows, radio and writing.

I really have been extraordinarily lucky. My parents gave me love, encouragement and an appreciation of music, books and movies. My husband Steve makes sure I don't take myself too seriously and is always there with his support, which I simply couldn't do without. I have very good friends and the people I work with make me laugh, give me their loyalty and work like Trojans to make sure the show is a success. And I try to follow the best advice I was ever given.

My old Granny Mac always said you should never keep anything for 'best'. If you gave her a new scarf, perfume or bubble-bath, she would use it right away and not save it for a rainy day. Every new day, in her book, should be treated as 'best'. Not a bad way to live your life.

My daughter Rosie is growing up to be a beautiful, funny and smart young woman. She is great company and I'm very proud of her. My favourite part of the week is just spending time with her, even if we're only doing maths homework or watching *America's Next Top Model* on the TV and shricking at how ghastly and bitchy the contestants are.

I think she will do something creative. She loves fashion and art and she might even end up on TV one day. You never know.

It's certainly been a fantastic career for me, and after so many years at the coal-face, I'm told I've become something of a 'cult'. At least, I hope that's how you spell it.

Epilogue

I have always been a worrier, even as a kid. I worried about
school. I fretted about getting top marks. I lost sleep over
whether I was good enough to do my job, and I still worry that
one day I'm going to be 'found out'.

I was brought up in the Gorbals, once considered to be the
poorest, roughest and most deprived area of Britain, but I had a
terrific childhood with parents who loved me. I'm married to a
wonderful man and we have a daughter who makes me smile
every day.

I have good pals and I love my *LK Today* show on GMTV,
writing my weekly columns for the *Sun* and the *Sunday Post*, as
well as being an agony aunt for *Best* magazine. It's a busy, rich,
full life and it's pretty damned good.

Even so, I still find plenty to worry about. When you have
been given so much, and then worked hard to build on that,

there is so much more to lose. I'm very realistic about the sort of work I do and I compare being on TV to being a footballer. It's a fantastic career, but it's short-lived and it will inevitably end one day. As I have been working on breakfast TV in one form or another since 1985, I'm a veteran player in anyone's book. I truly never expected still to be going strong after all these years and to be enjoying what I do more than ever. There are not many people who genuinely love their job, and are lucky enough to be surrounded by interesting, stimulating and often exasperating people all day.

Yet I still worry about whether the show is good enough, if people will still want to watch it – and what you will think now that you've got to the end of this book?

Index

2001 A Space Odyssey 31
Adams, Helen 240, 248
Alaska 57
Aldrin, Buzz 16
Allsop, Bill 54–5, 74
Amundsen, Roald 117
Anderston 6
Andrews, Julie 188–9
Ant and Dec 235, 236–8
Armstrong, Fiona 132, 133, 134
Armstrong, Neil 15, 16
Arnold, Richard 278
Attenborough, Sir David 110
Attitude 105, 106
Ayr 38
Aziz, Liza 97, 120, 134

Bacall, Lauren 70
Baker, Tina 191, 220, 279
Ballantine, Pammie 166
ballet 28
Bannon, Lorna 125
Barker, Sue 171
Barough, Nina 161–2, 163, 164–5, 166, 167
Barr, Eric 51, 53
Barr, Mike 51, 55

Barra 75
Barrowland Ballroom 46
Barrows market 46–7
Barry Eddie 2
Baxter, Stanley 245
Bay City Rollers 48
Bazalgette, Peter 114–15
BBC Scotland 60, 61, 63–6, 114, 289
Beckham, Victoria 194, 240–1
Berry, Halle 247
Best 222, 287, 299
The Big Breakfast 71, 133, 136
Big Brother 114, 240
Biggs, Ronnie 56, 57
The Bill 244
Birch, Ian 193
Black Wednesday (1992) 126
Blackburn, Tony 139
Bosomworth, Kate 162, 168
Botswana 57
Bowie, David 45
Boyz 104, 105
Brambles, Jackie 93–4
Brand, Russell 277, 282
Bravest Dog in Britain 110–11
Breakfast 71
breakfast TV 66, 71, 134

see also individual programmes
Breakthrough Breast Cancer 161, 175, 179
breast cancer and breast cancer charities 22, 23, 161–2, 164–5, 166, 167, 175, 179, 270
Brewster, Craig 143
Bridgeton, Glasgow 12, 38, 80
British Heart Foundation 55, 169
British Home Stores 46
Britton, Fern 249, 250, 252
Broadcast News 85
Brombley, Squadron Leader Pete 284
Brookside 141, 242
Brown, Bobbi 224
Brown, Gordon 186, 295, 296
Brown, Sarah 295–6
Brownies 17
Bryans, Allan 125
Buerk, Michael 90
Bullock, Sandra 282

Caldwell, Pete 70–1
car phones 79
Carey, Mariah 186
'Caring Christmas' Campaign 111–12
Carman, Dominic 255
Carr, Alan 291–2, 293
celebrity entourages 186–7
Celtic 80
Chalk, Tim 118, 119
Channel 4 133
Channel 4 Daily 71
Charles, Prince of Wales 78, 205, 207
Chelsea Girl 45–6
chocolate cigarettes 36
Christmases 210–12, 252
Churchill, Sir Winston 20, 21
The Clan 122, 124
Claremont High School 43, 44, 102
Clarke, Kenneth 141, 142
Clayderman, Richard 111–12
Cleaver, Sue 220
Clinton, Bill 43
Clooney, George 280–1
Collette, Toni 242–3
Collins, Justin Lee 291–2, 293
Collins, Mike 16
Collymore, Stan 215
comics 27
compassionate reporting 90, 198
Concannon, Joan 268
Connolly, Billy 245
Cookham Dean 130, 140, 212–13, 214, 215, 272, 276

Cookham Wanderers 213
Cooper, Alice 31
Corley, Paul 223
Coronation Street 246, 247
Cosgrove, Stuart 289
Costello, Elvis 54, 223
Cow & Gate 150–1
Cowell, Simon 187, 238
Cox, Brian 268
Cox, Mark 246
Cox, Tracey 240
Crawford, Betty 109
Crawford, Graham 51
Crawford, Joan 144
Crawford, Michael 84
Crean, Tom 118
Crosbie, Annette 244
The Cure 108, 109

Daily Mail 97, 183
Daily Mirror 260
Daily Record 105–6
Daleks 142
Davies, Annie 135
Davis, Bette 69–70, 144
Davis, Sammy, Jr 70
De Vries, Mark 290
Deayton, Angus 291
debriefings 137, 279
D'Elia, Ilaria 162
Dennistoun Palais 7
Desilu, Madame 43
Dexter, Colin 210
Diamond, Anne 69, 70, 83, 97, 183
Diana, Princess of Wales 55, 78, 158–9, 193–4, 207
Diaz, Cameron 242, 277
Dimbleby, David 294
discos and disco fashion 44–5, 48
Discovery (ship) 118, 119
Disneyland 126, 142
Donnellon, Kevin 255
Douglas, Kirk 107
Dr Who 142
Draperstown 5
Duchovny, David 189
Duffy, Keith 240
Dunblane massacre (1996) 195–207
Dundee 82–3, 118, 121, 267–8
Dundee United 79, 80, 81–2, 143, 213, 288–91
Dundee University 263–5, 267, 268–72
Dyke, Greg 67
Dynasty 91

earpieces 92–3
East Kilbride 20, 38, 39, 40–3
East Kilbride district council 52
East Kilbride News 49–56, 60–1, 76
Edinburgh 47–8, 53–4
Edinburgh Castle 77
Edinburgh Moonwalk 166–7
Edmonds, Noel 139, 235
'elastics' 35
Eriksson, Sven-Göran 216
Essex, David 31
Eurovision Song Contest 253–4

family parties 10
Ferguson, Miss (schoolteacher) 33
Fiennes, Ralph 95
Figure Happy 161
Figure It Out 159
Finnigan, Judy 183, 246
First Steps 149
Fisher, Gregor 245
fitness videos 158–61, 179
Fitzpatrick, Tony 191
Flatley, Michael 258
Focal Point 65
football 9, 79–80, 81–2, 103, 213–14,
    215–16, 295
Ford, Anna 132
Ford, Harrison 282
Fordham, Julia 190
Forsyth, Bruce 110
Foxx, Jamie 187
Frasers 18
Friday Night with Jonathan Ross 247
The Friday Night Project 291–3
Frizzell, Martin 184
Frost, David 96, 110, 132
Frost on Sunday 96
fruit dumplings 10–11
Fry, Stephen 263, 269
Fun in the Sun 184
Furnish, David 193, 194
Fyfe, Cameron 76

Gallagher, Kevin 81, 289
Gallie, Aileen 39
games, childhood 34–6
Garraway, Kate 101, 178
Gascoigne, Paul 133
Gates, Gareth 186
gay media 104, 105
Geldof, Bob 133
'Get Up and Give' week 185
Gish, Lillian 30

Glasgow Rangers 9, 79, 80, 290
Glenister, Philip 248
Glenrothes 73
GMTV 5, 15, 101, 115, 130–42, 145, 147,
    148, 149, 150–1, 161, 162, 178,
    181–94, 196, 198, 202, 209, 217, 222,
    223, 233, 234, 239, 245, 246, 247,
    248, 249, 250, 252, 260, 261, 265,
    267, 269, 272, 275, 276, 277, 279,
    286, 288, 292, 299
    see also individual programmes
GMTV Today 277, 279
Golden, Maurice 263
Good Morning Britain 69–79, 83–95,
    97–109, 110–13
goodie bags 112
Goodwin, Trudi 112
Gorbals 3–5, 6, 7, 11, 12, 299
Grampian TV 189
Grant, Hugh 265 6, 267, 285
Grant, Joan 166, 266, 267, 285
Green, Melanie 189
Greenhills 42, 43
Greig, John 80
gun crime 73
Gyngell, Bruce 67, 83, 91, 99–100, 109,
    114, 130

Haase, Pauline 277
Hagen, Mark 191
Hamilton, Ian 199
Hamilton, Jan 104
Hamilton, Liam 162
Hand, Helen 247
Hanley, Stephen 235
Hannah, John 102
Harley, Steve 45
Harridan, Janice 44, 45, 47
Harris, Rolf 214
Have I Got News For You 291
Heat 241
Hefner, Hugh 192
Hemphill, Greg 245
Henderson, Connie 63
Hesmondhalgh, Julie 220
Heyes, Mark 113, 156, 162, 164, 188,
    240, 267, 268, 279
Hislop, Ian 291
Hodgkins, Sophie 110, 189, 265, 267,
    275
Hogmanay 10
Holloway, Kathryn 131
Holmes, Eamonn 135, 141, 142, 144–5,
    147, 151, 181, 182–4, 198

Holt, John 213
Horne, Helen 184, 229
Hughes, Mark 82
Hunniford, Gloria 149
Hunt, Noel 289–90
Hunter, Angus 70–1
Hunter, Holly 85
Hunter, Rachel 133
Hurley, Liz 194
Hurricane Andrew 126
Hurt, William 85
Hyde, Connie 244

Independent Television Commission 75
interview techniques 51, 92
Ironside-Wood, Janey 120
Irving, Jayne 100
Islay 75–6

Jackman, Hugh 247
Jacobsen, David 83, 84
The James Gang 242–3
Jameson, Sue 278
Japan 57
Jardine, Sandy 80
Jay, Simon 91, 133
Jessel, Toby 136
John, Elton 192, 193–4
John Street Secondary School 37–8
Johnceline, Nikki 223
Johnson, Mo 103
Johnston, Linda 39
Johnstone, Derek 80
Jones, Dr Hilary 115, 151, 278
Jonsson, Ulrika 97, 103, 113, 129, 215, 216
Joyce, Michael 157, 257, 258, 261

Kellagher, Ian 71, 76
Kelly, Anne (née McMahon: mother) 1, 2, 3–4, 7, 8, 9, 10, 13, 17–19, 20, 21, 22, 25, 27, 29, 38–9, 42, 45, 52–3, 56, 57, 80, 99, 103, 105, 109, 123, 146, 148, 153, 154, 229–30, 267, 275
Kelly, Billy (great-uncle) 10, 60
Kelly, Billy (uncle) 5, 9, 38, 59
Kelly, Carol (aunt) 5, 27, 50, 220
Kelly, Catherine (great-great-grandmother) 6
Kelly, Danny (grandfather) 9–10, 41, 225
Kelly, Graham (brother) 13–15, 16, 18–19, 25, 27, 29, 38, 45, 50, 124–5, 154, 254, 274
Kelly, Granny 4–5, 10, 19–20

Kelly, Great Granny 11–12
Kelly, John (father) 1, 2–3, 5, 7, 9, 12, 15, 16, 29, 30, 31, 38, 41, 52, 53, 59, 80, 106, 123, 124–5, 146, 148, 154, 172, 214, 215, 267, 275
Kelly, John (great-great-grandfather) 5–6
Kelly, John (great-great-great-grandfather) 5
Kelly, Lena (great-aunt) 10
Kelly, Lisa 189
Kelly, Lorraine
  accent 66, 67, 95, 98, 107, 136, 183
  on ageing gracefully 219–20
  agony aunt 222, 299
  axed from GMTV 149
  ballet lessons 28
  BBC Scotland researcher 60, 61, 63–6
  birth 1–2, 4
  birth of Rosie 143–7
  bullied at school 25–7, 44
  cameo appearances 141, 242–6
  charity marathons and walks 55–6, 161–79
  childhood homes 4, 12–13, 17–18, 39, 40–3, 45
  childhood play and games 33, 34–6, 37
  cover-girl 103–4
  Daily Record 'exposé' 105–6
  East Kilbride News journalist 49–56, 60–1, 76
  Edinburgh college student 53–5
  education 25–7, 31–3, 37–8, 43, 44, 49, 80–1
  electric shock 41–2
  family background 1–23
  family language 30
  fashion and style 18, 44–5, 48, 54, 92, 119, 156
  first boyfriend 54
  first earnings 27–8
  fitness videos 158–61, 179
  flashed to the nation 112
  football fan 79–80, 81–2, 213–14, 288–91
  football reporting 82
  fortieth birthday 220–1
  'glam' occasions 77–9
  Glasgow flat 59–60, 64–5, 129
  golfing 266–7
  hair styles 144
  holidays 29–30, 38, 57

honeymoon 126–7
honorary law degree 271–2
joins GMTV 114–15, 130
joins TVam 66–7
laser eye surgery 239
love of reading 27, 39–40
love of Shakespeare 44
market stallholder 46, 47
marries Steve 116, 120–6
media awards 109–10
meets Stephen Smith 79
miscarriage 224–31
moves to Cookham Dean 130
movie buff 30–1, 280
musical tastes 31, 40, 45, 54, 63, 108
natural camera quality 95
nerves, performance 90–1, 92, 94, 95
newspaper columnist 106–7, 149,
    221–2, 238, 287–8, 299
nicknames 51–2
pet animals 274–5
photo-shoots 103–4
piano lessons 29
politics 43–4, 296
pregnancy 139–40
on press intrusion 240–1
public recognition 103, 241–2
punk phase 54
Queen of Hearts competition winner
    55–6
radio broadcasting 209–11, 217–18
rector of Dundee University 263–5,
    267, 268–72
reporting of Dunblane massacre
    195–9
reporting of Lockerbie bombing
    87–90, 94
returns home to Scotland 272–5
Saturday jobs 45–6
sexual assault accusation 257–62
shingles 113
on smoking and drinking 51–2,
    102–3, 154–5, 225
tidiness 25, 182
Tornado jet flight 283–5
waitressing job 61, 62–3
weekly schedule 286–8
weight problems 150, 153–4, 155–9,
    173, 179–80, 239
work ethic 141, 211
working mother dilemma 184–5,
    217, 286

youth hostelling 47–9
    see also BBC Scotland; GMTV;
        TVam; and individual television
        and radio shows
Kelly, Lydia (aunt) 5, 27
Kelly, Matthew 258
Kelly, Ross 186, 188–9
Kennedy, Brian 54
Kennedy, Kate 246
Keyes, Richard 70, 100–1, 113–14, 134
Keyes, Robert 132
Khan, Zafar 255
Kiernan, Ford 245
King, Ross 191, 192
Kirkbride, Anne 246, 247
Knitting Now . . . and Crochet Too 103–4
Knockout 27
Kutcher, Ashton 277

Lamont, Norman 126
lang, kd 279–80
Langland, Sir Alan 267
Lawley, Sue 66
Lawrence, Josie 185
Letford, John 269
Levien, Craig 288, 289, 290
Life on Mars 247–8
Lineker, Gary 82
Little, Alan 63, 64
LK Today 247, 249, 277–83, 291, 294, 299
LK in the USA 223–4
Lockerbie air crash (1988) 87–90, 94
London Fashion Week 112–13
London Marathon 168–74
London Palladium 185
Lopez, Jennifer 186
Lorraine 233, 234
Los Angeles 83, 189–92
Lovell, Jim 15
Ludford, Bill 82, 97–8
Lusardi, Linda 133

McAllister, Colin 289
McAlpine, Hamish 213
McCall, Stuart 103
McCarthy, John 83, 84
Macdonald, Sheena 64
McDonald, Sir Trevor 276
McHugh, Peter 202, 276
McKenna, Steve 240
McKenzie, Alison 285
MacKenzie, Kelvin 217, 218, 254–5, 256
McKerragher, Joanna 51
McLean, Andrea 186

McLean, Jim 81
McLean, Lex 3
McLellan galleries 28
McMahon, Helen (aunt) 8, 19
McMahon, Jacqueline (aunt) 2, 8, 121
McMahon, Jimmy (uncle) 8, 22, 39
McMahon, John (grandfather) 8, 22
McMahon, Josephine (aunt) 8, 9, 29, 125
McMahon, Margaret (grandmother) 2, 3, 4, 8, 20–3, 30, 39, 72, 162, 296–7
McMahon, Mary (aunt) 2, 8
McMahon, Patricia (aunt) 8
McMahon, Tony (uncle) 8
Macmillan, Harold 21
McMurray, Helen 185
McPhedran, Miss (schoolteacher) 44
Madeley, Richard 183
Madonna 279
Mains Castle, Dundee 121–2, 123–4
Major, John 126
makeup, studio 91
Mallett, Timmy 213
Malpas, Maurice 274
Marchioness disaster (1989) 96–7
Margaret Hopkins School of Dancing 28
Marlow 129
Mead, Geoff 96
Merrilees, Bob 130
Merrilees, Cynthia 130
Merton, Paul 291
Metcalfe, Michael 110, 265
Michael, George 282–3
Midler, Bette 107–8
Midnight Express 61
Millar, Craig 173, 174, 264, 266
Millar, Jacqueline 166, 226, 266
mixed marriages 9, 80
Monro, Matt 13
moon landings 15–16
Moonwalks 162, 163–7, 169, 266
Moore, Patrick 15
Morgan, Piers 187
Morley, Ken 132
Morris, Mike 69, 70, 94, 100, 101, 103, 113, 114, 115, 116, 120, 130–1, 134
Morris, Pete 189, 190, 191
Morrison, Jim 51
Moxton Girls 10
multiple sclerosis 273
Murray, Chick 245

Napier College, Edinburgh 54
Narey, Davey 213
Nasir, Claire 278

Nevin, Pat 289
New York 222–3
New York Marathon 175–8
Newmar, Julie 70
news/entertainment balance 132
Noel's House Party 139

O'Brien, Gray 245
O'Gorman, Siobhan 165–6, 167, 177, 178, 220, 222, 233, 239, 249, 254, 259, 265, 267, 285
O'Grady, Paul 112, 293
Oliver, Jamie 107
One Foot in the Grave 243–4
Open University 71
Orange marching bands 80
O'Reilly, Jimmy 157–8
Orkney Islands 48, 76
Osbourne, Jack 192
Osbourne, Sharon 192
Outer Hebrides 78
Owen, Nick 70, 183

Paris 29, 107–8
Parker, Dorothy 63
Parker, Sarah Jessica 277
Parkinson, Michael 132
Parlane, Derek 80
Paul, Dorothy 7
The Paul O'Grady Show 112, 293
Peck, Gregory 30, 70
penguin sculpture and painting 118–20, 215
Pentland, Paul 88, 89
Peterhead jail siege (1987) 86, 189
Peters, Davie 162
Peters, Maggie 162
Pfeiffer, Michele 189
The Phantom of the Opera 84
Phillips, Fiona 101, 184, 187
photo-shoots 103–4
piece to camera (ptc) 73–4
Pink Floyd 46
Piper Alpha oil-rig disaster (1988) 86–7
poker 51
polar exploration 117
Pollock, Jason 191
Pop Idol 239
Porter, Mr (schoolteacher) 43
Potts, Rodney Hilton 256–7
poverty 16–17
power-dressing 91–2
press interviews, pitfalls of 106–7
Priestley, Raymond 118

Prince's Trust 78
public baths 32, 39

QE2 108, 109
The Quarter to Nine Show 151
Queen 40
Question Time 293–5, 296
Quinn, Katherine 277

radiograms 13
RAF Leuchars air show 283–6
Ralston, Spencer 123
Ramsay, Gordon 171
Ravenscraig steelworks 70
Reeves, Keanu 282
regional accents 66, 67, 95, 98, 107, 136, 183
Reid, Mark 87
Renwick, David 243, 244
Riddoch, Lesley 263
Rifkind, Malcolm 77
Rio de Janeiro 56–7
Rippon, Angela 132
River City 244–5
Rivers, Joan 223
Rivett, Jenni 158–9, 160–1
Rocky the dog 274, 275
roller-skating 55–6
Rook, Jean 49, 101
Ross, Pam 199-202, 203–4
Rutto, Evans 172
Ryan, Justin 289

St James's Palace 78
Schofield, Philip 249, 250, 251, 261
science fiction 15
Scott, David 65
Scottish comic talent 245
'scraps', trading 37
Seamill 38
sectarianism 80–1
Semples 7
September 11 terrorist attacks 248–9
Sergeant, John 254, 255, 256
Shackleton, Sir Ernest 117–18
Shakira 187
Shannon, Dell 13
Shayler, David 263
Shephard, Ben 240
Shinwell, Emanuel 21
Simm, John 247
Sinclair, George 66
Singh, Fauja 173
Sixty Minutes 60

skiing 138
skipping 35–6
Sky TV 233, 239, 240, 248, 249
Slater, Oscar 30
Smith, Margaret 122, 123, 273, 274
Smith, Penny 151, 188, 278
Smith, Robert 108
Smith, Rosie (daughter) 33–4, 143–8, 151, 159, 163, 170, 172, 173, 180, 181, 182, 184, 185, 191, 193–4, 211, 212–13, 213, 214, 215, 216–17, 222, 225, 226–7, 228, 231, 242, 267, 272, 275, 285, 297
Smith, Stephen (husband) 79, 83, 85–6, 87–8, 89, 94, 98–9, 105–6, 116–17, 118, 119, 122–6, 129, 136, 140, 145, 146–7, 148, 150, 151, 156, 160, 164, 170, 172, 173, 174, 189, 191, 192, 213, 214–15, 216–17, 220, 225, 226, 228, 230, 260, 266, 272, 273, 275, 288, 296
Smith, Will 281
smoking 154–5
Snowdrop Campaign 204
social engineering 11
Sommers, Miss (schoolteacher) 44
Sommerville, Hamish 44
Soviet Union 44
Spark, Elizabeth 26, 29, 31, 39
Spears, Britney 186, 221
Speirs, Miss (schoolteacher) 32–3
Sportscene 289
Springer, Jerry 127
Springfield, Dusty 13
Stapleton, John 186, 188
Star Trek 15
Starr, Freddie 136
Stewart, Dixi 210
Stewart, Sian 150
Stigers, Curtis 109
Still Game 245–6
'stilts' 35
Stott, Grant 166
Strathclyde Primary School 25–6, 31–2
Stuart, Jackie 86
Suchet, David 110
Sun 106, 116, 179, 221–2, 238, 288, 294, 299
Sunday Post 149, 197, 222, 288, 294, 299
Sunrise 114, 115
see also GMTV
sweets 36–7, 39

T. Rex 31
Taggart 102
Talk Radio 209–11, 217–18
talkback 93, 94
Tamm, Mary 141
Tankell, Sarah 188
Tayler, Kathy 94, 97, 129, 130
Tayport 272, 273
television, early 7, 12–13
television franchises 113
Thames TV 132
Thatcher, Margaret 113
thinness, cult of 154
This Morning 249–52, 261, 269
Thompson, Eddie 290
Thurso 48
Tobermory 37
Tomlinson, Jane 270
Top of the Morning 115, 131–5, 137
Top of the Pops 31
transsexuals 104
Troon 38
TSW (Television South West) 132
Turnbull, John 215
Turner, Anthea 149, 150, 182–4
TV and Radio Industry (TRIC) 109
TV Times 103
TVam 66–7, 69–79, 82–116, 130–1,
    132, 133, 136, 137, 189, 213, 215,
    222
    see also individual programmes
TVS (Television South) 132
Twin Towers 224, 248

Ustinov, Peter 263, 265

Venables, Terry 82
Versace, Gianni 192
viewers' letters 77, 286
voice-overs 70

Vote for Me 254–7, 259, 263
vox pops 65–6

Waite, Terry 83, 84
Wake, Jane 169, 170, 171–2, 179, 286
Walk Off the Pounds 179
Walker, Colin 53, 54
Walker, Nancy 53–4
Wark, Kirsty 64
Webb, Lizzie 134
WeightWatchers 156
Weller, Paul 258
West Side Story 33
Whately, Kevin 110
Wightman, Reverend Bob 122
Willis, Bruce 242, 282
Wilson, Craig 239
Wilson, Michael 132, 135
Wingett, Mark 112
Woffenden, Gary 61–2
Wogan 70
Woman's Weekly 107
Wonder, Stevie 46
Woodrow, Joyce 47, 48–9, 63, 65, 121,
    122, 123, 147, 158, 163, 164, 165,
    166, 169, 170, 171, 172, 173, 174,
    175, 177
Woolford, Keo 185
working mother dilemma 184–5, 217, 286
Worsley, Frank 118
Wright, Jez 210

X Factor 254
The X-Files 189

Yewdell, Brenda 91, 102, 122, 123
Young, Lynn 47
youth hostelling 47–9

Zephyr car 38

Picture Credits

The author and publisher are grateful to all copyright holders, with particular thanks to Steve Smith.

Credits are listed according to the order the pictures appear on each page, left to right, top to bottom.

'LK' denotes photographs that are courtesy of Lorraine Kelly.

End Papers 1
All © Steve Smith

Section 1
Page 1: all LK; *Page 2*: all LK; *Page 3*: all LK; *Page 4*: all LK except last © W. M. Il Wraith; *Page 5*, all LK; *Page 6*: all LK; *Page 7*: © Doug McKenzie, © DC Thomson & Co Ltd, © TVam, © TVam; *Page 8*: © Steve Smith, © Steve Smith, © Steve Smith, LK, LK

Section 2

Page 1: © Best Magazine/Bill Morton; *Page 2*: © Allan Olley, GMTV, © Steve Smith, © David Cheskin/PA Photos, © DC Thomson & Co Ltd; *Page 3*: © Walk the Walk (www.walkthe walk.org), © Steve Smith, © Siobhan O'Gorman, © Steve Smith, © Steve Smith; *Page 4*: © Steve Smith, LK, © Peter Morris, © Steve Smith, © Steve Smith; *Page 5*: Courtesy of Hat Trick Productions Ltd, Courtesy of So Television; *Page 6*: © Steve Smith, LK, © Steve Smith, © Steve Smith; *Page 7*: LK, LK, © Steve Smith, © Steve Smith, © Rosie Smith; *Page 8*: © Nicky Johnston, GMTV

End Papers 2

LK, © Vikki Grant, Top Santé, © Steve Smith, © Steve Smith, © Steve Smith